*Less Than a Treason*

# LESS
# THAN A
# TREASON

*Hemingway in Paris*

PETER GRIFFIN

New York  Oxford
OXFORD UNIVERSITY PRESS
1990

Oxford University Press

Oxford   New York   Toronto
Delhi   Bombay   Calcutta   Madras   Karachi
Petaling Jaya   Singapore   Hong Kong   Tokyo
Nairobi   Dar es Salaam   Cape Town
Melbourne   Auckland
and associated companies in
Berlin   Ibadan

Published by Oxford University Press, Inc.,
200 Madison Avenue, New York, New York 10016

Oxford is a registered trademark of Oxford University Press

Library of Congress Cataloging-in-Publication Data
Griffin, Peter, 1942–
Less than a treason : Hemingway in Paris / Peter Griffin.
p.   cm.   ISBN 0-19-505332-X
1. Hemingway, Ernest, 1899–1961—Biography.
2. Hemingway, Ernest, 1899–1961—Homes and haunts—France—Paris.
3. Americans—France—Paris—History—20th century.
4. Paris (France)—Intellectual life—20th century.
5. Authors, American—20th century—Biography.
I. Title.  PS3515.E37Z6115  1990
813'.52—dc20 [B]   89-26606

1 3 5 7 9 8 6 4 2
Printed in the United States of America
on acid-free paper

*To my wife,*
*Penelope*

# *Preface*

Since the publication in 1985 of my *Along with Youth: Hemingway, the Early Years,* much has changed. Mary Hemingway, my first benefactor, is dead. Carlos Baker, the official Hemingway biographer, in whose work I found a gold mine of information, is dead. Bill Horne, who generously allowed me to read his private collection of letters written to him by Ernest just after they returned from World War I, is now dead, too.

As I submit this second volume of my biography to the reader, I recall Bill Horne's self-admonition during one of our interviews. Eighty-eight or eighty-nine years old at the time, Bill had told my wife and me the true story of Ernest's break with William Smith, his best boyhood friend. In doing so, Bill had spoken harshly of Smith's sister-in-law, "Doodles," who, he said, had caused all the trouble. Then, suddenly, Bill seemed embarrassed. Then he looked right at me, yet another biographer of his friend, and said, "Remember, speak well of the dead."

Of course, no biographer can speak only well of his subject, living or dead. And Bill knew this. But perhaps he meant something more by "speaking well" than telling just the good things. Perhaps he meant that the dead should be afforded the same compassion, understanding, and tolerance, should be approached with the same generosity with which, at our best, we meet the living.

During the Twenties in Paris, Ernest lost much of the boyish charm that made him so appealing in the years of *Along with Youth.* To replace it, he nurtured a pragmatism founded on the question "What to make of a diminished thing?" It was defined by his first fictional antihero, Jacob Barnes of *The Sun Also Rises,* in this way: "I did not care what it was all about. [Barnes says to himself during one of his long, sleepless nights.] All I wanted to know was how to live in it. Maybe if you found out how to live in it you learned from that what it was all about."

Most likely, Ernest considered this change of heart a strategic retreat, an attempt to limit his casualties as the battle of life went on. But the longer he assumed this persona, the more it became for him the only way to live.

Since *Along with Youth* appeared, several excellent studies of Hemingway have been published, by Jeffrey Meyers, Kenneth Lynn, Michael Reynolds. Each adds insights and worthwhile information. In *Less Than a Treason,* I do not analyze this well-examined life; I try instead to recreate it. In *Death in the Afternoon,* Ernest wrote that the function of art is to "Make all that come true again." In this book I have told a story of Ernest's Paris years.

I wish to thank my friends Jack Hemingway, Michael V. Carlisle, William Sisler, Curtis Church, the late Raymond Carver; my mother and father, Anna and Milton Griffin, both now deceased; and David Wise, at the National Endowment for the Humanities.

*Fall River, Mass.*                                                            P.G.
*December 1989*

# Contents

*Less Than a Treason*

Ah, when to the heart of man
   Was it ever less than a treason
To go with the drift of things,
   To yield with a grace to reason,
And bow and accept the end
   Of a love or a season?

ROBERT FROST
"Reluctance"

# 1

## The Innocents Abroad

Down at the Fourteenth Street dock, at the French Line's New York terminal, Ernest looked over the ship that would take him and his bride, Hadley, to France. He had read in the line's brochure that this solid, German-built freighter, twenty years old, a war prize, now hauled four hundred passengers to Europe and back every two weeks. The *Leopoldina* was slower than most of the transatlantic liners, but broad abeam and almost vibration-free. There was something appropriate, Ernest thought, about crossing this time on her. In the French Line schedule, she sailed a few days after the *Chicago,* the ship that had carried Ernest and his fellow Red Cross volunteers to France in 1918, and a few days before the *La Lorraine,* which had brought his first love, nurse Agnes von Kurowsky, to Italy, and their romance at the Red Cross hospital in Milan.

At boarding time, Ernest still clutched a letter written at the last minute on complimentary hotel stationery and with the hotel pen. He had not yet mailed it because he believed that the ship's postmark would be exciting to his "folks" back in Oak Park, Illinois. In this letter, Ernest thanked his parents, Clarence and Grace, for their going-away presents—father's dates and apples, mother's check—and for the good-humored letters they'd sent along, from his sisters "Nunbones" and Marcelline. He warned the family that, because of the stockyard strike, they should stay away from the West End of Chicago. Being cautious himself, he had been down to look over the ship that would take him and his wife across. Twice he called everything "very lovely."

3

He signed the letter "Ernest," then added, "My dear love to all of yez."

By dinnertime first night out, December 8, 1921, the *Leopoldina* had reached open ocean. The sea was unusually calm for winter, the weather mild. Ernest and Hadley traveled first class—in a stateroom with all the comforts of an inexpensive hotel. Besides the twin beds with pillows tightly rolled, there was a dresser, a nighttable with lamp, and a couch. There were little curtains on both portholes, a sink with running water, and an oscillating fan on the wall. But the walls, even the ceiling, were paneled in oak, and that made the air seem close and hard to breathe. Out in the dining area, actually a hall in the center of the ship, Ernest felt much better. There was plenty of space between the sets of small round tables and wicker chairs. And red napkins stood in crowns, four to a table.

Because the *Leopoldina* was first of all a freighter, much of the deck space was taken up with strapped-down, canvas-covered cargo. The staterooms, the social hall, the promenade, the veranda café, were all clustered amidships in decks below the bridge. There were no steerage passengers, and the atmosphere was informal, more like a local excursion, or a cruise.

Hadley was happy to find pianos in both the smoking room and the veranda café. Soon her affectionate renditions of the classics and her skill with popular tunes made her the center of attention. Hadley spoke French fluently and, with her bobbed auburn hair and vivacious smile, she attracted a crowd. But it distressed Ernest when good-looking young men stood about the piano, encouraging Hadley to play. In a letter he wrote in the stateroom while Hadley was "off entertaining," he called these men "Argentineans," because W. H. Hudson, whose work Ernest admired, had made that country and its people sensually romantic in his current novel, *Far Away and Long Ago*. Ernest did not say anything to Hadley about his jealousy, but he decided to put on a show of his own—and in the knitted boxing shorts that Hadley once said were all too revealing of his "manly form."

Not long after Ernest came aboard the *Leopoldina,* he had met a professional boxer, Henry Cuddy of Salt Lake City. Cuddy said he was crossing over to fight in France and Italy. People didn't think much of European fighters anymore, Cuddy said, not since Jack Dempsey had destroyed Georges Carpentier that past June. Ernest mentioned that he himself had lost big money on the Carpentier fight. Neverthless, Cuddy said, fighting in Europe was still a way to get some publicity back in the States. When Ernest told Cuddy he had soldiered in Italy during the war, Cuddy acknowledged he was Italian, and the two became shipboard friends. With Cuddy's willing assistance, Ernest concocted a plan.

There was, Ernest told Cuddy, a beautiful young Frenchwoman on board whose AEF husband had deserted her. Ernest had heard she was down to her last ten francs, and she had a baby to care for. Why not put on a benefit for the woman? Three rounds in a roped-off part of the dining room. Cuddy should not worry about hurting him, Ernest said. He had sparred with Sammy Langford in Chicago.

For the next few days, Ernest and Henry Cuddy trained together, doing roadwork on the promenade deck, shadow boxing in front of the smoking-room mirrors. The captain of the *Leopoldina* liked the idea of the benefit and had crew members remove three tables from the dining-room floor. Ernest knew Cuddy had all the advantages: the professional's sense of timing that would make his punches feel like hammer blows; the skill to slip opponents' punches; the professional fighter's tolerance for pain. But Ernest, with his long arms, his good left jab, and his powerful right, thought he could keep Cuddy off him, at least for three rounds.

To Ernest's surprise, he was more than a match for Henry Cuddy. Ernest resisted the temptation to come out swinging, as amateurs usually do, and thereby punch himself out in the first round, and he fought carefully and well. In round three, Cuddy stepped into a solid right, and Ernest saw his friend's eyes flicker. But Cuddy would not go down. After the captain announced that more than one hundred dollars had been collected for the charity, he awarded Ernest the unanimous decision.

The fight was a success for Ernest in more ways than one. He became a shipboard celebrity; Cuddy complimented him with a suggestion that he fight professionally in Paris; and Hadley, who had been Ernest's "corner man," had watched her knight do battle for another lady fair.

The last leg of the southern route across the Atlantic brought the *Leopoldina* past the coasts of Portugal and Spain. The weather was warm and the sky a deep Iberian blue. Ernest and Hadley spent hours each day walking the sunny decks and standing quietly at the ship's rail. There was something in the wake of the ship, Ernest said, that reminded him of plowed land. But Hadley's eyes were off toward the Spanish mountains. Weren't they lovely, she said. To Ernest they looked like dinosaurs with bare brown, wrinkled skin. The sea gulls that followed behind the ship and held steadily in the air looked like stage-prop birds to Ernest, raised and lowered by wires. Hadley said that Spain looked long and brown, and very old.

There was something splendid about the *Leopoldina*'s first port of call. A powerful Atlantic storm had drawn away with it all the heavy winter coastal clouds, and Vigo, a bright little fishing village, shone in the afternoon sun. Ernest watched schools of tuna, churning in the harbor.

The hillside town with its narrow, friendly streets filled with cozy places to drink and eat seemed to Ernest a young man's paradise. Wine was cheap, brandy was cheap, and, down on the ancient dock, a lateen-sailed boat cost a dollar a day. His future lay in Paris, Ernest said, and he would go there and work it out. But wouldn't it be wonderful if one day he could write in Spain?

The *Leopoldina* docked at Le Havre on December 20, 1921, and Ernest and Hadley were soon aboard the boat train for Paris. Just before they'd left Chicago, Sherwood Anderson, whose subtle simplicity in *Winesburg, Ohio* made him one of the few contemporary American writers Ernest admired, had given Ernest letters introducing him to Ezra Pound and Gertrude Stein. Ernest wanted to write to thank Anderson soon after he arrived, and he wanted to write well. As the train rolled through the Normandy countryside, Ernest carefully noted details: there were manure piles smoking in the damp morning air and "long fields and woods with the leaves on the ground and the trees trimmed bare of branches way up their trunks"; the train passed through "Dark stations and tunnels"; the third-class compartments were filled with "boy soldiers." As the train neared Paris, Ernest, the only one in his compartment still awake, felt something he knew would please Anderson, if he could manage to get it clearly stated: "There's a deathly, tired silence you can't get anywhere else except a railway compartment at the end of a long ride."

Ernest and Hadley Hemingway had traveled from Chicago to New York—from New York to Le Havre—from Le Havre to Paris—by boat and train, five thousand miles in fourteen days. When they got to the Left Bank hotel Anderson had recommended, Hotel Jacob et D'Angleterre, they were "tired unto death." Ernest was moved to tears when he found Sherwood Anderson's warmhearted note of welcome waiting at the reception desk.

Ernest and Hadley spent their next three weeks at the intimate little hotel, just behind the Musee des Beaux Arts and a few minutes' walk from the Tuileries Gardens. Their room was clean and well-heated.

There was hot and cold running water, and a bathroom on the same floor. In America, Ernest and Hadley would have considered these the most meager of accommodations. Yet they were intent on being tough-spirited and open-minded, and insisted to each other that mastering inconvenience was part of learning about the world.

Sleep had never come easy to either Ernest or Hadley, especially in unfamiliar surroundings, and this held true for their first week in Paris. And so, despite a persistent December rain, night after night they went out to walk. But there was something pleasant in this, too, because they were happy to be alone, or nearly alone, in the ancient city. Pausing now and then under a streetlamp, Ernest would read something to Hadley from the fifteenth-century poet Francois Villon, whose favorite café was still in business, not far from the Hotel Jacob. Villon had killed a man in a duel, Ernest said, and had lived with bandits. His passionate and wise *Confessions* were written in his twenties; he was hung at thirty-two. Ernest loved Villon's most famous line, "But where are the snows of yesteryear?"

Striding down the narrow cobblestone streets, pitched unevenly by generations of patchwork repairs, Ernest and Hadley soon earned the legs to take them however far they wanted to go—once all the way to the Madeleine where Ernest pointed out the statue whose head he had seen knocked off by an artillery fragment in 1918. On the way home, in the early morning, they often passed the famous cafés of Montparnesse: Le Dome, Le Select, La Rotonde. At many of the tables were the Russians of Paris, refugees of the Revolution of 1917. These Russians did not fit the mold of refugees Ernest had seen during the war in Italy. These were aristocrats who had lived very well under the czar. Hadley found them attractive, and Ernest did too, except, he said, they seemed childish, drifting along, hoping that things would somehow be all right again.

On Christmas Day, 1921, Ernest and Hadley went to dinner at a small second-floor restaurant on the Rue Jacob. It was called "The Veritable Restaurant of the Third Republic." There were two rooms, four tiny tables, and a cat. A Christmas special was offered. The meat consisted of a taste of turkey, a lot of gristle, and a large piece of bone. When Ernest and Hadley finished eating, the proprietor came in with a partly burned dessert and a small bottle of red wine. He had forgotten the wine for dinner, he said. Ernest put his arm around Hadley; she was on the verge of tears. Homesickness, Ernest suggested. Hadley agreed.

But dining out was usually a happy affair for the Hemingways. Almost every evening, Ernest and Hadley ate just down the street from their hotel at a working-class restaurant, "Le Pre aux Clercs." The menu was a wonder to Ernest: roast beef, veal cutlet, lamb mutton, thick steaks, all served with the most delicious potatoes he'd ever tasted, and brussels sprouts in butter, creamed spinach, sifted peas, and salad. Soon Ernest and Hadley got to know the waiters, and the waiters got to like them. At Ernest's insistence, Hadley would make a ceremony of preparing the salad dressing at their table. The bill, with a bottle of wine, came to less than a dollar a day.

Ernest and Hadley knew they were still living like tourists in Paris, and that it was time to find an apartment. But it would have to be a flat not too far from the neighborhood they had gotten to know living at the hotel. Ernest got in touch with someone Sherwood Anderson had recommended: Lewis Galantiere, an American who knew Paris like "the back of his hand." When Ernest called, Galantiere suggested a get-acquainted dinner at the Restaurant Michaud.

Dinner with Galantiere turned into something of an ordeal for Ernest. The little man—no more than five-foot three or four—ordered the food, flirted with Hadley, and entertained his guests with his skill in mimicry. Each time Galantiere finished a routine and peered over his rimless glasses, Hadley would laugh and laugh. When Galantiere mentioned that he had done some boxing in his time, Ernest took him up on it.

The bout at the Hotel Jacob did not last long because Galantiere sensed that Ernest wanted to knock him out. After one round, in order to signal he'd quit, Lewis put on his glasses. But Ernest had not yet satisfied himself. With one sharp left, he broke the glasses, and then, mortified, helped pick up the pieces.

Soon after Christmas, Galantiere told Ernest that he had found a clean and cheap apartment at 74 Rue du Cardinal Lemoine. What kind of a neighborhood was it? Ernest asked. The street ran up Montmartre from the Seine near Pont Sully, and ended in a little cobblestone square called the Place de la Contrescarpe—a working-class neighborhood, Galantiere said.

Ernest and Hadley moved themselves into the flat on January 9, 1922—he straining under the weight of the footlockers which held all their possessions, she guiding him through the narrow entrance, up the four flights of narrow, spiraling stairs. Unlike rooms in American apartments, these two were all corners and angles; it was impossible, Hadley said, to walk a straight line from here to there. To make matters worse, the apartment was stuffed with ugly furniture: the bed, gilt-trimmed, fake mahogany; in the dining room, a crude oak table and chairs. Heat would come from a small fireplace in the bedroom. Hadley asked Ernest if he had seen their neighbors. They were the salt of the earth, she said, with a little dirt mixed in.

Still, the rooms were in a good part of town, Ernest said. Good, that was, for a writer. Yes, Paris was inexpensive; Paris was glamorous. In Paris there was the freedom to live as one wished. But there was something more. Ernest had heard Americans, especially those who had managed to get themselves past the tourist sights and over to the Left Bank, say that Paris was a shabby, unfriendly city, dirty and old. It had none of the gregariousness of Chicago or the cool elegance of New York. But Paris had what was far more important for an artist. There was, Ernest said, a decayed, fermentative quality to Paris, like a compost heap. Walking up the Rue Mouffetard, the market street congested with the smells of food and people, to the Place Contrascarpe with its clochards warming themselves on the sewer grates and its whores lounging outside the Bal Musette, Ernest felt transplanted into a truly fertile soil, one rich with the presence of life upon life.

But for the artist who sent down his roots there, Paris held danger, too. For Ernest this was embodied by the nearby Café des Amateurs. It was a sad, evilly run place, where the drunkards of the quarter gathered. Ernest hated the smell of their dirty bodies and the sour smell of drunkenness that came out onto the street even on a cold, windy day. To him, this café was a cesspool. But unlike the cesspool beneath the house where he and Hadley lived—which was pumped out every night into a tank wagon, that, in the moonlight, looked like a Braque painting—nothing ever emptied the Café des Amateurs. Ernest believed that, as an artist, he could be nourished by the fermentation of life. But he'd best leave death's residue alone.

Before Ernest left the States, he had managed to land a job as a foreign correspondent for the *Toronto Star,* a paper he had sent articles to, off and on, since his return from the Italian Front in 1919. By the second week of January 1922, less than a month after the Hemingways had arrived in Paris, Ernest had written three articles for the *Star:* "Living on $1,000 a Year in Paris"; "Poincaré's Folly," a piece on the new prime minister of France; and "Tuna Fishing in Spain," his recollections of visiting Vigo on the trip across. Ernest had also worked at his Nick Adams novel, the one he'd started in Chicago, in 1921, while he was courting Hadley.

When he finally sent his three stories off to John Bone, his editor at the *Star,* Ernest felt relieved. There would be money coming back, maybe by return mail. But he felt a pressure building, too. Aroused by the sights and sounds and smells of Paris, Ernest wanted to empty some of himself into his art again.

Ernest had discovered that while he could do his journalism with Hadley around, he could not write his stories. It had nothing to do with Hadley's "interfering" in any way. It was just that he worked with the intensity of a monk at devotions, and he felt the tension of his shutting Hadley out. To make them both comfortable, Ernest took a room in a tall, cheap hotel at 39 Rue Descartes. The hotel's distinction lay in the fact that the famous poet Paul Verlaine had died there in 1896. Ironically, Verlaine, a homosexual and the lover of Arthur Rimbaud, was, at the time of his death, widely despised for his drunkenness and debauchery. Ernest admired Verlaine's musical and powerfully imagistic poetry. In his own way, he wanted to do the same sort of thing in prose.

Ernest took a room at the Verlaine, on the top floor. It cost him sixty francs a month (about five dollars). Most days his tiny fireplace and the chimneys coming up through the center of the room gave him a cosy and comfortable retreat. But occasionally his fireplace would not draw, and Ernest had only a cold room full of smoke.

One such morning Ernest walked down to the Boulevard St.-Germain to a warm and clean café on the Place St.-Michel. He hung his waterproof on the coat rack and ordered a café-au-lait. Then he spread his notebook—the pages bound with thread, the outside cover blue—on the table before him and began a story about his boyhood in Michigan. In writing the story, Ernest discovered something.

It was wild, cold, and blowing outside the café. So he made it that sort of day in the story. Writing about two boys drinking made him thirsty, and he ordered a rum St. James. A beautiful girl came into the café, and he wished he could put her into the story, or into his life for that matter. But it was obvious that she was waiting for someone. Yet, because he had seen her with the eyes of the artist at work, she belonged to him. In a quiet epiphany, Ernest saw that for him art and life moved side by side, each imitating and affecting the other.

The transitional seasons, spring and fall, had always distressed Ernest, especially the fall. Like most people, he sensed in autumn the end of something and was reminded of death. But for him the attendant melancholy had no appeal. If anything, he hated it because it seemed perilously close to boredom and despondency, which he believed to be sins.

Perhaps it was the season then, Hadley thought, that caused Ernest to suddenly bother himself about money. She knew there was no good reason for it. With her income—from a trust fund her St. Louis grandfather had established—and the money Ernest would get from the *Star* for his articles, the Hemingways had enough to be comfortable in their "young artists'" life. Nevertheless, Ernest would now economize, especially on the things that gave them pleasure. There would be no more restaurant lunches, he said. An egg, a glass of wine, and some boiled potatoes would do. Hadley, who had fallen in love with French cooking in general, and French pastry in particular, thought Ernest was being silly, and told him so. But he said that hunger was good discipline, for both the artist and his wife.

Ernest also complained that he found it difficult to get the exercise he needed in Paris, and his stomach had begun to resemble a washboard again. Hadley suggested walking, but Ernest said that walking the damp city streets was depressing and would probably make him sick. Didn't she remember that he had been plagued with severe sore throats ever since childhood, and that his mother had once gone blind from rheumatic fever, which begins as a sore throat? Besides, he had seen men die, horribly, of influenza, and that disease began with a sore throat, too.

At this point, Hadley knew that Ernest needed a rest. There had been too many changes for him, in too short a time. Why not, she asked, try Chamby sur Montreux, in the Swiss Alps just above Geneva? They would go third class, and, she had heard, the pension would cost little more than they spent in Paris. Ernest groused about the inconvenience of the move, so soon after they had just settled in. But he finally agreed.

In Chamby the Hemingways found rooms in an ancient chalet, nestled in pine trees on the side of a mountain. As they had done when they first got to Paris, Ernest and Hadley walked everywhere. Only this time, with the frost-hardened rutted roads, always going either up or down, they called the walk, hiking. The road in front of their chalet went up the mountain, slow but steady, through a forest to where there were meadows. In the crisp, cold air their voices sounded strangely clear to them, as if they could whisper to each other from yards away. Sometimes Ernest led Hadley off the road, and the forest floor was as soft and free of undergrowth as in the pine woods back of his family's summer place in northern Michigan. But there were mountains here, sharp and steep and snow-topped. And the lake was a gray steel-blue.

Sometimes Ernest and Hadley walked down from the chalet, into the town of Montreux. On the way they passed an old square-built stone chateau with terraced fields of vines. After the odors of Parisian streets, the air of Montreux calmed the Hemingways. Wherever they went, it smelled of snow. There was, however, one form of rushing about in Montreux: the favorite Swiss pastime sport, lugeing.

The luge, Ernest discovered, was a small hickory sled steered with one's feet. If the sled swerved off to the right, you dragged your left leg in the snow; if to the left, you dropped your right leg. Most of the British colony on Lake Geneva were avid lugers. In fact, the ex–military governor of Khartoum had become a hero to the Swiss children because he luged with abandon down the mountain and into the streets of Montreux.

Back at the chalet, after an early supper, Ernest and Hadley went right to bed. Ernest's father, Dr. Clarence Hemingway, had taught him the virtues of winter's night air, and Ernest opened their bedroom windows wide. The next morning, Mrs. Gangwisch, the proprietor's wife, would come into their room and shut the windows and start a fire in the tall, porcelain stove. Then she would come back with big chunks of wood and a pitcher of hot water. Then she'd bring in breakfast.

Ernest and Hadley returned to Paris in late January 1922. Now the air was clear and cold, the wind sharp, the trees bare against a brightened sky. Hadley saw that Ernest felt better. He was ready to get to work.

Each morning, after a breakfast eaten quickly and most often in silence, Ernest would dress lightly enough to feel the cold and then hurry to his room at the Hotel Verlaine. If the writing went well, or sometimes if it would not go at all, Ernest would refresh himself with mandarin oranges, peeling them slowly and then spitting their seeds into the fire, or with a small sack of roasted chestnuts he'd bought from the old woman vendor at her brazier across the street.

When Ernest finished writing for the day, stopping before he had written himself out so that there was always something to prime the pump with tomorrow, he would put his notebook into the table drawer. Then he would fold his new story into his jacket pocket and walk down the long flights of stairs and home through the cold city streets as if he were carrying a prize. Hadley saw that Ernest needed this ritual and the illusion of small adventure it created, and she didn't complain about the hours she spent alone.

Ernest knew that making himself a writer meant more than learning to write the best he possibly could. Much of the time he was romantic about art and life, but he was practical, too. Stories he knew were good had been rejected by popular magazines. To be published right off, you had to be both mediocre and lucky. Other than that, you had to have influential friends.

Ernest and Hadley had been in Paris for two months before they used the letters of introduction Sherwood Anderson had given them. They wouldn't admit it, except to each other, but they were a little afraid of Gertrude Stein and Ezra Pound. Hadley had never cared much for eccentrics, she said. And Ernest had less confidence in his charm here, in the "big leagues."

What did Ernest know about Ezra Pound? Hadley asked. Pound was in his late thirties, Ernest said. He was a westerner, from Idaho. His family had money. How else could he have afforded the University of Pennsylvania? But, Ernest said, Pound had no degree. How much had he written? Hadley asked. Most of his work was translation, Ernest said. From Oriental languages. He'd be pretty safe from critics there, Hadley said. In fact, Ernest had heard that Pound's translations had gotten some terrible reviews. But, Ernest said, Pound had published two works of significance: *Hugh Selwyn Mauberley,* an attack on the "tawdry cheapness" of modern civilization; and three *Cantos* of what he called a modern epic. What made Pound interesting to Ernest was the affiliation with William Butler Yeats. Pound had been Yeats's private secretary.

Ernest told Hadley that the literary world was divided into those who "counted" and those who did not. Ordinarily, he would have dismissed Pound as a congenital dilettante. But he had heard from Sherwood Anderson that Pound could be useful in two ways. First, he had that priceless critical attribute: he took other people's work more seriously than he did his own. Second, he was well-connected in publishing.

At their first meeting, Ernest thought Pound, with his wild red hair and open Byronic collar, a pretentious fool. Not content to talk about writing, which was all Ernest wanted to hear from him, Pound presented what Ernest considered "big ideas"—all about the sickness and health of society, and how the misuse of capital had corrupted human affairs. When Pound fixed Ernest with sharp blue eyes, and spoke in tones low and reverential, apropos of profundity, Ernest could hardly resist laughing.

The day after his meeting with Pound, Ernest wrote an acidic character sketch of him. Then he called on Pound, and they walked down to the gym on Boulevarde Raspail, where Ernest had earned money sparring. Although Ezra was clumsy and ineffectual in the ring (he would quickly exhaust himself swinging at Ernest with great, looping blows), Ernest could not help but admire him for not once "slacking it" in four hard rounds. Ernest also liked it that Pound, fifteen years his senior, would, with good humor, tolerate the indignity of being dumped on his pants now and then. Behind Pound's nonsense and affectation, there was someone worthwhile.

Like Ezra Pound, Gertrude Stein had a colossal ego. (She once said that Paris was "the place that suited those of us that were to create the twentieth century art and literaure.") As of 1922, Gertrude Stein had written *Three Lives,* stories of women absorbed in the lives of other women; *Tender Buttons,* prose poems full of original images and ideas; and *The Making of Americans,* a sprawling experiment in the novel that had degenerated into self-indulgence.

Like Pound, Gertrude Stein was what Ernest would later call "lazy," meaning that without finishing up what she had started, she was always starting something new. Although considered a brilliant student at Harvard College (William James, who taught her philosophy, had said so), she had left Harvard without a degree. After traveling extensively in Europe with her brother, Leo, she enrolled in Johns Hopkins Medical School. Five years later, she failed her final exam. Next it was Europe, this time to her brother in Italy and then, on her own, to London. Finally, in 1903, Gertrude settled in Paris at 27 Rue de Fleurus, where she would live for the next thirty-seven years.

When Ernest met Gertrude Stein, in March 1922, she was fat and in her late forties. She had thick, beautiful hair and the face of an Indian man. Miss Stein and her lover, Alice Toklas, a tiny, hatchet-faced woman with a soft, pleasant voice, came to visit the Hemingways at Rue du Cardinal Lemoine. After struggling up the four flights of narrow stairs, Gertrude seated herself on the mahogany bed (the most comfortable piece of furniture for her in the flat) and reviewed all the work Ernest showed her. She said she "rather liked" his poems, but she did not care for his Nick Adams novel. She told him that his " .escription" was not good, and that he should "begin over and concentrate."

Because Ernest was proud of his ability to render the natural world (the editors at the *Toronto Star* had praised this in his work), this criticism made him furious. Ernest knew Gertrude was a lesbian, and so he brought out the most "sexual" story he had. Gertrude read "Up in Michigan"—a delicate presentation of the irresistible desire women feel for men—and pronounced it *inaccrochable* ("it can't be hung"). Ernest would always feel he stimulated something in Gertrude, as she did in him. But that night, he was sure Gertrude knew he wanted to make love to her. That she clearly enjoyed this knowledge was worth more to Ernest than all the talk.

The third person Sherwood Anderson had told Ernest to look up in Paris was another American, Sylvia Beach. Sylvia ran a rental library and a bookstore, Shakespeare and Company, at 12 Rue de l'Odeon. Miss Beach, as Ernest called her, was, like Gertrude Stein, a lesbian, but petite, with sharp features and piercing black eyes. Ernest told Hadley Miss Beach reminded him of a small animal, self-sufficient, but friendly. He found Sylvia's hair very attractive, "cut thick below her ears and at the line of the collar of the brown velvet jacket she wore." He noticed that she had lovely legs.

Sylvia Beach knew of Ernest before he came into the shop—probably from a letter from Sherwood Anderson—and she did everything she could to make the "shy, hesitant newcomer," as she called him, feel comfortable. Ernest told Sylvia that he had no money with him for the customary deposit. Sylvia said that that was all right. He could bring in the money anytime. She filled out a card for him, and said he could take books with him that day.

From the ceiling-high shelves of books, Ernest picked Turgenev, two volumes of *A Sportsman's Sketches,* and D. H. Lawrence's *Sons and Lovers.* Sylvia asked if that was all he wanted. Because he had not paid yet, Ernest was embarrassed about taking anything more. But when Miss Beach seemed annoyed at his timidity, he took the Constance Garnett edition of *War and Peace* and *The Gambler and Other Stories* by Dostoyevski. Ernest had heard that Miss Beach had published James Joyce's new novel, *Ulysses,* and he asked her when Joyce might come in. In the late afternoon, she said. Ernest did not particularly like the Irish. He felt they were sentimental and enjoyed being pitied. Under the guise of innocence, they were very shrewd. Nevertheless, he knew how good he would have to be to match Joyce's *Dubliners,* and that maybe *Ulysses* was beyond his range.

Before he left, Ernest told Miss Beach about a book he had just reviewed for the *Toronto Star*. It was the first book review he had ever done. The book was the novel *Batouala,* which had recently won the prestigious Goncourt Prize as the best novel of the year. While most of the literary community of Paris praised the book for its rendering of life in the African village that gave the book its title, others—the "patriots," the politicians, the critics who saw literature primarily as propaganda— were furious. In telling the story of *Batouala,* the author, René Maran, born in Martinique and educated in France, presented an incontestable indictment of French policy in Africa. There was no polemic in the book—only facts, presented by a man who had been there, written in the plain, understated prose Ernest admired. Ernest had written, "You smell the smells of the village, you eat its food, you see the white man as the black man sees him, and after you have lived in the village you die there. That is all there is to the story, but when you have read it, you have seen Batouala, and that makes it a great novel."

When Ernest had worked well in his top-floor room at the Hotel Verlaine, he would walk down to the river toward the book stalls on the quai opposite Notre Dame. There was one particular book stall, behind the Tour d'Argent restaurant, where he could find recently published American books, books that had been left by American tourists in the rooms above the restaurant. Since they were printed in English, the proprietress of the stall thought these books of little value and sold them to Ernest for a few centimes. During friendly chats, the bookseller expressed what Ernest knew was a popular approach to literary criticism. "First there are the pictures," she said. "Then it is a question of the quality of the pictures. Then it is the binding. If a book is good, the owner will have it bound properly. All books in English are bound, but bound badly. There is no way of judging them."

Ernest found something else of value on the quais of the Seine. If he was having difficulty writing, and could not put his troubles out of his mind, he would walk down to where the fishermen of Paris fished for *gougon*. These fishermen were very serious about their sport and usually were fishing for their food. Using long, jointed cane poles and fine leaders, and baiting their piece of water, they'd end the day with a bucketful of the little fish, "plump and sweet-fleshed with a finer flavor than fresh sardines." Seeing people work with confidence and skill for what they needed to survive inspired Ernest, and gave him confidence he could also work that way.

In early April, just when the winter rains softened and the Luxembourg Gardens started to bloom again, Ernest heard from John Bone, his editor in Toronto. Bone wanted Ernest to cover the International Economic Conference about to begin in Genoa. All the world powers, except for the United States, would be there, and the future of international trade would be decided.

The assignment to Genoa reminded Ernest of all the reasons he had for hating journalism. He would use up great chunks of his time, his energy, and whatever talent he had on work that would be discarded in a day. Besides, he'd have to travel south in a cattle car of reporters and, because of his inexperience on the "European scene," be deferential and friendly to men he didn't even know. Then there was the weather. Genoa was always as damp as a swamp and, in April, was as hot as Chicago in July. He told Hadley that, mark his words, he'd come home very sick from this trip. As he raged against the injustice of it all, Hadley burned with frustration. Yes, it was horrible, but, by God, what could she do?

Pressure usually drove Ernest to reckon up his resources. He had to be sure about one thing, he told Hadley—that he'd never ask his parents for a dime. Before he and Hadley had left for Paris, they had given Kate Smith, Ernest's former lover and one of Hadley's best friends, all the money they had saved for a trip to Italy, a trip they'd planned during their courtship. Katy had put the money in her safe-deposit box—more than eight hundred dollars' worth of lire. Ernest wrote to Kate immediately. He told her all about how happy he and Hadley were, and what a beautiful place they had found to be alone together in the Swiss Alps. Then, apparently as an afterthought, he gently reminded Kate of the money and asked her to send it right away.

The night before the Hemingways' wedding in 1921, Kate, who had been Hadley's maid of honor, had predicted that the marriage would not last. And she had made clear to Ernest that she did not want it to last. Kate never answered Ernest's letter. But she did write this poem on the back of the final page:

> You have brought me
> Sudden long gusts
> Bowing full wet leafed trees
> Under a lightning shattered sky
>
> I am not of the eagle's race
> But you have sent me high

High into the loveliest sky-deeps
High into the coldest airless places,

I am not of the eagle's race
But you have driven me up
Alone
I do not even know
If you are above me
Or below

Weight of snow
Bending the pine boughs to earth
Would be light to me
Weight of still snow
Bending the pine boughs
To snap.

The trip south was just what Ernest had expected. The older reporters were drunk most of the time and played mentor to the younger
ones, willingly servile and fawning. On his first day in Genoa, Ernest
was "blown up" by a gas water heater. The pilot light for the burners
beneath the copper coil had gone out, and when Ernest tried to relight
it with a cigarette, the seeping gas exploded. His wounds—an eight-inch
gash in his right shin, a badly bruised left hip, a sprained wrist—were
bad enough, he wrote Hadley. But the skin had been burned off the
palm of his right hand. How was he going to take all those notes when
he couldn't even hold his pencil?

To transcend his "rotten luck," Ernest decided not to think about
misfortune. In fact, he would no longer use that word. He would now
divide life into times of action and times of contemplation. Bad luck,
in times of action, had to be thought of as if it were bad weather. One
had to tighten up and focus in. Taking his cue from the Canadian
representative at the conference, Sir Charles Gordon, who said upon
his arrival, "Canada's chief interest in the Genoa Conference is the
recognition of Russia," Ernest fixed his attention on the inscrutable
Soviet delegation and its leader, George Tchitcherin.

Ernest first met Tchitcherin at the end of a hot, eighteen-mile ride
from Genoa to Rapallo. Tchitcherin was tall and blond, and dressed in
new clothes. He looked like an up-and-coming businessman to Ernest,
except that there was a red rectangular badge on his lapel, signifying
the Soviet. Ernest noticed that Tchitcherin talked with a purr because
of missing front teeth.

Ernest admired George Tchitcherin because he could speak French and German and English, and spoke to the reporters in their own languages. Also, he ignored the photographers, even though rumor had it that czarist sympathizers used bombs disguised as cameras.

Tchitcherin was cool under questioning, giving a clearly stated, unapologetic response to questions about the persecution in Russia of moderate socialists, about the Russian famine (he said that four years of blockade had made the famine, but that all of Russia was being taxed to help the starving), and about the rights of foreign capital in Russia (it would be perfectly secure, but Russia would resist all attempts by consortiums to make it a colony).

Most of Ernest's stories about the Genoa conference were about Tchitcherin and the Russians. He knew his editor at the *Star* wanted it that way. But there was something else, too. More than any other delegation—the pompous, bitter Germans, the ineffectual Italians, the belligerent and vindictive French—Ernest admired the Russians for their single-minded devotion to duty. Much as he was revolted by communism as a system of government, a way of life, he was deeply moved that these men had fought for years to become the leaders of a country they could not even enter without risking death. Finally, there was "the way the light shone out from under the crack at the base of the door of their council room at three o'clock in the morning."

While Ernest found much to like about the serious, devoted professionalism of Tchitcherin, the most attractive diplomat he saw at the conference was the British prime minister, David Lloyd George. Ernest described the prime minister's departure from the Royal Palace in Genoa this way: "The magnificently uniformed carabinieri stiffened to a rigid attention, a big limousine slipped quietly into gear and rolled forward from the row of cars parked in the hot sun of the palace courtyard, three photographers squatted and aimed their Graflexes and David Lloyd George, smiling, assured, and beautiful with his fresh young face, his smooth-brushed white hair, and his smile-wrinkled eyes, climbed into the car, leaned back, bowed, and the car slid down the driveway and into the street."

Ernest wrote to Hadley that he saw in Lloyd George the kind of man he hoped one day to be. "George," as the cognoscenti called him, had the two things Ernest, because he felt he did not have them, valued most: aristocratic charm and self-assurance. Ernest said that Lloyd George carried the magic of grandeur with him wherever he went.

When Ernest returned from the Economic Conference at Genoa, he brought with him some fresh ideals. One was the professionalism and the dedication of the Russian, Tchitcherin; another was the grace of the Britisher, Lloyd George. But Ernest had also discovered something that was directly applicable to his writing.

The performance of the diplomat was, in fact, a work of art. The presentation was full of nuance and suggestion, full of signals to the informed, attentive audience. It had to be decorous and professional—the illusion of sincerity created and sustained. Ernest saw that what was not said in these meetings was often more important than what was. And with this "style," diplomats changed the world.

# 2

## His Heart to School

As Ernest had predicted, he returned from Genoa sick with the worst "spring throat" he said he'd had since childhood. He was certain of fever, and in the mirror he could see, at the back of his throat, two big sacs of pus and many white patches. Before lying down, Ernest would scrape his throat with a toothbrush, and then gargle with alcohol and water. Hadley thought the toothbrush a bad idea and said so. Ernest settled for a gargle, and rest in bed.

Propped up on pillows, with his Corona on his lap, Ernest spent each afternoon of his convalescence writing letters and watching the steady cold drizzle that, he told Hadley, would probably keep on and ruin May. As soon as his fever was gone, Ernest said, they should head for the mountains again, for Chamby. Their week there in January had been "lovely"—they both agreed to this—and they'd had, Ernest said, a "wonderful" time. Besides, the mountains were the best cure for his throat.

Hadley knew her husband was right. Chamby was a good idea. And yet she was less pleased than, for his sake, she appeared. Hadley remembered that on their last trip to Chamby Ernest had become restless, agitated, not quite satisfied with anything she said or did. Hadley knew it wasn't their lovemaking. In the mountains especially, they'd always had a "fine time" in bed. It was just that Ernest needed something more than she, alone, could give. Although he liked to speak of "us against the world," Hadley knew better. She was not surprised when Ernest announced that for this trip he would invite a wartime friend to join them—a tall, handsome Irishman, an officer in the British service, Eric Dorman-Smith.

When Ernest met Dorman-Smith in Italy in 1918, "Chink," as Ernest called him, was a twenty-three-year-old lieutenant in the Northumberland Fusiliers. A braggart and an anglophile, he affected the clipped manner of speaking of the English officers and their studied nonchalance. Even then, Ernest recognized Chink for what he was. But Ernest enjoyed creating heroes as much as he delighted in nicknaming his friends. As he had done with Agnes von Kurowsky, Ernest made up a persona for Dorman-Smith. To Ernest, Chink would be a cultured warrior, possessed of that rare synthesis of imagination and courage Ernest hoped one day to achieve himself.

During the week of preparation for the trip to Chamby, Hadley nurtured her enthusiasm. She had recently discovered that the delicious liquors Ernest kept in good supply—rum, Asti Spumante (her special favorite), and Cinzano Vermouth—could make almost anything fun.

In mid-May, Ernest and Hadley left Paris for the Gangwisch pension at Chamby. Dorman-Smith, now stationed in Germany, had arranged a furlough, and he joined them there. Chink met the Hemingways in full dress: a safari hat, two natural wool sweaters, short suspendered pants, and hobnailed boots—the "uniform" of the British mountaineer. Ernest thought Chink quick-witted and loquacious, and urged his friend to put on a show for Hadley. Dorman-Smith cheerfully complied, and fell to treating Ernest as he had in Milan—with good-humored condescension, calling him "Popplethwaite," a word that Ernest, because he could not clearly pronounce his *l*'s, had trouble saying. Hadley was not as charmed as Ernest thought she'd be. She resented Chink's immediate assumption of a superior familiarity with her. She should have been Mrs. Hemingway or, at least, Hadley, and not "Mrs. Popplethwaite," especially to a stranger four years younger than she.

Ernest and Chink, and Hadley, too, drank their way through the next two weeks. First there was a climb of Cape au Moine, then "lugeing" down through the snow fields on their backsides. A few days later, they climbed the Dent du Jaman. Then, before dawn one morning, Ernest left the inn in Aigle and went fishing in the yard-wide Rhone Canal. Not to be outdone that day, Dorman-Smith went off climbing alone. According to the report he gave Ernest, as they sat drinking beer after beer at a smoky café in Bain des Allaiz, he once had to cross a torrent so wide and deep he had almost been drowned. Ernest beerfully lauded Chink's daring, while Hadley slept on the grass just out-side the windows.

For their last two days together, Ernest suggested they all hike over the Grand St. Bernard into Italy—fifty-seven kilometers, on bad road, in wet spring snow. Halfway there, the air became so thin Hadley had to stop again and again, and breathe deeply, and endure the pa-tronizing of the men. Ernest and Chink had on their hobnailed boots. But Hadley had forgotten hers in Paris, and so she sloshed along in low American Oxfords.

At the Hospice of St. Bernard, contrary to myth, the dogs that greeted Ernest, Hadley, and Chink had no brandy casks tied around their necks. But, in their big-pawed, slack-jowled way, they couldn't have been more friendly. That night, the monks served hot tea mixed with wine, hot soup, bread, and cheese, and told their guests the story of St. Bernard.

In the first century, the monks said, the Romans built the roadway through the pass, and, not far from where the hospice was now, erected a temple to their chief god, Jupiter. For many years this was the safest and most-traveled route through the mountains. Then, with the fall of Rome, the barbarians—Huns, Vandals, Saracens—took over. Still, Char-lemagne had been able to travel the road in safety, on his way to be crowned in Rome. But, eventually, the pass fell under the control of marauders and thieves and was hardly used at all.

In the tenth century, a wealthy young nobleman, Bernard de Men-thon, returned from his studies in Paris and announced he would be-come a monk. His father, a great feudal baron, was furious. He had, he told his son, arranged a marriage. Then he jailed Bernard to ensure his presence at the ceremony. The night before the wedding, according to legend, Bernard tore the bars from his cell and escaped.

Within a few years Bernard had earned a reputation as a Christian hero, a defender of the weak, and an agent of the Lord's justice. He was gentle as a dove, the people said, but strong as a lion. He feared nothing.

One night, a handful of pilgrims came to ask Bernard's help. The pass had been blocked by Procus, a barbarian giant who worshipped Jupiter. Bernard led the villagers up to the Plain of Jupiter, as it was called, and challenged Procus. During the fight, the pagan changed himself into a dragon. Bernard threw his cape around the dragon's neck, and it became a chain which held the dragon down while Ber-nard, like the great snows of winter, smothered him. Freed of Procus, the villagers destroyed the statue of Jupiter and the pass was cleansed.

After the storytelling and the evening prayer—the medieval chants rolling out over the moonlit snow—Ernest and Hadley and Chink were led through arched stone corridors, lit dimly and then only at long intervals. Their rooms were clammy cells, their beds hard. With the legend of the saint to dream of, Ernest felt they would spend the night at the end of the world.

Two days later, when Ernest and Hadley saw Chink off at the Garibaldi Station in Milan, Ernest took pride in telling Dorman-Smith how he planned to go on to Italy. Hadley listened to this with dismay. She was exhausted; her feet were still blistered raw. Nothing now seemed better to her than those little rooms on the fourth floor at 74 Rue du Cardinal Lemoine. But Ernest insisted on taking a backward look. Come what may, he would see his wartime barracks at Schio again and stand on the bank of the Piave River, on the spot where, in 1918, he'd been wounded and nearly killed.

Before he and Hadley left for the Dolomites, Ernest said he'd had an idea. The Italian Fascist Mussolini was the most infamous man in Europe, and Ernest had been fascinated by what he'd read about him. In 1914, when war broke out, Mussolini was the editor of *Avanti,* a paper in Milan. Because he was a strong supporter of the Allies, and the socialist owners of the paper were not, he was fired. By begging and borrowing, Mussolini raised enough to start his own paper, *Popolo d'Italia.* When Italy entered the war, Mussolini immediately joined the Bersagliere, an elite corps noted for their extraordinary bravery under fire and for the cock-feathered hats they wore.

Like Mussolini himself, Ernest had been severely wounded in Italy, and had received the Silver Medal for Valor. That was the connection, Ernest believed, that would get him an interview. Ernest thought he might even wear his own Bersagliere hat for the meeting—the hat he'd worn when he stepped off the troop ship that brought him home from Italy in 1919.

Just as Ernest expected, Mussolini said he would be happy to talk to a young American who had shed his blood for Italy. During the two-hour interview, he told Ernest how it had all gotten started. Back in 1915, when the Communists were about to take over all of northern Italy, Mussolini had organized his own anti-Communist shock troops, the Fascisti. In two years they had not only succeeded in defeating the Communists but had become the most powerful political party in the country. Mussolini impressed Ernest as a strong-willed, surprisingly intelligent man who, with the same deliberation he used in speaking simple Italian to Ernest, was deciding the fate of his country for years to come. Ernest did not especially like Mussolini, but he admired him for his love of country, his belief in himself, and the loyalty he inspired.

By the time Ernest had arranged, conducted, and then written up the interview with Mussolini, Hadley was "sick" of Milan. Ernest said he was tired, and sick too—the throat again. Nevertheless, he insisted on taking Hadley to see the old house on the Via Bacheto, the Red Cross "hospital" where he had recovered from his wounds and where, Hadley knew, he had made love to his nurse and had asked her to marry him. Later, Ernest took Hadley to Biffi's in the Galleria, for sentimental reasons, he said. It was the place he and Agnes often dined. Hadley hated all this, and Ernest knew it. But he could not resist living through it all again.

At eighteen, during the war, Ernest had thought of Schio as "one of the finest places on earth. It was a little town in the Trentino, under the shoulder of the Alps, and it contained all the good cheer, amusement and relaxation a man could desire." Going back there four years later, Ernest found that everything had changed. Ever so carefully, he recorded this change and the sadness and disappointment that it caused him. He wrote for the *Star:*

> . . . Schio seemed to have shrunk. I walked up one side of the long, narrow main street looking in shop windows at the fly-specked shirts, the cheap china dishes, the postcards showing about seven different varieties of a young man and a young girl looking into each other's eyes, the stiff, fly-specked pastry, the big, round loaves of sour bread. At the end of the street were the mountains, but I had walked over the St. Bernard Pass the week before and the mountains, without snow caps, looked rain-furrowed and dull; not much more than hills. I looked at the mountains a long time, though, and then walked down the other side of the street to the principal bar. It was starting to rain a little and the shopkeepers were lowering the shutters in front of their shops.

At the place where he had been wounded on the Piave River, the change was even more dramatic than in Schio. The grotesque reconstruction of the war-shattered town was a desecration:

> We stopped the car in Fossalta and got out to walk. All the shattered, tragic dignity of the wrecked town was gone. In its place was a new, smug, hideous collection of plaster houses, painted bright blues, reds, and yellows. I had been in Fossalta perhaps fifty times and I would not

have recognized it. The new plaster church was the worst looking thing. The trees that had been splintered and gashed showed their scars if you looked for them, and had a stunted appearance, but you could not have told in passing, unless you had known, how they had been torn.

Ernest and Hadley were back in Paris when he wrote these beautiful lines. They were a part of an article that the *Star* entitled "A Veteran Visits the Old Front." Everything on Ernest's long-awaited trip to Italy had been a disappointment. And the two weeks with Dorman-Smith in the Alps had been a farce. Yet from these mistakes, this waste of life, had come a firsthand knowledge of the pain and the permanence of change. To his old friend and roommate and groom man at his wedding, Bill Horne, Ernest wrote: "Horney we've got to go on. We can't ever go back to old things or try and get the 'old kick' out of something or find things the way we remembered them. We have them as we remember them and they are fine and wonderful and we have to go on and have other things because the old things are nowhere except in our minds now. I suppose this sounds like all sorts of Merde from the good old manure spreader." From then on, Ernest knew that the only way to make the past come true again was through his art.

After the sadness of Italy, Hadley knew that Ernest needed cheering up. She tried pretending that it really had been great fun crossing the St. Bernard with Chink, and she said all the sensible things about how good it was, really, that Italy had rebuilt so quickly. She took Ernest for long walks to make him hungry, and then suggested they dine at that "wonderful place," Michaud's. Unfortunately, nothing helped— that is, until Bastille Day, the fourteenth of July, came around.

Bastille Day, 1922, was something more than the usual celebration. That year it began on Wednesday night, the thirteenth, went on all that night, all day Thursday, all Thursday night, and so on—until Sunday night, the seventeenth. Everything, except the liquor stores, was closed for four days. The government spent millions of francs on the party. Flags were everywhere; fireworks went off at all hours of the day and night. Every two blocks, streets were closed to traffic by a party.

In the Place de la Contrascarpe, just below the Hemingways' flat, an accordionist, two drummers, a cornetist, and an honest-to-goodness bagpiper played indefatigably. Their stage was a wagon set on four wine casks and covered with branches broken from trees in the Tuileries Gardens. Shop girls, butchers, bakers, laborers, tram conductors, laundresses polkaed round and round.

Hadley knew that Ernest loved to dance, and she took him down to the crowd in the streets. There was much good-spirited partner changing, and Ernest appeared to have a wonderful time. Eventually, some of the dancers moved into the nearby Bal Musette, where the "apaches" of the Quarter hung out with their girls. Ernest and Hadley sat on a long bench in the heavy, smoky air, and listened as another accordion player, seated on the small stage between two white lamps in the shape of dice, played love songs. At the wall tables, young women, apparently without partners, hunched over their drinks; a grinning, drunken man stood by the door. Suddenly, Hadley told Ernest that she was frightened. Ernest took her up to their apartment and soon rediscovered how lucky he was to have such a girl.

Ernest was doing well with his journalism, but he had made no progress toward his real goal: to publish a book of fiction. Although nothing had come of his "connections" so far, Ernest felt he must still pursue people who ran the small presses, people who were willing to take a chance on an unknown.

On the trip to Genoa, Ernest had met a young man with a degree from Trinity College in Connecticut. His name was Bill Bird; he had plenty of family money, and he had talked of starting a press. Ernest told Hadley he thought it would be a good idea to invite Bill Bird and his wife, Sally, for a hike through the Black Forest.

In part to impress the Birds, in part because he had loved the idea of flying ever since he'd watched biplanes strain over the Duomo from his hospital-room window in Milan, Ernest bought two tickets on the Franco-Rumanian Aero Company's flight into Strasbourg. The trip would take two and a half hours, he told Hadley, compared to ten hours by express train.

Ernest first saw the plane from the window of the taxi he and Hadley took to the field. It was a silver biplane with a tiny cabin with portholes, and a seat for the pilot in the rear. Ernest bought the tickets at a counter in the plane shed, and had them checked by an attendant who stood just ten feet away, by the door to the field. Then, with cotton stuffed into their ears, Ernest and Hadley climbed aboard the plane and sat one behind the other. The pilot, a short, little man with his cap on backwards, shouted contact, and the mechanic gave the propeller a spin.

As the little plane climbed straight east from Paris, the landscape slowly became yellow and brown and green squares, and the forests looked as soft as velvet. Over St. Mihiel, Ernest saw the trenches zigzagging through a field, and the shell holes of the Front. Sometimes the pilot flew so low that Ernest could see bicyclists rolling like pennies down a narrow white strip of road. As the plane drove through a misty rain, the foothills of the Vogues seemed to swell up to meet it.

On the ground at Strasbourg, Ernest totaled up. Except for the strong smell of castor oil from the engine, the trip had been all he'd expected. And it gave him a certain advantage with the Birds. They had chosen the safety of the train.

In Italy, Ernest had found that the effects of the war had all but disappeared. But this was not true in Germany. Defeated in war, the German people now suffered the scourge of reparation. The European Allies, led by the French (who were perhaps the most vengeful because, fighting alone, they had been crushed by the Germans), insisted that the Germans should "pay" for the war. To this end they set about extracting everything of value the German people had to give. Naturally, the Germans grew to hate the French, and then, finally, all the *Auslanders*.

In one way, travel in Germany was cheap—cheaper than Ernest believed possible. It cost eighty cents a day for the Hemingways and the Birds to stay at a Freiburg hotel. But in another way, travel in Germany cost a great deal. Wherever the two couples went, they encountered rudeness, hostility, and abuse.

Ernest was furious at everything: the obstructionist local officials who made getting a fishing permit an excruciating ordeal, the offensive young men with shaved heads or hair cut like porcupine quills, who toured the countryside in bands of six or eight, "their knees bare, cock feathers in their hats, sauerkraut on the breath, the wanderlust in their eyes and a collection of aluminum cooking utensils clashing against their legs." At his first overnight stop, Ernest endured the stupid, camel-like wife of the innkeeper, the bad wine, the sour black bread, the manure piles smoking below the bedroom windows.

Then, to make matters worse, Ernest behaved in a way he considered disgraceful. It happened one night in the dining room of some "sauerkraut inn." Ernest and Hadley, Bill and Sally had a table for five. (They had been joined by a pathetic American woman who had studied opera in Berlin.) Two blond German men sat close by, at the end of a long table. When Hadley and Sally Bird wished to pass on their way to the ladies' toilet, the young Germans refused to move their chairs. The girls had no choice but to walk the long way around.

While the Hemingways and the Birds dined, the Germans insulted them, making sure their gestures conveyed what the Americans might miss in the language. When the Germans decided to leave, they pushed at Ernest's chair, and, before he could stop himself, he rose to let them pass.

But then came the rage. Ernest turned on the Germans. "Du bist ein schweinhund," he said. Bill Bird grabbed a bottle by the neck, and the Germans retreated. Although Hadley "understood" everything Ernest said about why he'd moved that "goddamn chair," Ernest couldn't let go of the incident for months.

Toward the end of the trip, Ernest wrote to the "Dear Folks" back in Oak Park, Illinois. But the letter was really for his father, who had sent him handkerchiefs for his birthday. He wrote about how good trout fishing in the Black Forest had been. His old McGintys, he said, seemed to have an international flavor. Then he spoke of the German money he'd enclosed for "Dad." The notes were worthless, but very beautiful. He had saved some better ones for his father for a long time. But then he'd had to spend them.

Ernest and Hadley weren't back in Paris a week when a cable arrived from Ernest's editor at the *Star*, ordering him to Constantinople to cover the Greco-Turkish war. This time, Hadley said, she'd had enough. Why did Ernest have to run off to these terrible places and leave her alone? They had enough money to live on; her trust fund gave them that. As it turned out, the journalism money was, really, "extra." So why should Ernest choose to be at John Bone's beck and call?

Ernest knew these were good, hard questions. He knew he had his own writing, his poetry and fiction, to do. Why indeed should he waste his time and energy on journalism? But the truth was that he needed, more than anything else just then, an appreciative audience. A month earlier, with Ezra Pound's assurances, Ernest had sent six poems to Scofield Thayer at the *Dial*, and one of his best stories, "The Three-Day Blow," to Margaret Anderson and Jane Heap at *The Little Review*. Margaret Anderson had rejected the story, and Scofield Thayer had turned down the poems. John Bone, on the other hand, had praised Ernest's work and said he would publish in the *Star* anything Ernest wrote. When Ernest left for the Gare de Lyon, September 25, 1922, Hadley had not spoken to him for three days. Hadley knew she was in the wrong, but this time, she told herself, she just didn't care.

The four-day trip on the Simplon-Orient Express gave Ernest an unexpected pleasure, and an insight that took his mind off the troubles at home. As the long, brown train rolled across fields and mountains, Europe in September looked green and golden and ripe. The bleak-sounding Balkans turned out to be the most beautiful country Ernest had ever seen. Then on the flat, rich, green and brown plain of Lombardy, there were rows of poplars, thick mulberry hedges, dry riverbeds with pebbles as big and white as hen's eggs. At twilight, Ernest watched white oxen moving along dusty roads, and the white shaft of a campanile against the evening sky. In the morning, a blue late-September haze covered fields of yellowing tobacco. Flocks of sheep and herds of cattle grazed among beech groves, and heaps of yellow pumpkins sat ripening in the shocked corn. Now and then came a cottage, with peat smoke rising from the chimney. Yes, Ernest decided. There were just wars, wars to be fought as long as one people held the land of another people. It was all a matter of mine and thine.

Ernest shared his compartment on the Simplon Express with a Serb. The young man spoke what he considered "American" English. He had been to school in Boston, he said. In one of the blue notebooks, Ernest recorded the Serb's drunken conversation: "Say. Wattaya think I paid for this coat in Paris? Hundernfiftey francs. Pretty good? Huh? Wanta see picture my girl? Some girl? Huh? I got a better-looking girl but her picture's in my trunk. Say, look at that Italian officer. Don't he look just like a woman? I bet he wears corsets. Don't tell me a guy dresses like that can fight. Say, ain't he a scream?"

Ernest saw that the Italian, who wore a monocle, had three wound stripes and a British Military Cross. The Serb's boorishness reminded Ernest of all the worst things about his own country and yet, in some strange way, made him miss it very much.

Ernest got his first look at Constantinople as the train wound down a "sun-baked, treeless, rolling plain to the sea." Across the blue water there was a big brown island, and beyond that the bulk of the Asian shore. Suddenly there were high stone walls and then dilapidated wooden tenements. A Frenchman standing, looking out the window with Ernest, cried, "Stamboul."

Ernest had seen the Chicago stockyards, the jails in Kansas City, the naval yard districts of New York on the Lower East Side. In Milan there'd been squalor, on the Left Bank in Paris plenty of filth. Yet nothing had prepared him for that morning vision of "storied East."

In "Stamboul," Ernest found himself immersed in the dirty, foul-smelling, pathetic, crowded, and poor. The city was like a great ancient carcass, yielding itself to the maggots of modern life. Rumor had it that Constantinople would soon be put under siege by a quarter of a million Turkish troops under the command of the short and stolid, blond and blue-eyed bandit named Kemal. Kemal—absurdly, Ernest felt—called himself "Pasha."

As Ernest rode to his hotel in a taxi, he passed over a long bridge. The boats were packed so close on both sides that he could not see the water. "What's that?" he asked the interpreter he had hired, "the Golden Horn?" "Yes," the interpreter answered. Ernest thought it looked like the Chicago River.

To Ernest, all the foreign buildings in Constantinople—the American Embassy, the Allied police commission, the British Embassy—looked like Carnegie libraries. At the Rumanian and Armenian consulates, lines of refugees seeking visas and passports wound out into the street. In the face of the threat from Kemal, governmental assurance of safety meant nothing to these people. They remembered the atrocities the Turks had committed at Smyrna, and they had, Ernest believed, the racial memory of a thousand years of abuse besides.

After the long train ride, Ernest cleaned up as best he could at the filthy little Hotel de Londres. Then he "stood on the dusty, rubbish-strewn hillside of Pera . . . and looked down at the harbor, forested with masts and grimy with smoke funnels and across the dust-covered hills on the other side where the Turkish town sprawled in square mud-colored houses, ramshackle tenements with the dirty-white fingers of minarets rising like gray-white slim lighthouses out of the muddled houses." Ezra Pound had dismissed the West as "an old bitch gone in the teeth, / . . . a botched civilization. . . . For two gross of broken statues, / For a few thousand battered books." What a fool Pound was, Ernest thought. How false and petulant that estimate seemed beside the true corruption of the East.

On the seventeenth of October, Ernest left for home. A hundred and thirty miles later, his train pulled into Adrianople. Under the threat of the Turk, the entire Christian population of eastern Thrace had left their homes and were now crossing the Maritza River. On the main road, close by the track, Ernest saw astonishing sights. The column of refugees was twenty miles long. Despite severe chill and fever (Ernest was certain he had malaria), he covered himself with two blankets from the compartment and went out into the road. In the rain, he watched the ghastly procession, herded by Greek cavalry, pass by.

Ernest learned something about communal terror that day. First, when panic has long since passed, terror is silent. No one has enough

strength of body or spirit for displays of any kind. A look at the faces
told him everyone was in despair. Then there was the evidence of dese-
crated pride. The peasants, when they began the march, had dressed in
their finest, most colorful clothes. Now, soaked and draggled, gaunt-
eyed, no better off than the pigs that slopped beside them in the mud,
they had lost even the dignity that suffering gives. While Ernest looked
on, a woman delivered a baby in the back of a moving wagon, her
husband trying to protect her with a blanket that kept flapping in the
wind.

When Hadley brought Ernest home from the Gare de Lyon at half
past six the morning of October 21, he was as sick as she had ever seen
him. More than anything else, Ernest said, he wanted to go to bed. But
Hadley said no. She saw that Ernest was indescribably filthy, and
since he was too tired to wash himself, she'd do it for him. Then there
was the problem of lice. The horrid little things were in Ernest's hair,
all over his clothes, and in his luggage. He would have to soak in a tub
of hot water and creolene. Then another tub and more creolene for his
clothes.

While Hadley used the fine-toothed comb on Ernest's hair, he told
her about Madame Marie, a fat, slovenly Croatian, whose hotel he'd
stayed at. She was, like the lice that covered his room, a parasite. She
had the only hotel on the main road, Ernest said, and she made money
off the officers of whatever army passed through. The Turks after the
Greeks one way, then the Greeks after the Turks again. What about
the poor people out on the road? Ernest had asked the Madame. "It is
always that way with the people," she said. *"Toujours la meme chose."*
Then she recited a Turkish proverb: "It is not only the fault of the
axe but of the tree as well." She said this was a good proverb. Later on,
Ernest said, she got drunk with him and tried to show him her softer
side. She knew that one hundred drachmas were too much for her
rooms. "But I have the only hotel here," she said. "It is better than the
street? Eh?"

Hadley told Ernest that the fever he had was probably not malaria,
and then she put him to bed. Ernest slept for twenty-four hours; then
he slept the better part of every day for a week. To his surprise, Hadley lay with him. It was time for a baby, she said.

Not long after Ernest returned from Constantinople, the effort he
had made to know useful people began to pay off. Ezra Pound told
him he intended to make "an inquest into the state of contemporary

English prose," and planned to edit a half-dozen small books to that
end. Of course, Ernest would contribute something. William Bird, Ernest's friend from the Black Forest trip, would be the publisher. Bird
had set up shop at 29 Quai d'Anjou. He'd named his company "Three
Mountains Press," after the three "hills" of Paris.

Another contact paid off, too. Harriet Monroe, the Chicago dowager
who published the prestigious magazine *Poetry,* had taken, most likely
at the urging of Sherwood Anderson, six of Ernest's poems. Printing
this poem, born of Ernest's brief experience at Mount Grappa, must
have been especially difficult for her:

*Riparto d'Assalto*
Drummed their boots on the camion floor,
Hob-nailed boots on the camion floor.
Sergeants stiff,
Corporals sore.
Lieutenants thought of a Mestre whore—
Warm and soft and sleepy whore,
Cozy, warm and lovely whore:
Damned cold, bitter, rotten ride,
Winding road up the Grappa side.
Arditi on benches stiff and cold,
Pride of their country stiff and cold,
Bristly faces, dirty hides—
Infantry marches, Arditi rides.
Grey, cold, bitter, sullen ride—
To splintered pines on the Grappa side
At Asalone, where the truck-load died.

Despite being in Paris, and the appreciation for his work he got
from John Bone, and the financial cushion Hadley's trust fund gave
him, Ernest found himself, in his poetry, drawn to images of frustration, futility, and despair. He thought very much about the war and
wrote many poems he kept to himself,

All armies are the same
Publicity is fame
Atillery makes the same old noise
Valor is an attribute of boys
Old soldiers all have tired eyes
All soldiers hear the same old lies
Dead bodies always have drawn flies

*Shock Troops*
Men went happily to death
But they were not the men
Who marched
For years
Up to the line.
These rode a few times
And were gone
Leaving a heritage of obscene song.


Arsiero, Asiago,
Half a hundred more,
Little border villages,
Back before the war,
Monte Grappa, Monte Corno,
Twice a dozen such,
In the piping times of peace
Didn't come to much.

For one strange poem, Ernest took on a female persona:

*Poem*
only
The first man I ever loved
Said good bye
And went away
He was killed in Picardy
On a sunny day.

I have slept with many men
wakened in the night and cried . . .

Ernest left off writing here, drew a cat, a snake, a fish, and a caricature of a carabinieri, an Italian military policeman.

Ernest knew he must be "nice" to many people he didn't like, all for the sake of publication. One was Ford Madox Heuffer, who, since the war, had said his name was Ford Madox Ford. Ernest couldn't stand Ford, physically. He hated Ford's yellowish-white, old man's hair, his pale-blue, watery eyes, his thick and dirty mustache. Ernest thought that Ford, barely forty, seemed to enjoy having prematurely gone to seed. Ernest had also seen that Ford's wife bullied him, and that Ford cultivated his submission to her until it appeared to be the best thing a gentleman could do. Despite this, Ernest had a measure of respect for

Ford. After all, Ford had earned a friend like Joseph Conrad and with *The Good Soldier* had proven himself a novelist.

While Ernest found Ford Madox Ford obnoxious, there was one type of "artist" Ernest hated: the literary poseur. Because Ernest felt art was sacred and believed in the artist's calling, he considered the fakers who ordained themselves and then drank and talked away their days no better, and just as dangerous, as counterfeit priests. Privately, and even publicly (in the *Toronto Star*), he called them "scum."

One such poseur arrived in Paris just after Ernest had recovered from his weeks in Turkey. He was Dave O'Neil, a forty-eight-year-old St. Louis native, a lumber dealer with a million dollars behind him and, he presumed, a career as a painter ahead. Ernest told Hadley, who had been close friends with O'Neil in St. Louis years before, that he believed in first impressions and that he considered O'Neil a pretentious fool. When Ernest was angry about something, he wrote to Ezra Pound, because Pound was usually angry about something, too.

[Dave O'Neil] is also writing a number of new poems. His system is to write a few words about something he doesn't understand. Anything he doesn't understand. The less he understands it the more "magic" the better the poem. He has re-acted sufficiently from your aroma, I think you were an aroma to him, a "magic" aroma to tell me that the words in a poem, i.e. cliches, Byronic phrases, Matthew Arnoldania; don't matter. It's the "magic" that matters. He also says that Rose O'Neil, who draws cupies, no Kewpies, has written much better poetry than Yeats. It is in the O'Neil blood. I suggested that he meant she had drawn better Kewpies than Yeats. This was not well received.

According to Ernest, another poseur of the first rank was Ernest Walsh. When Ernest met him, Walsh was only twenty-five years old. Yet he affected the role of "a man marked for death." Walsh had thick, black hair cut so it fell, conspicuously, over his forehead when he talked with passionate intensity, as he almost always did. His black Irish eyes sat deep in his sallow face, and his big-toothed smile charmed certain women. Walsh called himself a poet, and these ladies, especially, believed him. His current companion, Ethel Moorhead, was a rich, middle-aged American, trying to learn to paint.

Ernest felt sorry for Walsh. It was clear he had consumption, and would probably die of it. And Ernest was touched by the sincerity of the affection Miss Moorhead—as Ernest always called her—had for Walsh. It seemed as if she would forgive him anything. Walsh told Er-

nest that he and Ethel Moorhead planned to bring out a literary magazine, and he would want Ernest to contribute.

Holidays had always meant a lot to Ernest. They were occasions for
summing up, taking stock, for an inquest into the state of his life. By
Thanksgiving, 1922, Ernest and Hadley had been in Paris almost a
year. According to their plan, Ernest was to have become a full-time
artist and a part-time journalist. But it had turned out the other way
around. From January to October, Ernest had sent eighty-two articles
to the *Star*. That meant sixty-four thousand words. On the other hand,
Ernest had written only a few poems and stories. The poetry had had
some success: six pieces to Harriet Monroe's *Poetry,* one to the *Double-
Dealer* in New Orleans. But Ernest hadn't yet placed a story.

Besides the weeks spent on writing for the *Star*, Ernest had done a
lot of traveling: Genoa, the Balkans, Constantinople. Ernest said he
was sure he'd spent a month, at least, sleeping on trains. His faith in
journalism as the best training for a writer, he now thought misplaced.
Yes, it had worked for Richard Harding Davis and Stephen Crane. But
they had lived at a time when it took less effort to get through the daily
traffic of life. Ernest could recreate each thing he saw or learned only
once. After a year of journalism, he must begin to "economize"; he
must use his knowledge and experience in his fiction, where it would
do him the most good.

The second week in November 1922, John Bone ordered Ernest to
the Lausanne Peace Conference. Its work was, ideally, to end the Greco-
Turkish war, and to alleviate the suffering of people Ernest had seen
in those columns in the rain and mud in Adrianople. Ernest had
learned enough about international politics to be pessimistic about the
conferees' chance for success. Yet he knew there would be some good
men there, and that anything could happen. This time, Hadley did not
make a scene about Ernest's leaving. But it was terrible timing nevertheless. It came just during those days of the month when Hadley believed she had the best chance of becoming pregnant. The disappointment made her ill. Fortunately, she told Ernest, she had a good nurse
to take care of her—a female friend from Chicago, one of long standing. After an unhappy love affair at home, "Letticia" was traveling
alone in France.

Ernest got to Lausanne on November 22. The conference was to be
held not in the city itself, but rather in the nearby little town of
Ouchy. Lord Byron, Ernest learned, had once stayed there, at the lo-

cal inn. Ernest imagined the poet, resting his bad leg on a chair, at work on *The Prisoner of Chillon*. Ernest was fascinated by Byron—the handsome, talented aristocrat, irresistible to women, contemptuous of death—and by his poems. Unique in the literature Ernest knew, Byron had portrayed the hero as living just the sort of emotional life Ernest believed his had been. The Byronic hero, a born idealist, learns early and through pain that faith in anything or anybody usually ends with betrayal. He survives by force of will and comes "to love despair."

Ernest met another of his heroes at the Lausanne Conference, the Russian, George Tchitcherin. Tchitcherin had come with his usual message: the Dardanelles and the Bosporus must be closed to warships, otherwise Russia would be at the mercy of any nation that sent a fleet into the Black Sea. Ernest knew that this was the same old message Tchitcherin had had for the conference at Genoa. He saw how the Russian spoke with "the tired intensity of a man who is saying a thing for the hundredth time, who believes it and is as impassioned about it as the first time, but has become wearied from not being understood."

During a brief interview, Ernest actually got to shake Tchitcherin's hand, and he was shocked. The hand was cold and flaccid, and no matter how hard, how long Ernest squeezed, Tchitcherin would not respond. Gossip among the reporters had it that the high-minded, tough-talking Russian was as timid, physically, as a child. And he had a special weakness, too. Dressed as a girl for the first twelve years of his life, Tchitcherin now insisted on playing the soldier. He'd even had a German tailor fit him for a uniform that looked, to Ernest, like a costume for *The Nutcracker*. With this knowledge, Ernest observed the fragile, red-bearded Russian, inhuman in his capacity for work, distrustful of women, indifferent to publicity, public opinion, money, or anything else except his work and Russia, and admired him even more.

From Paris, Hadley wrote to Ernest every day. But Ernest seldom replied. Hadley accused Ernest of "stalling," and suggested that he didn't care if she came to him in Lausanne. Ernest wrote back immediately that he'd been "crazy" for her to come. But then he added, "if you say you are too miserable for the trip you know best." It was terrible, Ernest wrote, that Hadley had gotten so sick. But then he continued: "Anyway both being laid out with colds we haven't lost so much time on the time of the month because you've probably been too sick."

Ernest had some news, too, he said. His "old friend" from back home in Oak Park, Isabel Simmons, a sprightly dark-eyed twenty-year-old, would be coming to the Gangwisch pension in Chamby. Ernest called Isabel by pet names, and Hadley read between the lines. She decided to leave for Lausanne immediately, sickness or no.

To keep Ernest's mind on his fiction, the "first cause," as they had always called it, and to remind him of what she believed they were committed to, Hadley decided to bring along all of the stories she could find. She stuffed Ernest's manuscripts, typescripts, and carbons into a small valise, and carried it tightly under her arm, in the taxi, at the station, and onto the train. Relieved to be safely on board, she left the second-class compartment for a moment to buy a bottle of Vittel water. When she returned, the valise was gone.

The trip from Paris to Lausanne took seven hours, and they were, Hadley felt, the worst hours of her life. She had meant to bring with her all that was important to Ernest: her love and his work. Instead she came sick and empty, with the worst news her husband could hear. When she first saw Ernest, Hadley could not tell him what had happened. She just cried and cried. Ernest tried to comfort his wife by telling her that no matter what it was, it couldn't be that bad. Then she told him, and saw that for him it was as bad as it could be. But wasn't this the "Train Bleu"? Ernest asked. Even second-class compartments on this train were as safe as a bank. Nevertheless, the valise had been stolen, Hadley said. Did she check "Lost and Found"? Ernest asked. Did she contact the police? But no, of course not. She would not have gotten there, on that train, if she had. Ernest took the next train for Paris, hoping, he said, that she had not brought all the carbons. Hadley thought she would go mad.

Ernest could never bring himself to believe Hadley's story of the lost manuscripts. While they were courting, a doctor had told Hadley that if she became pregnant she would risk insanity. Perhaps this was it, Ernest thought. Perhaps, against the odds, Hadley had conceived during their last few days together in Paris, and had gone crazy. Years later, Ernest would write:

> Inside the room he opened the big Vuitton suitcase. The pile of cahiers that the stories had been written in was gone. . . . He closed and locked the suitcase and searched all of the drawers in the armoire and searched the room. He had not believed that the stories could be gone. He had not believed that she could do it. . . . Now he knew that it had happened but still thought it might be some ghastly joke. So, empty and dead in his heart, he re-opened the suitcase and checked it and after he locked it he checked the room again.
>
> Now there was no danger and no emergency. It was only disaster

now. But it couldn't be. . . . No one could do that to a fellow human
being.

When Ernest came back from Paris, he had that air of lighthearted
acceptance, that cynical flippancy Hadley knew meant the hurt was
bitter and deep. To punish his wife, Ernest took Hadley up to the
Gangwisch hotel again, for more of the masculine "fun" she had suffered through when they had crossed the St. Bernard Pass with Dorman-Smith. Ernest coerced Hadley into skiiing almost every day. Occasionally, Ernest skied with the young son of Dave O'Neil. His name
was George, and Ernest put him in a story about how marriage (and
pregnancy) reduces a young man's life.

> "Is Helen going to have a baby?" George said, coming down to the
> table from the wall.
> "Yes."
> "When?"
> "Late next summer."
> "Are you glad?"
> "Yes. Now."
> "Will you go back to the States?"
> "I guess so."
> "Do you want to?"
> "No."
> "Does Helen?"
> "No.
> George sat silent. He looked at the empty bottle and the empty
> glasses.
> "It's hell, isn't it?" he said.
> "No. Not exactly," Nick said.
> "Why not?"
> "I don't know," Nick said.
> "Will you ever go skiing together in the States?" George said.
> "I don't know," Nick said.
> "The mountains aren't much," George said.
> "No," Nick said. "They're too rocky. There's too much timber and
> they're too far away."

Another part of Hadley's punishment was young Isabel Simmons.
Ernest had written at length to Isabel, advising her as to the most comfortable train to take, how to handle the customs, and charming her
with a lyrical rendering of the trip from Paris. He wrote of how much
fun it had always been for him (and would be for her, because she was
so like him) to stay up to watch the moonlight on the French countryside, eating sandwiches made in Dijon. If anyone tried to come into

the compartment during the night, he said, the occupants would point to a sleeping person and say, "shhh—Malade!" Ernest told Isabel it was a lovely trip; he had made it "about twelve times this year."

Then he wrote about clothes. He was sure Hadley had been advising Isabel, but Ernest had some ideas of his own. It was riding breeches for the skiing and a sweater and tam for bobsledding. No one dressed for dinner; part of the fun was eating in your "tough clothes." Hadley wore riding breeches, puttees or golf stockings, a white flannel shirt with a sweater or her riding jacket with a belt. Ernest wanted Isabel to be as comfortable as she could be. All this, Ernest knew, his young hometown friend would eventually relate to his wife.

Finally, Ernest did what he knew would hurt Hadley most of all. He wrote a "why-not-let's-be-friends-again" letter to Agnes von Kurowsky. Agnes's reply was less than he'd hoped for. In a letter dripping with condescension, she played a woman of the world, reminding Ernest that her jilting him had been all for the best, as even he could see, "now that you have Hadley."

Ernest hated himself for doing these things to Hadley. But he was powerless against his need to be cruel. He had to let his cruelty run its course, and then give whatever gods may be a chance to punish him.

At the Gangwisches' pension one morning, Ernest announced that he would retrieve a ski young George O'Neil had lost on the Dent de Jaman the day before. A heavy, wet snow was falling; by ten o'clock, it had changed to rain. Ernest had heard all about the horror of avalanches from the brothers at St. Bernard. While Hadley and Isabel waited all through that long afternoon, fourteen avalanches thundered down. Then, just before sunset, there was Ernest, struggling up the slope toward them, knee deep in the wet snow, the lost ski in his mittened hand.

Ernest and Hadley stayed on at Chamby long after their friends had departed, after the cold spring rains had turned the snow to slush. Each morning, the clear and deep blue skies turned slowly gray, with clouds over the lake and the valley. To walk in the roads, Hadley wore heavy overshoes; Ernest borrowed Mr. Gangwisch's rubber boots. Hadley knew it was the wrong time for announcements. She knew that Ernest thought the change of seasons dangerous, a time for living on the defensive. Nevertheless, he had to know. One morning, after breakfast, Hadley told him they were going to have a baby. Ernest said very little. But he soon stopped making love to Hadley, claiming that the altitude had made his glands inoperative. Hadley felt humiliated when Ernest wrote to Ezra Pound about his condition.

# 3

# Paradoxes and Problems

While Ernest could write to Ezra Pound about all the things that made him angry and be sure of a sympathetic response, he was mistaken to think that Pound would ever write back with the sympathy of a true friend. Ernest's reference to impotence, so clear a signal to Pound that something had gone very wrong, was ignored. Pound replied only that he and his wife, Dorothy, needed company, and that he had decided that Ernest and Hadley were the best he could find. Pound's subsequent letters to Ernest had only one consistent theme: when were Ernest and Hadley coming down to Rapallo?

Pound had been hard at work, he said, discovering the literary potential in the life story of one Sigismondo Malatesta, a patron of the arts in Renaissance Italy and a bitter enemy of the papacy. Dante had immortalized a part of the Malatesta family in *The Divine Comedy* when he told the story of the hunchback, Gianciotto, who killed his wife, Francesca da Rimini, when he learned of her love affair with his brother. Ezra proposed that as soon as the Hemingways arrived, he would take them on a tour of the battlefields where Sigismondo fought the pope.

Hadley had had more than enough of walking tours, and she didn't care much for Ezra or Dorothy Pound. Ernest, who had once prided himself on his endurance—at sixteen he had hiked some hundred and forty miles, half the length of Michigan's lower peninsula—now worried about his heart. He told Hadley that he'd been getting the same sort of chest pains he'd had in Chicago when he and Hadley were courting. It must be angina, Ernest said, a heart condition his father,

Clarence, had been suffering with for almost two years. Also, Ernest suspected that the Hemingways were invited to Rapallo merely to keep Dorothy occupied while Ezra had his rendezvous in Rome with Nancy Cunard, the English shipping heiress. Still, it wouldn't hurt to do Ezra a favor—in the cause of the Hemingway career.

Pound's other guests at Rapallo were to be the painter Henry (Mike) Strater and his wife, Maggie. Ernest and Hadley had met the Straters at Pound's flat in Paris. Ernest and Mike, who, like Ernest, was a natural heavyweight, had boxed a few even rounds and had drunk a lot of wine together. But the Straters had a small, undisciplined child, and Ernest said he found Maggie "Pushy."

Ernest and Hadley got to Rapallo on the eleventh of February, 1923, and took rooms where the Pounds were staying, at the Hotel Mignon, the second-best hotel in the town. At their first dinner together, Strater vowed, winefully, that he would do portraits of both Ernest and Hadley. Ernest, in turn, chose his usual form of reply to someone he felt was showing off. He challenged Strater to box again.

Ernest found Rapallo as damp and humid as Genoa. And the Mediterranean, with its one-inch tide and waves that broke with the sound "of ashes being dumped from a scow," fit Ernest's mood. A week later, when Pound announced he was off to Rome, Dorothy decided to accompany him.

Once the Pounds were gone, Ernest and Hadley moved into the best hotel in Rapallo, the Hotel Splendide. The rooms were on the second floor, facing a square, a war monument, and the sea. At the Splendide, Ernest met a writer he felt had some honest-to-goodness talent. Robert Menzies McAlmon was three years older than Ernest. He stood five-feet ten inches, had a John Barrymore profile, and, because of his athletic build, had once worked as an artists' school model. Born in Clinton, Kansas, brought up in the Dakotas, McAlmon was, like Ernest, a midwesterner.

"Mac," as Ernest soon called him, had missed the world war (his pilot training in California ended just before the Armistice was signed), but he had worked with surveying gangs in the Dakotas, laid track in the Plains, and sailored on the Great Lakes steamers. He had even spent a year punching cattle.

Like Ernest, McAlmon admired Lord Byron, both the man and his work, and had published six poems, done in his own interpretation of the Byronic style, in Harriet Monroe's *Poetry*. McAlmon was married to a lesbian heiress, Annie Winifred Ellerman, who wrote under the name of "Bryher." But Annie spent more time with the poet Hilda Doolittle ("H.D.") than she did with him.

Ernest found it difficult to act tough around McAlmon because Mac knew as much of low life and of low-life patois as Ernest did. Even worse, Mac could tell a good story. But since McAlmon had been a publisher of sorts in New York and, with his wife's money, intended to revive his Contact Editions of American poetry and prose in Paris, Ernest tried to make him another useful friend.

Some of the gossip McAlmon told Ernest during their bar-hopping found its way into a poem. Ernest called it "The Lady Poets With Foot Notes." It characterized, among others, Edna St. Vincent Millay, "a nymphomaniac" who "wrote for *Vanity Fair*"; Sara Teasdale, who "wanted her lover, but was afraid of having a/baby. When she finally got married, she found she couldn't/have a baby"; and Amy Lowell, who was "big and fat and no fool," but her "stuff was no good." Ernest sensed McAlmon's homosexuality. He was the severe, dried-down "British military" type, Ernest thought, with nothing at all effeminate about him.

Back in his room at the Hotel Splendide, Ernest took some notes for a short story that would become, "Cat in the Rain." Years later he claimed that the story concerned another young American couple staying at the hotel. But with the tension Hadley's pregnancy had caused and the loss of the stories, Ernest was writing autobiography all the same.

Much of "Cat in the Rain" focuses on the young wife's demands. She wants "to eat at a table with my own silver," she wants candles, she wants to brush her hair out in front of a mirror, she wants new clothes and for it to be spring. The wife sounds silly and childishly selfish, but she is not. She is simply unaware. She does not know, or cannot feel, the meaning of the bronze war monument, glistening in the rain in the square outside their window. For her, life should be fulfillment. But for her veteran husband, lying there on the bed, trying to read, half listening to her, life is mostly denial.

The elderly padrone, tall, dignified, taking his position as hotel keeper very seriously, stirs in the wife something akin to new life. He makes her feel, for a moment, "supremely important" by giving her a tortoiseshell cat she had seen crouched under a patio table, avoiding the rain. Ernest knew that Hadley wanted, needed, him to be like the padrone—to give her something to treasure. Why, Hadley would say, couldn't her pregnancy be a beginning rather than an end?

As soon as Pound and his wife got back to Rapallo, Ezra began again to plague Ernest with demands for the walking tour. Ernest suggested, instead of the haunts of Sigismondo, a place he had come to love during the war. In Calabria, Ernest said, lemon orchards and orange groves crowd along the right-hand side of the railway, and the hills are terraced with yellow fruit shining through the green leaves. Then come the darker green olive trees on the hills, and the streams with wide dry pebbly beds cutting down to the sea, and the old stone houses. Over on the left-hand side, is the sea, a lot bluer than even the Bay of Naples. Pound, however, was a stubborn man, and the Hemingways ended up going on his tour. Always taking an early-morning train, they visited, successively, Pisa, Piombino, Orbetello, and Grosseto.

Although Ezra was fifteen years older than Ernest and with a career of sorts in London and Paris behind him, he had been unable to feel superior, to comfortably assume a tutorial role. But for this trip, he was prepared.

Each morning, as soon as they started, Ezra began to talk learnedly of Malatesta, quoting from appropriate tomes, making esoteric allusions, enriching his monologue with Italian idioms and Italian names. Naturally, Ernest tried to keep up with Ezra. He matched Pound's long-legged stride around the spots where Sigismondo had won his reputation, listened attentively while, like a monk at a holy place, Ezra read the military histories. Then, having finished off a flask full of Gordon's gin, Ernest made his contribution by trying to reenact, as Pound described them, Sigismondo's famous battle scenes.

At the end of two weeks, the Hemingways and the Pounds had had enough of each other. One easy way to separate would be to take a trip together, and then one couple would decide to "continue on." Ernest suggested Sirmione on Lake Garda. There the Pounds and the Hemingways parted: the Pounds for Rapallo, the Hemingways for the resort town of Cortina D'Ampezzo, just north of Venice.

At Cortina, Ernest and Hadley felt as if they'd drawn back the season. Instead of landscape dissolving in raw late-winter rain, as it had in Rapallo, there was dry morning cold, a late-arriving sun, and then long shadows and freezing again as early as three o'clock. The first friend Ernest and Hadley made in Cortina was the concert pianist Renata Borgatti, a tall, dark-eyed beauty with a graceful, boyish figure. Renata was especially attracted to Hadley, and soon they were walking and shopping friends.

Ernest spent his mornings in Cortina working over one-paragraph sketches, the first things he'd done since the loss of his manuscripts. Like "Crossroads"—the collection of character sketches of people in northern Michigan written more than two years before, just after Agnes von Kurowsky—these miniatures revealed a compression that simple cutting could not give. Writing now was a forced march for Ernest, each word, each sentence, resisted its place on the page. But the power that finally put it there showed.

One of the sketches grew to be much longer than the others. At seven paragraphs, three manuscript pages, there was enough to call it "A Very Short Story." Aside from the purely fictional last sketch of "Crossroads," this was Ernest's first attempt to put into his art the heartbreak he felt at Agnes von Kurowsky's faithlessness.

In "A Very Short Story" Ernest tells of a love affair between an American wounded on the Italian Front and his hospital nurse. The theme is that, "in our time," a man learns through pain, and only through pain. The plot is based on the story of the biblical Jacob.

Autobiographical in most details—the setting is a hospital in Milan; the nurse's name is "Ag"—"A Very Short Story" involves a young man who has suffered, like Jacob, a wound in the leg. But while Jacob had been wrestling with an angel, this soldier was wounded by an artillery shell. Like the biblical Jacob, the soldier has come to a foreign land and has found a woman to marry. In order to secure Rachel's hand, Jacob agrees to work fourteen years. The soldier "agreed he should go home and get a job so they could be married." Both the biblical Jacob and Ernest's hero have "visions." But while Jacob's vision is of heaven and God's messengers, the soldier sees only the roofs of a wartime city and the beams of searchlights seeking enemy airplanes. While Jacob hears the wonderful promises of divine commitment, the soldier hears only the bottles at the party going on in the hospital's music room downstairs. Jacob, through his visitation from God, is made into a new man, the founder of a people. Ernest's young hero is made—by the Austrian artillery shell, by his nurse in Milan, by a whore in a taxi back home in Chicago, from whom he contracts gonorrhea—into a "new man," too, a cripple who embodies the effects of life in our time. (Years later, Ernest would make clear his intention by renaming the nurse "Luz," after the place where Jacob learned of his destiny, and by changing the setting to Padua, the "City of Learning.")

In late March, a cable arrived for Ernest from his editor at the *Star*. John Bone wanted him to travel to the Ruhr, formerly the heart of industrial Germany but now under French control, and to report on the efficacy of French administration. En route to Germany, Ernest wrote to his father, Clarence: "I hope you have some good fishing this spring. I appreciate your letters so much and am dreadfully sorry I don't write more, but when you make a living writing it is hard to write letters. I've been 38 hours on the train and am awfully tired. . . . Your loving son, Ernie." Although Ernest felt closer to his father than to anyone else in the family, he did not tell him that Hadley was going to have a baby.

The first story Ernest filed from the Ruhr was saturated with irony as bitter as any since his work at the *Kansas City Star*. Affecting the voice of an "observer," Ernest dissected an incident in which thirteen German workingmen had been killed in a factory courtyard in a confrontation with French soldiers.

Ernest began by acknowledging the difficulty of getting valid information. (The troops in question had been transferred, and the workingmen, he knew, could have been lying.) So far as Ernest could discover, a thick crowd had pressed tight around the soldiers. The soldiers had fired, first a volley into the air, and then randomly into the crowd. The whole incident, Ernest implied, had been instigated by German industrialists who wanted the French out and their profits restored.

The horror lived for Ernest in the grotesqueries of legalistic "truth": "The Funeral at Essen was delayed . . . because French and German doctors could not agree on the nature of the bullet wounds. The Germans claimed eleven of the workingmen were shot in the back. The French surgeon claimed that five were shot in the front, five bullets entered from the side and two in the back." Ernest concluded, "I do not know the claims of the two men who died since the argument started."

When Ernest returned to Cortina in mid-April, Hadley was past the first three months of pregnancy, and she seemed happy. She was, in fact, quite proud that she was "showing," and she liked having Ernest see her progress. While Ernest was away, Hadley said, she had become fond of Renata Borgatti. Renata loved to walk, and Hadley took her on the short, lovely hikes she and Ernest had discovered. Hadley said she had been unhappy, rather than surprised, when Renata asked her to make love.

The next day, Ernest began a story that recalled a fishing trip he and Hadley had attempted in Cortina just before he'd left for Germany. It was straight autobiography, injected with all the frustration, bitterness, and self-disgust he'd distilled from the past year.

The chief character of Ernest's story "Out of Season" is Peduzzi, hired as a fishing guide by a young couple staying at a Cortina hotel. Peduzzi is an old drunkard and the laughingstock of the town. The fishing he promises to take the young couple to is illegal, because it is out of season.

On their way to the fishing, the young couple stop at a wine shop. Peduzzi wears an old military coat; he says he wants a little marsala. The wife in the story is revolted by Peduzzi, so he waits in the street. When the young couple come out of the shop, the wife, looking scornful and bemused, carries the bottle of marsala.

As they walk through town, Peduzzi is proud to have clients. He points to a girl in a doorway. "My daughter," he says. The wife, who, like the wife in "Cat in the Rain," is dissatisfied with her marriage, misunderstands. "His doctor . . . has he got to show us his doctor?" she asks. The girl had gone into the house as soon as Peduzzi pointed. Peduzzi talks in a Tyroler German dialect, then in a d'Ampezzo dialect. The young man and his wife understand nothing.

Finally, the three of them get to the stream. It is brown and muddy, discolored by the melting snow. Off to the right there is a dump heap. Peduzzi now speaks in Italian and the young man understands. The young man tells his wife, "He says it's at least a half hour more." The young man suggests that his wife go back. She's cold, and it's been a rotten day. "All right," the wife replies, and she begins to climb the grassy bank. Peduzzi is desperate. He is afraid that the young man will leave. Yes, Peduzzi says, the fishing is good a half-hour further on, but it is good here, too.

Unfortunately, the young man has forgotten his "piombo," a little lead to keep the line submerged. Peduzzi sifts in vain through the cloth dirt in his military pockets. His day is "going to pieces before his eyes." The young man, however, is relieved; he will not have to violate the law. He offers Peduzzi the marsala; they drink, and agree to fish the next day. With eyes glistening, Peduzzi tells the young gentleman that he, Peduzzi, will come with everything—"Pane, salami, formaggio"—at seven in the morning. He calls the young man "caro," darling.

Suddenly, the young gentleman says, "I may not be going . . . very probably not." Ernest ends the story here. But, in reality, his and Hadley's guide for their "out of season" fishing had hung himself in the town stable after Ernest complained about the guide's incompetence and lost him his job.

By early summer 1923, Ernest was sick of traveling. The idea of gaining "continental experience" had lost all its romance. He longed to get back to his writing, in Paris, at the flat in Rue du Cardinal

Lemoine. And yet, he told Hadley, he needed to go to Spain. Why Spain? Hadley asked. Ernest told her a story.

The *Giuseppi Verdi*, on which Ernest had returned from Italy to the United States in 1919, had docked for a while under the shadow of Gibraltar, at the little town of Algeciras. Just before he'd left Milan, Ernest and Agnes von Kurowsky had had a fight about her coming home with him. They had not yet "made up" when they said goodbye. The winter winds had blown hard at Gibraltar, and Ernest had climbed into the hills during his hours ashore to rid himself of the staleness Agnes's "common sense" attitude (he'd have to earn a certain salary before she'd come home and marry him) had engendered. The wind, he hoped, would blow all the disappointment away.

But to his surprise, Ernest returned to the ship filled with something new. Seen from these hills, Spain was frightening to him, and yet irresistible. The brown land seemed acquainted with death, with a slow dying under relentless wind and sun. The houses, the people of Algeciras, extruded out of the land, like geological formations, independent of seasons, having nothing to do with fertility or growth, but rather with slow, implacable, elemental change. In Spain, Ernest believed, a man died well who was worn away in living.

Then Ernest told Hadley of a portrait of Gertrude Stein done by the Spaniard, Pablo Picasso. It had taken almost ninety sittings, Gertrude said, and finally Picasso had chosen to finish it in her absence. The portrait reminded Ernest of Van Gogh's "L'Arlesienne," in which the stolid permanence of Madame Ginoux obscures all but essential human features. Ernest said that the Picassos he saw in Gertrude Stein's rooms were mostly from the painter's early work—studies of poverty, hunger, and heartbreak, involving especially lonely and pitiful women and sad, impotent men. There were, however, two startling paintings, expressing masculine power, evoking the analogy of the Spanish fighting bull. One was "Portrait of Guillaume Apollinaire," the other "The Two Giants." Ernest had taken note. Poets and warriors: these were the Spaniard's heroes.

Before the birth of his baby, Ernest wanted desperately to become what he himself would consider a man. In Italy, four years before, Ernest had bet his life on Agnes von Kurowsky. He had given up everything for her because she was his ideal. He would be her knight with or without armor. For her the dragons of this world could be slain. When Agnes left him, Ernest said he was crushed like a hermit crab in its borrowed shell. The dreams of youth, the long, long thoughts

of the young man, the enchanted world of love—he'd had to burn all of
this from his heart. To himself, he'd called it "hardening"—an act of
self-sacrifice to toughen his spirit the way, in soaks of brine, Jack Dempsey toughened his face.

And yet, his efforts had failed. Under pressure, as he had been that
night at dinner with the Germans sitting nearby and insulting him,
Ernest still could not do "the one thing, the only thing for a man to
do, easily and naturally."

Ernest had heard about the bullfight from Gertrude Stein. It was a
ritual, she had said, one that could, if the participants were worthy,
turn fear into courage, ugliness into beauty, death into life. Ernest told
Hadley that Robert McAlmon's father-in-law had made Mac a gift of
seventy thousand dollars, and McAlmon was looking for things to do
with the money. Ernest suggested that, on a borrow-and-pay-back plan,
he and McAlmon might go to Spain to see the bullfight and test the
toughness they said they possessed. Ernest remembered that William
Bird, his other potential publisher, had been ready to fight the surly
Black Forest Germans, and he asked McAlmon to invite Bird, too.

After his third goodbye to Hadley in less than a year, Ernest left for
Spain with McAlmon and Bill Bird. He knew that the prospects for
trouble among the men were enormous. And the first chance for confrontation came soon.

The train had stopped at a wayside station on the road to Madrid.
Ernest wore a stingy brim hat, turned up at the front, the three-piece
Brooks Brothers suit he had bought in Chicago to impress Hadley with
during their courtship, and a big carnation in his lapel. For the photo
Bill Bird insisted on taking of his two companions, Ernest grinned
easily, showing his big, white teeth, while Mac looked solemn. (Ernest
thought McAlmon's teeth were gnarled and twisted like the tines of a
northern Michigan plow.) On the tracks beside the passenger car was
a flatcar, and on this lay the maggot-eaten corpse of a dog. Ernest saw
that McAlmon, with his rakish hat pulled down to the bridge of his
nose, was trying to avoid looking at the dog. McAlmon claimed he was
tough. All right, Ernest said. A man had to "back it up when he put it
on the line." "Hell, Mac," Ernest said. "You write like a realist. Are
you going to go romantic on us?" To his surprise, McAlmon took this
"lying down."

Ernest knew how much he needed McAlmon. Getting a book published was now the most important thing in the world. But when he

saw McAlmon's performance at the bullring, he looked on with undis-
guised disdain. McAlmon couldn't stay in his seat. All during the
bullfight, McAlmon "reacted": first to what he called the "tremendous
violence" of the "black velocity and force" of the bull. Then he was up
in his seat, "yelling," when the bull charged into the horse. Carried
away by the bull's assaults on the belly of the horse (on one occasion
the horse was disemboweled and, in hysteria, trampled upon its own
entrails), McAlmon missed the work of the matador. It was the
"cruelty" of the spectators, hurling seat cushions down into the ring,
that next caught his eye.

Then there was McAlmon's literary taste. Not long into the trip, Ernest discovered that McAlmon believed Sherwood Anderson couldn't
write. McAlmon claimed that Anderson assumed the emotional attitude "of an older person who insists upon trying to think and write as
a child." He mocked Anderson's tone—"the hurt-child-being-brave"—
and his dialogue—"lone words and staccato phrases." Ernest knew that
one of the stories he had left, "My Old Man," sounded to McAlmon
just like Sherwood Anderson's "I'm a Fool." Of course, it would not be
politic to tell McAlmon that the pristine, "innocent" voice of the good
observer of life always sounds "childlike" to the essentially stupid or
corrupt. And yet, Ernest could have told McAlmon anything. After their
week together, McAlmon was in love with Ernest and would publish
him no matter what he said.

Years later, McAlmon wrote that he had resented Ernest's smug condescension, and that this was the chief reason for their broken friendship. Yet the break came because, in his early twenties, Ernest found
homosexuals disgusting. He wouldn't write about them, he said, because they were predictable. Given certain and usually unavoidable
circumstances, they would act according to their perversion. One of
their characteristics, Ernest believed, was the tendency to overreact or,
better, to misreact, because their emotions were somehow short-circuited.
Usually afraid to let their genuine feelings show, they would either am-
plify or suppress their response—keeping up a static of excitement, or
affecting ennui—in order to hide themselves. In speech and writing, everything for them had to be more, or less, than it was.

When Ernest got back to Paris, he found Hadley very upset. She had
gotten bads news from home. Helen Breaker, a maid of honor at their
wedding and Hadley's best friend, had written that the principal of
Hadley's trust fund, managed by Helen's brother, George Breaker,

had "somehow been diminished" by fifty percent. Starting with nine-teen thousand dollars in the bull market of the early twenties, George Breaker now could offer Hadley dividends on assets of only nine thousand dollars—a fifty percent loss in less than two years.

When Hadley told Ernest the news, he became hysterical. He had mistrusted Breaker, Ernest said, ever since he'd laid eyes on him. Breaker was short and furtive, he dressed like a dandy, he was slick with women, and he liked making cheap show. Ernest said he believed Breaker wasn't losing the money; he was stealing it. The question was, what to do?

Hadley said she would write to Breaker, or rather that Ernest should compose letters under which she would sign her name. Ernest could use all his skill to convince Breaker that Hadley's income was the foundation of their world. Security would be the essential theme. Ernest needed the money to write; the marriage needed it now that a baby was coming. The next day, Ernest began a series of letters to George Breaker, each asking for "hard information," each sounding a bit more desperate than the one before.

Unfortunately, the weeks dragged on, and George Breaker did not reply. There was nothing to do for it, Ernest said. He and Hadley must get back to America. He would wire John Bone at the *Star* requesting a job as staff writer in Toronto. He could make a steady salary, and oversee their finances with easy trips to New York. Hadley resisted. She knew what Ernest had thought of Canada before they left home. Having lived in Paris, what would he think of it now? But, Ernest argued, there could be no Paris, no Switzerland, no Spain for that matter, unless the money held up—now with the baby. When Ernest wrote of his plans to John Bone at the *Star,* Bone replied with enthusiasm, offering to make Ernest a feature writer.

Ernest told Hadley that before they left for Canada they must see at least one bullfight together. Gertrude Stein had recommended Pamplona, where the Fiesta of San Fermin was held in early July. Hadley, now six months' pregnant, worried about the Spanish sun and the heat.

The bullfights at Pamplona were everything Ernest hoped they would be. And he enjoyed making Hadley feel all his own strong emotions. Ernest said that the morality he brought to the bullfight was his own. What is moral, you feel good after; what is immoral, you feel bad after. That was the only way for an artist to function. And the bullfight demanded that its spectators be artists in this way.

While the bullfight was going on, Ernest said, he had the "feeling of

life and death," and, afterward, he felt "very sad but very fine." Hadley
had heard about what happened to the horses. Ernest told her that he
didn't mind the horses—not only in principle, but in fact he did not
mind them. Outside of the ritual of the bullfight, he could not see a
horse down in the street without rushing to spread sacking, unbuckle
harnesses, and, dodging shod hoofs, help get the animal onto its feet
again. But in the bullfight the horses were not themselves; they, like
every other participant, played a role. And life and art were blurred.
Though the "characters" in fact suffered and died, in the imagination
of the crowd they did so not as individuals but as part of a sacrificial
drama. It was like the Catholic Mass, Ernest said, if you took tran-
substantiation seriously. The cushion throwing that could come at the
end of an unsatisfactory performance was not an act of barbarity,
but a fair admonition to the matador who had promised, and failed,
to earn his audience a brief salvation.

There was one harsh note for Ernest at Fiesta San Fermin. Hadley
could not help falling in love with a handsome bullfighter. His name
was Nicanor Villalta, and Hadley said she wanted to name their baby
after him.

With his great expectations unrealized, and Paris already a place he
was leaving, maybe for good, Ernest worked desperately to complete
the vignettes he'd begun in Cortina for Bill Bird's publication of *in
our time*. In each vignette Ernest treated what had become his central
concern: how to live "right" when everything is going wrong. For his
subjects, Ernest chose men under terrible stress. There was Sam Cardi-
nella, a Chicago hoodlum about to be hanged, losing control of his
bowels, unable to walk to the gallows, the rope placed on his neck
while he sat strapped in a chair on the trap door. There was the soldier, Nick, lying wounded with Rinaldi against a wall, Austrian dead
in the rubble, more dead up the street. The day was very hot. Nick's
legs stuck out awkwardly. He had been hit in the spine. "Senta Rinaldi.
Senta. You and me we've made a separate peace," Nick says. "Rinaldi
lay still in the sun breathing with difficulty."

Then there were the bullfighters Ernest had just seen in Pamplona.
He wrote five miniatures about them. One was a "kid" who, because
he was third in a three-man field, had to kill the bulls the other two
had failed with. When he started there were five bulls left, and after
the fourth the young man was so tired he could hardly lift his arm.
Five times he tried to kill the fifth bull, and then, finally, he did it.

The reward? "He sat down in the sand and puked and they held a cape over him while the crowd hollered and threw things down into the bull ring."

Then Ernest chose a hero for himself, a man who knew well the mystery and the invincibility of fate, and yet had the courage to go on. Ernest did not portray Maera in the midst of victory, but burdened rather with his final defeat. Like the young bullfighter who had killed the five bulls, Maera takes as his duty the cleaning up of the mess matadors who came before him have made. He knows that doing this may cost him his life. But he makes that of no consequence. After killing the savages' bulls, the drunkards' bulls, the riau-riau dancers' bulls, he lies, sticky in his own blood, and feels the horn go through him and into the sand.

On August 5, 1923, Ernest's mail included the proofs of his first book. It would be published by Robert McAlmon and entitled *Three Stories and Ten Poems*. It would contain "Up in Michigan," the story that Gertrude Stein had found offensive, "Out of Season," Ernest's autobiographical rendering of the fishing trip with the suicide, Peduzzi, and "My Old Man," a story of a young boy who discovers after his father's death at the track that his horse-racing father was corrupt. The poems were written about, and just after, the war.

To himself, Ernest admitted this volume was hardly impressive—no bigger than a greeting card, the binding stitched with thread. Still, he worried over the cover. He said he wanted the titles of the stories and poems printed on the cover. They were, he wrote McAlmon, very good titles. Even Bill Bird had agreed. Ernest wanted the title of the book printed taller and leaner, but just as black. He wanted blank pages included at the beginning and end. "Nobody will buy a book if it is too goddamn thin," he said.

Finally, on August 17, 1923, Ernest and Hadley set sail from Cherbourg. It would be a quiet, late-summer trip of blue skies and gentle swells. It made going home seem a pleasant, almost appropriate thing to do. And yet each time the sun rose over the stern of the small freighter, everything Ernest wanted seemed farther and farther away.

# ⁂ 4 ⁂

## Since There's No Help

Soon after Ernest arrived in Toronto, he wrote to Ezra Pound: "It couldn't be any worse. You can't imagine it. I'm not going to describe it. But for Christ sake if anybody pulls any more of that stuff about America, Tom Mix, Home and Adventure in search of beauty refer them to me." A postwar tune seemed appropriate: "How you gonna keep 'em down on the farm, after they've seen Par-ee?" Toronto wasn't exactly "the farm." But compared to Paris, it had the look of a second-rate city in the States.

In his letter to Pound, Ernest blamed the trip on the pregnancy. Hadley had been worried about the competence of French doctors, he said. But in Canada, obstetrics was "specialite de ville." Ernest even made a disgusting remark for Ezra's benefit, about the lack of attention to birth control: "I can hear you, 'but my dear Hem what about the old syringe?'"

In this ugly mood, Ernest wrote contemptuously of Lloyd George, calling him "Prince Charming" and hinting at homosexuality. Now Lloyd George was "the fair-haired bugger." Greg Clark, a friend at the *Star* since 1920, had sent Ernest a fine welcoming note. Ernest mocked him to Pound. John Bone's encouraging letter, outlining Ernest's "wonderful" prospects at the *Star*, he ignored.

There was, however, a reason for his rudeness to Bone. His first week in Toronto, Ernest had been invited by John Bone to a *Star* party at an estate on a hill in the best part of town. When he arrived with Hadley, Ernest saw a vast crowd dancing. Then he spotted

Bone, and was given a "man-to-man" smile. Later, Ernest gained admittance to the house's private bar, open only to the quality of Toronto. To his surprise, he was given the cold shoulder by his boss, the host, and all the "distinguished-looking men." Choking with humiliation and rage, Ernest returned to the dance floor, to Hadley in her maternity dress.

During the winter and early spring of 1920, Ernest had worked for the Ralph Connables, a wealthy Toronto family associated with the Woolworth stores. He had been a companion and guardian for their retarded son, Ralph Jr. Harriet Connable, the mother, was, Ernest maintained, the finest woman he knew. And the daughter, Dorothy, was his "true female friend."

Ernest said he considered it lucky that Greg Clark had found an apartment for him in the new red-brick Cedarvale Mansions, because it was just across the ravine from the Connable estate. The new apartment had only two rooms, but its floor space was at least twice what he'd had in Paris. And there were those big windows that looked out over the ravine. But the apartment still smelled of cheap paint, Hadley said. How did her husband really feel about all this? After a year in Canada, Ernest said, he'd be ready for suicide.

The early weeks in Toronto were especially hard on Hadley. First there was the loss of Ernest's manuscripts, and now the pregnancy. It was her fault that they were in Canada and that Ernest couldn't write. Even her income, the money her grandfather had left her, which she had entrusted to a good friend, was being stolen by the friend's brother. Hadley was desperate. She felt that now she was everything Ernest didn't want, didn't even need. She was so relieved when Ernest found someone else to blame for how badly being in Canada made him feel.

Harry Hindmarsh, the city editor of the *Toronto Star* in 1923, was fat and loud and arrogant. He bullied his reporters, considered himself an artist, and talked like a jingoistic patriot. He was jealous of Ernest's ability, his youth, and, most of all, the reputation he'd gained from his work in Europe. Ernest hated Hindmarsh, especially Hindmarsh's eyes—bright blue and seemingly made of glass.

For weeks Ernest tried for a confrontation. He wanted to box, and he asked, almost begged for that. But Hindmarsh would have none of it. He knew he could destroy Ernest a slow, safe way. Every week there would be an exhausting assignment. Then every possible obstacle would be placed in Ernest's path. Finally, there would be snide and sarcastic criticism of the work. The first time out, Hindmarsh sent Ernest six

hundred miles away, to investigate mining problems in the Sudbury
Basin, north of Georgian Bay.

When Ernest returned a week later, exhausted from the ordeal of
interviewing miners who suspected he was a "government man," Hindmarsh ordered him south, to New York, to cover the arrival of the
British prime minister, Lloyd George. Ernest's first reaction was to tell
Hindmarsh to go to hell, to take his job and "put it where the sun
don't shine." But Hadley suggested they should think about it. Didn't
Ernest need to get to New York to check on what George Breaker was
doing with their money? Wouldn't this be a fine opportunity to use
the *Star,* and Harry Hindmarsh, for their own ends?

Ernest agreed, and came up with a plan. He would ask his friend,
Isabel Simmons, now enrolled at Barnard College in New York, to
cover a Lloyd George speech for him. Ernest had met "George" at
Lausanne, and he could always fill in details from memory. Mean-
while, Ernest said, he could search the valleys of Wall Street, find
George Breaker's brokerage house, and see what was what.

Both Ernest and Hadley agreed that Ernest should go to New York.
But Hadley's time was drawing near, and she and Ernest were very
afraid to be apart. Although they did not speak of it, they both
knew that at thirty-two years old Hadley was well past the best and
safest years for childbearing. And Ernest, with something of an in-
sider's knowledge of medicine (Clarence Hemingway had practiced
obstetrics for years), had no illusions about the safety of "modern"
childbirth. On the other hand, Hadley's Canadian doctor had assured
her that everything so far had been normal, and the baby wouldn't
come for at least a month. Ernest called Harriet Connable. Could
Hadley stay for a week with her? Mrs. Connable was as kind and
generous as Ernest remembered her, and she welcomed Hadley as a
cherished friend.

Ernest got to New York on October 5, the day Lloyd George arrived
on the largest and fastest of the Cunard liners, the *Mauretania.* The
ship, as it lay off quarantine just outside the harbor, looked as tall as a
cliff to Ernest. At the Genoa Conference, Lloyd George had been one
of Ernest's heroes because, of all the participants, he seemed the most
truly idealistic. Now Ernest portrayed the prime minister as a "short,
thickset, ruddy-faced little man with a thick, patriarchal mane of white
hair" who, because he was vain, spent too much time dressing in his
cabin.

The piece Ernest wired to the *Star* that day also chronicled the
deaths of the men who, along with Lloyd George, had tried to make

economic peace in Genoa. First, there was the German minister, the intellectual Walter Rathenau, who had been "shot in the back in his town motor car as he drove to the foreign office in Berlin." Then there was "Vorovsky, the Russian, scholarly and kindly . . . murdered at the table as he drank his after-dinner coffee in a hotel in Lausanne." Ernest had admired Stambouliski, of Bulgaria, very much. He was "a roaring bull of a man who worked only for the good of Bulgaria [and] was hunted down and killed in a field by his own soldiers while he tried to hide in a straw stack." Most sad and pitiful was the Greek premier, Gounaris, who "was carried from his bed sick with typhoid to stand before the firing squad in a drizzling rain in the courtyard of the military hospital." "All this," Ernest added, had happened "within a year."

The ironies of fate were on Ernest's mind as he walked the streets of New York, especially down on Broad Street and Wall, "where there is never any light gets down except streaks." In front of the Stock Exchange, Ernest watched a man drawing on the sidewalk with yellow and red chalk. The man shouted, "He sent his only begotten son to do this. He sent his only begotten son to die on the tree. He sent his only begotten son to hang there and die." A big crowd stood around, listening. Then one of the crowd, a messenger boy, said, very seriously to another messenger, "Pretty tough on the boy."

Ernest thought that New York, despite its beautiful new buildings, wouldn't last. In three hundred years, it would be "Dead and deserted like Egypt," and be "Cooks most popular tour." In this mood, Ernest quit his search for George Breaker.

On October 9, Ernest left New York, on the same northbound train to Toronto that carried Lloyd George. Ernest had already filed six good stories on the prime minister's visit. But the day he'd wasted on his quixotic search of Wall Street, the day Isabel Simmons was "covering" for him, New York deputy mayor Hulbert had publicly lectured Lloyd George on British ingratitude for America's help in the war. All the New York papers got the story. But Isabel Simmons, somehow, had missed it, and Ernest had filed nothing with the *Star*. Ernest knew that this "failure" would put a whip in Hindmarsh's ready hand.

All through that day, October 9, Hadley had struggled with the worst sickness she had ever endured. She had pains that seemed like labor, but they were irregular, and it was weeks before the baby was due. Nevertheless, she could not eat her supper, and at nine o'clock she went to bed.

Just before midnight, Hadley walked into Mrs. Connable's room. It was time for the baby, Hadley said. She was absolutely sure. Mrs. Connable, who had had two children herself, tried to calm Hadley with her quiet efficiency—getting things together, helping Hadley to dress. At two o'clock in the morning, with the help of laughing gas, Hadley delivered a seven-pound, five-ounce boy.

Seven hours later, Ernest rushed into the hospital. He was distraught. He had promised Hadley he would be there when she had "all that suffering to go through." Hadley was nursing the baby when Ernest came in. She asked the nurse to take the boy away. When the baby was removed, Ernest threw himself on Hadley's knees and wept. They had not been together when it counted most, he said. And it was the fault of that son-of-a-bitch Hindmarsh. And because of George Breaker, it was money again, too, just as it had been with Agnes.

But this was not at all as it had been with Agnes, Hadley said. Now there was a child to bind them together, come what may. And never mind her "suffering alone." Hadley said that childbearing was overrated. The laughing gas had made it easy.

Dry-eyed, Ernest admitted he was impressed with his son, who, all the nurses agreed, was very handsome. But he was annoyed at the biting way the baby had nursed his mother. That was all right, Hadley said. This was natural for boy babies. And her breasts would get used to it. Now it was time to change direction. Ernest should quit journalism, once and for all. They should leave Toronto as soon as possible and return to Paris. They'd all bet their future on Ernest's talent.

With the holidays approaching, Ernest felt the tug of conscience. Clarence Hemingway had been writing to him regularly, all during the time overseas. He had sent Ernest little gifts, personal things like handkerchiefs that he thought Ernest, with his chronic throat and nasal inflammation, could use. Ernest knew that his father was very ill with coronary artery disease. There was a chance he might suddenly die. Now and then, Clarence would send Ernest a small check, money Ernest knew had come from what Clarence had managed to keep his wife, Grace, from requisitioning for the general household funds. When Ernest got still another letter with a check from his father, he wrote immediately that, just before Christmas, he would come to Oak Park.

As he usually did, Ernest began his letter to Clarence with an apology, his excuses for not writing: too much work, too little time, too tired. In fact, Ernest thought nothing of writing long letters to everyone he knew, as much for recreation as to convey sentiments or news. But writing to Clarence or Grace Hemingway was an ordeal. To protect his parents from the shock of reality, he had to affect a particularly awkward persona. He had to be their "good boy," trying his best to make them proud. Ernest tried hard not to lie to his parents, except by omission, except by giving them only what he knew they could comfortably tell their neighbors. And yet, now and then, Ernest revealed his deepest feelings in these letters home.

After thanking Dr. Hemingway for the check (the hospital expenses for the baby had been one hundred fifty dollars, and Clarence had covered it), and telling "Dad" just how well he had been doing, professionally—"traveled with Lloyd George," "had two articles on bull fighting, full page, with picture on the front page"—Ernest complained bitterly about the baby: "All the gang [Greg Clark] went deer hunting last Friday but not me. The Baby has taken to squawking and is a fine nuisance. I suppose he will yell his head off for the next two or three years." He and Hadley, Ernest said, had "made a mistake to come back here. But the only way to do with mistakes is to pay for them and get out of them as soon as possible."

Ernest also wrote that he would be happy to travel the six hundred miles to Oak Park, just before the holidays. Clarence should understand that Hadley and the baby could not be brought along. Ernest knew that this decision appeared "cold-blooded," but Hadley had to nurse every four hours. When she didn't, the "kid bawls," Hadley gets upset, and the milk stops altogether. It's a "vicious cycle," Ernest said. He was even worried about their "crossing over," going back to France. (They had already booked passage for January 19 on the *Antonia*, the smallest ship in the Cunard line.) "You can cross the ocean," Ernest wrote, "with a *nursing baby* but not with a baby on a bottle because of the constant changes of milk in different countries. We cannot risk Hadley's milk giving out and we have had a great deal of anxiety about it lately."

Ernest said he would come to Oak Park for Sunday and Monday, the twentieth and twenty-first, and then get back to Hadley for Christmas. He would not accept Clarence's offer to pay for the ticket to Oak Park because he knew his father really wanted to see the baby, "John Hadley Nicanor." Ernest closed the letter with, "I certainly look forward to seeing you all again. I can hardly wait." Then, in a bold, extravagant script, he signed with, "Love to you all, Ernie."

When Ernest got to Oak Park, on December 21, the whole family was waiting: his favorite sister, Ursula, who had slept with him after he'd returned from the war, comforting him when he dreamed of his wounding, night after night, and woke in terror; his sister "Sunny," sullen, inconsiderate, hypocritical, self-centered like their mother; his eldest sister, Marcelline, now happily married, still jealous of his talent, resenting that he'd had some kind of true success; his kid brother, Leicester, to whom Ernest, ever since he'd come back from the war in 1919 with all those knives and guns, was a hero.

At dinner that first night, Ernest felt suffocated. Clarence and Grace spoke in clichés: all about the advantages of an upbringing in a "Christian" home, and how the truths instilled there should last a man a lifetime no matter where he chose to live. Ernest bit his tongue at all this, smiled quietly, kept eating, and offered only hints that he did not quite agree.

But when the family gathered in the parlor, Ernest could not restrain himself. He exhorted his parents to be tolerant, to not be so quick to condemn. Other people, Ernest said, face different problems from the Hemingways, usually because they have come to see the world in a different way. He had been all over Europe now, and there were plenty of decent people everywhere, even in Germany. It was always good to be tolerant, to listen, Ernest said, to alternative points of view.

In his pocket, Ernest carried three copies of his *Three Stories and Ten Poems*. He intended to make them one of his Christmas gifts to the family. But at supper that night he sensed what a mistake that would be. Later, he quietly gave one copy to Marcelline.

Marcelline did not read the slender volume until she and her husband were on the train back home to Detroit. Lying in her lower Pullman berth, she read first "Up in Michigan," the story Gertrude Stein had called *inaccrochable*. The next morning, she told her husband, Sanford, that Ernest's story of Jim Gilmore and Liz Coates's lovemaking on the end of a lakeside dock was "sordid," "vulgar." It even made her feel nausea. (Marcelline considered herself a writer and had composed in her senior year at Oak Park High the story of an insidious black snake, both terrifying and irresistible to the young girl he visits at night.) The whole family should thank God, she said, that *Three Stories and Ten Poems* would not be published in the United States.

When Ernest got back to Toronto, he had some serious business to attend to. For many reasons—one being Harry Hindmarsh—he knew he must break with the *Star*. Some sort of confrontation would be both appropriate and satisfying. Ernest thought it a stroke of good luck that he soon got his chance.

Not long after Ernest returned from Oak Park, Harry Hindmarsh ordered him to interview the traveling Hungarian diplomat, Count Apponyi. The count, notoriously hostile to journalists, was having little success convincing Canadian officials to act as go-between for Hungary and the United States. Perhaps because of Ernest's war record, and his ability to listen well and to ask original and intelligent questions, he charmed the Hungarian, and the interview went "splendidly." Apponyi even gave Ernest some important official documents. But, quite reasonably, the count "extracted a promise that they would be returned later in the day."

Hindmarsh, after reading the documents and Ernest's note about returning them, tossed the papers into the wastebasket, from which they were collected and burned. The next day, Ernest went to the count humiliated, and tried to explain. The count surprised Ernest with his graciousness. Nevertheless, Ernest decided, Hindmarsh would have to pay.

As soon as he returned to the *Star*, Ernest wrote to John Bone. Ernest said that he, Bone, was the best man on the paper. Unhappily, Bone's subordinate and Ernest's superior, Harry Hindmarsh, was "neither a just man, a wise man, nor a very honest man." Ernest explained all about Hindmarsh's jealousy, and about his "inferiority complex." But when Ernest looked at the letter the next morning, he knew how sick and tired he was of explaining himself to people, of defending everything he did. Instead of writing to John Bone, Ernest would tell Hindmarsh, face to face, that he held him and "all his bunch of masturbating mouthed associates" in "utter contempt." If Hindmarsh so much as "opened his trap" while Ernest was talking, Ernest would knock him down. Yes, Ernest would quit the *Star*, but it would be Hindmarsh he was quitting.

The letter of resignation Ernest finally did send to John Bone read: "I regret very much the necessity of tendering my resignation from the local staff of the *Star*. This resignation to take effect January 1st., 1924 if convenient to you. Please believe there is no rudeness implied through the brevity of this memorandum. . . . Ernest."

Just before Ernest and Hadley boarded the train to New York, Ernest was stunned by word from his mother. Grace wrote that she could not have been prouder of Ernest, that he was just like her father, Ernest Hall. She had interpreted Ernest's parlor speech the night he tried and failed to create an occasion in which he could present the copies of *Three Stories* as a plea for "World Patriotism," a belief, she said, that her father and Ernest shared. Ernest was a thoroughbred, Grace affirmed. And what a wonderful difference it made to discover him so. Ernest's special gift for his great-uncle, Tyley Hancock, the traveling salesman of brass beds, had moved Tyley to tears. Grace wrote that she and Tyley were so touched by "your generous gift" that "we cried in each others arms, off in a corner of the music room."

As Ernest and Hadley prepared to sail for France again, they felt they had failed in almost everything they'd come to Canada for. They had left Paris because it had seemed the practical, the sensible thing to do. With the baby coming, Ernest needed to secure a steady job; he had to stop George Breaker from stealing the money in Hadley's trust fund; and without fear of going broke, he had to get on with his writing. Yet the apartment they had taken in Toronto cost the equivalent of eighteen-thousand francs a year, three times as much as they had paid in Paris.

To make matters worse, Ernest had discovered nothing in New York about George Breaker's manipulations, and Hadley's trust fund had continued to depreciate. Because Hindmarsh had worked Ernest day and night, he had neglected his fiction. To Ezra Pound, Ernest wrote: "Feel so full of hate and so damned bitchingly, sickeningly, tired that anything I do will be of little value." There was always hope, though, as Ezra knew. At the close of the letter Ernest added" the diseased oyster shits the finest pearl, as the palmist says."

There was one bit of good news those last days in Canada. Edward O'Brien, an expatriate Bostonian, a lady's man whom Ernset had met with Ezra Pound in Italy, intended to dedicate to Ernest the next volume of an annual he edited, *The Best Short Stories of 1923*. He would include, as Ernest's contribution, "My Old Man," the race-track story everyone, except Ernest, said was derived from Sherwood Anderson. O'Brien also mentioned his connection with Boni and Liveright, a well-known and respected American publisher who, he said, might be interested in Ernest's short stories. This all sounded wonderful, except that Ernest had no new short stories to send. When *The Best Short Stories of 1923* finally came out, Ernest saw that O'Brien spelled him "Hemminway" throughout the publication.

Ernest was so disoriented by all this that he tried to reestablish his equilibrium by appealing to the goodness of heart of a professional critic. Ernest had seen his name mentioned in Burton Rascoe's column, "Social and Literary Notes," published in the *New York Tri-bune*. Rascoe had written that Edmund Wilson had shown him some "sketches" in *The Little Review*. They were the work of one Ernest Hemingway, a young American now living in Paris, and they contained "much life." Ernest sent a cordial note to Wilson, and one of the copies of *Three Stories and Ten Poems* he had expected to give his family. He asked for Wilson's opinion. If Wilson thought the stories good, could he, Ernest asked, send along the names of four or five people who might do a full-length review?

Wilson, a shy, aloof Princeton graduate, only four years older than Ernest, but as well-respected, nationally, as a good critic of forty would be, wrote back by return mail. Wilson said he wasn't much impressed with the book, but he thought Ernest was doing something very worth-while in those sketches Margaret Anderson had published in *The Little Review*. Wilson offered to mention *Three Stories and Ten Poems* in the *Dial*. Ernest suggested that Wilson hold off until he could get to him a copy of *in our time*. This second book contained eighteen sketches of the kind published in *The Little Review*. Perhaps Wilson could review both books at once.

When he returned to Paris, Ernest intended to take up his various roles: with Pound, the vigorous young student who would challenge his teacher, but always with respect; with Gertrude Stein, the student again, self-disciplined and devoted to his craft, who would champion her aesthetics and make her "proud"; with McAlmon, the worthy opponent who could demand the best from others because he demanded it of himself. But just before he left Toronto, Ernest would take the time to write a long letter to his former commanding officer at the Italian Front, his close friend, James Gamble. It was Gamble who had found Ernest lying wounded outside the operating tent at Fornaci and had seen him safely back to Milan. Later, Ernest and Jim had spent two weeks together in Sicily, at the hillside resort Taormina, just before Ernest sailed home in January 1919.

With Jim Gamble, Ernest was at his ease. He did not have to be tough or shrewd or even "worthy." Recalling his time with Jim in Italy, Ernest wrote: "Didn't we have fun in Milan and when I visited you at Taormina? It seems so very long ago and I haven't seen you since. That trip to Milan from the Piave had all the bad part smoothed out by you, I didn't do a thing except let you make me perfectly comfortable." Ernest did not feel he'd had much comfort in his life since then.

# ◁ 5 ▷

# *Is Fancy Bred?*

The train from Toronto arrived at Grand Central Station a few days before the little freighter *Antonia* was due to sail for France. It was the second week of the new year. Twice before Ernest had left New York for Europe filled with great expectations; twice he'd returned with cherished illusions gone. But this time would be different; he was a much changed man. The war had made words like *glory, sacrifice,* and the expression *in vain* obscene to Ernest. Now, to words like *prudence* and *security,* fate had done the same.

Back in Toronto, the Hemingways had vowed to risk everything on Ernest's talent. But in New York, with Hadley overweight, exhausted, feeling, she said, much more than her thirty-two years, with the nights spent walking the baby, carried on a pillow in a shabby hotel room, with a horrid winter crossing on that tiny ship ahead of them, Ernest knew he needed a new kind of strength—the will to keep his spirits up, the courage, in spite of everything, to be "cheerful."

On one of his last nights in New York, Ernest invited Margaret Anderson and Jane Heap, publishers of his sketches in *The Little Review,* to a boxing match at Madison Square Garden. Miss Heap, who dressed like a boulevardier, and Miss Anderson were lesbians. But, unlike Gertrude Stein and Alice Toklas, they'd made themselves a handsome pair. Miss Anderson found she was enchanted with Ernest, with his enthusiasm for the boxing and his knowledgeable analysis of it, blow by blow. Ernest in turn promised to send her the first things he wrote in Paris.

When the *Antonia* sailed on the nineteenth, a contrite Isabel Simmons was there to say goodbye. Unfortunately, because Ernest took it as an omen, his sad-faced cousin, Walter Johnson, was there, too. With things at their worst, Ernest made a gesture of confidence. For his embarkation attire, he wore tweed golf pants, woolen stockings, a beret, and carried the walking stick he'd learned to use gracefully when he was hobbled by his wounds in Milan.

Cunard's *Antonia* took ten days to cross the North Atlantic, and each day it was tortured by the sea. Too small to ride the swells, the little freighter rolled with nauseating rhythm, and Ernest preferred the freezing gale on deck to that awful turning of the cabin walls. To Hadley, the Hemingways' cramped cabin, far amidships, catching the engine vibration, seemed like steerage.

Then there were the smells: "The ship smelled of bilge and oil and the grease of the brass portholes and of the lavaboes and the disinfectant they used that was in big pink cakes in the pissoirs." The dining room smelled of cheap English cooking and cigarette butts left in ashtrays overnight. But worst of all were the English themselves; they all had a peculiar odor. Ernest found he could keep down only dry, sparkling Devon cider, and he drank it all the way across. After the tedium of customs at Le Havre came the deadly train ride to Paris.

Just before he'd left New York, Ernest had heard from Ford Madox Ford. Ford had written that, since the Pounds were traveling, the Hemingways could spend a few weeks in the Pounds' flat at 70 Rue Notre Dame des Champs. But Ford had made a mistake. When Ernest arrived at Pound's apartment, he learned that, although Ezra was, as Ford said, traveling, he had left no key. Ernest, exhausted and desperate, trudged through the wet snow toward the noise of a band saw, a few buildings down the street. In a small square of black, dripping trees and narrow old wooden houses, he found Pierre Chautard, a carpenter.

When Ernest asked if the carpenter knew of a place to stay, Chautard showed him a five-room flat over the sawmill. The kitchen had a slimy slate sink and a gas stove, with piles of burnt matches beneath the two burners. The place was furnished, Chautard said. But Ernest saw little more than a big bed in one room and a big table in another. Still, there was the pleasant smell of fresh-cut lumber, and windows all around. Madame Chautard, a foulmouthed, henna-haired harridan, sneered at the young couple and suggested she was doing them a favor—especially with the baby. Though he wanted to, Ernest did not haggle over the rent. For himself, his wife, and his son, nothing mattered more than a good night's sleep.

Not long after Ernest and Hadley had unpacked and settled into the apartment, a note arrived from Ezra Pound. He would be back in Paris within the week, and he wanted Ernest to meet with Ford Madox Ford. According to Ezra, Ford planned to publish a high-quality literary magazine. It would give talented young artists, especially those with a "transatlantic" connection, the chance to be read. Ford intended to call his magazine *transatlantic review*—the absence of capitals a tribute to one of his favorite American poets, e. e. cummings.

Hadley warned Ernest against putting too much faith in Ezra Pound. He was, after all, jealous of Ernest, she said. Ernest said that he knew Ezra had terrible judgment when it came to anything besides literature. But he was truly kindhearted and the one person in Paris he considered a friend.

When Ernest arrived for his meeting with Ford Madox Ford, he found Ezra, with his wild and bristly hair, his bandana tied around his neck, his large, sockless feet in shoes as big as Ernest's, ensconced on the pillow-and-blanket-covered divan he kept at the foot of the bedroom stairs. Ford, in winged collar and spats, looked the fatuous Edwardian. The first time Ernest had seen Ford, more than a year before, he had noticed a lack of convergence in Ford's eyes. It was impossible to tell if Ford were actually looking at you, or just past.

After giving Ford's limp hand a firm American shake, Ernest noticed Ford's breath and moved quickly away. To cover this, he took to moving about the room, shadowboxing before Ezra's collection of Buddhas. Ford thought Ernest strange, but Ezra said that Ernest was "an experienced journalist. He writes very good verse and he's the finest prose stylist in the world." Unfortunately, Pound had said the same thing about Ford a few weeks before. Miffed by this, Ford became haughty— he would have to be persuaded to take this unpredictable youth on as subeditor. Ezra talked and talked, and soon Ford was placated. There was, however, nothing said of remuneration. When, at Ezra's suggestion, Ford and Ernest shook hands again, Ernest felt he had somehow been taken.

Ernest accepted Ford's offer of subeditorship for one reason, and one reason only. He knew it would mean he could get some of his own stories published in the magazine. And now he had a few to choose from. One story he was very proud of he called "Indian Camp." Its setting was the Ojibway settlement just down the road from his family's summer cottage, Windemere, in northern Michigan. As a young boy, Ernest had often accompanied his father when the Indians needed Dr. Hemingway's care.

As Ernest first conceived it, "Indian Camp" began with a boy recalling how he was left alone one night in the tent while his father, a doctor, and Uncle George go to fish for supper with a jack light. Nick, perhaps eight or nine years old, walks down to the shore of the lake with his father and Uncle George. As his father rows off—Uncle George sitting in the stern, trolling—Nick waits until he can no longer hear the oars on the lake.

> Walking back through the woods Nick began to be frightened. He was always a little frightened of the woods at night. He opened the flap of the tent and undressed and lay very quietly between the blankets in the dark. The fire was burned down to a bed of coals outside. Nick lay still and tried to go to sleep. There was no noise anywhere. Nick felt if he could only hear a fox bark or an owl or anything he would be all right. He was not afraid of anything definite as yet. But he was getting very afraid. Then suddenly he was afraid of dying.

In his terror, Nick fires three shots (the prearranged signal of danger), and his father and Uncle George return. Nick says, under questioning, that he heard a sound something like a fox or a wolf, or maybe a cross between a fox and a wolf. The men smile at each other, and Nick is humiliated. His father calls him a child; Uncle George says he's a coward. Nick's father tells him, "You don't want to be ever frightened in the woods, Nick. There is nothing that can hurt you." "Not even lightning?" Nick asks. "No, not even lightning," his father says. "If there is a thunder storm, get out into the open. Or get under a beech tree." The doctor has satisfying answers to Nick's questions. The boy feels safe.

For some reason, probably because he found he was embarrassed about publishing his own work and wanted to take up as little space as possible in the *transatlantic review,* Ernest cut this beginning and started instead with two Indians coming for the doctor to take him across the lake to the Indian camp. A young woman there is trying to give birth. She has been trying to get the baby born for three days. It is a breech birth, and the woman is in agony.

Dr. Adams brings Nick along to watch the delivery. It seems appropriate to him because the mother is a "squaw." To the doctor it's not much different from showing his son a bitch giving birth. Also, the doctor wants Nick to be an "intern"; he wants him to learn to control his emotions in the presence of pain, to be "affectively neutral" as a doctor, in order to function, must be.

But Nick becomes an "intern" of another kind. The woman's screams, the cutting and the blood terrify him, and he internalizes what he hears and sees. Nick begs his father, "Oh, Daddy, can't you give her something to make her stop screaming?" The doctor insists that the woman's screams are not important, and so he does not hear them. He has only to perform well, technically.

After the Caesarean, done with a jacknife and gut leaders, Nick's father is elated—until he discovers that the Indian husband, lying in a bunk against the wall, his foot festering with an axe wound, has slit his throat. When the doctor tips back the Indian's head, Nick sees everything in the lantern light. The doctor's hand comes away wet from the blood pooled in the blanket.

As his father rows back to their camp in the early morning, Nick asks questions (as he had in the pages Ernest cut), searching again for the safety his father had provided when Nick's fear had been caused only by something he sensed in the woods after dark. Nick asks about suicide. "Why did he kill himself, Daddy?" "I don't know, Nick. He couldn't stand things, I guess. . . ." "Is dying hard, Daddy?" "No, I think it's pretty easy, Nick. It all depends."

As the doctor rows on, Nick trails his hand in the lake water, warm to his hand against the chill morning air, as the suicide's blood was warm to the doctor. Too young to "internalize" all he'd seen that day— too young to live with the knowledge that the danger he sensed in the forest is real and part of what a man must learn to endure—Nick shrinks from a truth that would obsess Ernest Hemingway throughout his life. The boy has discovered that he lives in the valley of the shadow of death, and that there is really no one to call for help. To get his fear under control, Nick embraces a childlike illusion: "In the early morning on the lake sitting in the stern of the boat with his father rowing, he felt quite sure that he would never die."

Although Ernest disliked having Ford Madox Ford around, Ford found Ernest attractive. He noticed that Ernest spoke hesitantly, that he had a tendency "to pause between words and then to speak gently but with great decision." To Ford, Ernest gave the impression "of a person using restraint at the biddings of discipline." Ford liked Ernest's work, too, and with a novelist's insight, and a bit of hyperbole, he wrote: "I did not read more than six words of his before I decided to publish everything that he sent me."

All his life, Ernest loved ritual for its satisfying sense of harmony and control. Most attractive to Ernest was Christian ritual, especially in the Episcopal and the Roman Catholic Mass. Ernest loved the fluency, the coherence of the Mass, and the feeling that, however old this ceremony, it seemed always fresh and young. Ernest told Hadley he wanted their son baptized a Christian and, he thought, in the Episcopal church. He said he'd asked his old friend from Chicago, Bill Horne, to be the godfather. But Bill could not make the trip. So he would ask "Chink" Dorman-Smith instead. For the godmother, Ernest said he wanted Gertrude Stein.

Shortly after his son was christened "John Hadley Nicanor Hemingway," Ernest met a young writer-publisher from the States. His name was Harold Loeb, and he had in tow a tall and blond woman, given to tight satin dresses and wisecracking conversation. Ernest dismissed the woman, but Loeb disturbed him. By and large, Ernest was accustomed to being in the company of men not nearly as handsome as he. Walking down the street, sitting in a café, talking in someone's parlor while a party went on, Ernest expected to be listened to, and looked at, and touched, by women who wanted his attention. But with Harold Loeb around, things were different. Loeb, at thirty-two, retained the physique that had made him a varsity wrestler at Princeton. He had black hair, curled thick, and the nose and chin of a Greek statue. Even Hadley told Ernest that Loeb was "handsome."

In his years at prep school and at Princeton, Loeb had acquired an expensive tennis game, with a good "lawford," and an American twist serve. Each afternoon, he cheerfully beat Ernest at a small clay-court club in the shadow of the Parisian prison that harbored the guillotine. Loeb made Ernest the gift of a cat, a tabby he had found among the ruins in Rome. Ernest called her F. Puss, after the successful young American author F. Scott Fitzgerald. Ernest gave the big yellow cat to his son, now called Bumby, and she immediately lay quiet in Bumby's tall cage bed. People told Ernest that a cat would lie close to his son, while he slept, and suck the baby's breath away. Others said that the cat would lie across the baby's face and smother him. But, to Ernest, this was all nonsense. In fact, F. Puss took a proprietary interest in Bumby and would snarl and hiss if someone strange approached the baby's crib.

Ernest could not help liking Loeb, especially for his hard-won athletic skill. But he felt that Harold had three liabilities: he was slow-witted, he was clumsily sentimental, and he tried too hard to make friends. Ernest also resented Loeb's money—his mother was a Guggenheim.

While Hadley cared for Bumby most of the day, and made friends with Loeb's mistress, Kitty Cannell, Ernest found it did him good to earn some money boxing at a club on the Rue Pontoise. The pay was ten francs a round for sparring, and there was usually at least six rounds of work. At a thin 170, Ernest still looked a big man, and it was the heavyweights that hired him. Ernest could take a punch well, especially on the jaw where, luckily, he was one of those for whom it does not disconnect. The professionals worked on their speed and usually spent the rounds head-hunting. That meant there weren't the next-day body pains, but they did "thicken an ear" and "un-Greek" Ernest's nose.

Ernest had been drinking more than he should have, and felt good about "sweating the poison out" at the gym. Also he liked to watch a five-foot-four-inch Italian boxer named Paolino. Across the shoulders, Paolino was as wide "as the Arc de Triomphe," but he had "little legs like a sandpiper." Paolino ate raw fish, swung his eyes closed, and looked bad against anyone until he knocked them out.

On off days, Ernest spent his time in the backyard garden a waiter friend cultivated behind the Closerie des Lilas, a quiet café just down the street from Ernest's flat. When the barman at the Closerie was forced by the management to shave off a mustache he'd earned as a dragoon in a cavalry regiment, Ernest watched him work at his garden for three straight days.

With their return to Paris, Ernest and Hadley knew they must be hard on themselves, more disciplined perhaps than they'd ever been before. Everything they did now had a new dimension to it, the urgent need to economize. Where they lived, how they dressed, what they ate and when was determined by the scale of profit and loss. Everything was measured in the same way—did it help make it possible for them to go on, for Ernest to continue his writing?

Most mornings, Ernest closeted himself in the small room he and Hadley had first thought would be the baby's. But the drafts in the apartment did not bring the fireplace heat that way, and Bumby slept in his crib in his father and mother's room. To keep warm in the small room, Ernest bought a kerosene heater. Hadley worried about Ernest spending hours behind a closed door and, for all she knew, a closed window with that heater going strong. How could he write anything being "asphyxiated" that way? When Ernest emerged, often with a story in hand, Hadley would breathe a sigh of relief, and sit down and listen.

Depite everything he told his friends, and the impression he created around Montmartre—that he worked most of the time—Ernest could do no more than four hours of writing each day. After that, he became facile, or he resorted to the kind of self-indulgence (having "fun" with writing) that marked, he felt, the true amateur. After his work, Ernest would walk alone in the Luxembourg Gardens—"cooling off," he called it—on the fresh-washed gravel paths, in the clear, sharp wind. Like much of Paris, the gardens seemed full of life, unforced, immediate, in the process of being lived. Thoughts of the future, or the past, thoughts about the "meaning" of things, were lost in the friendly salute of a gendarme, or the sight of a boy in his hooded wool coat, launching his toy sailboat on the frigid waters of the pond.

When Ernest left the Luxembourg, he would walk down the narrow Rue Ferou to the Place St.-Sulpice. There he could sit on the benches of the square, before the great fountain of bishops and lions. In the square, shops sold religious articles, and there was a small hotel. Standing by these shops and this hotel, named for the notorious Madame Recamier, the cathedral looked a sheer cliff, with spires domed like churches in the pagan East.

In his twenties, Ernest loved to eat, and delicious food was cheap and plentiful in Paris. Yet he still suspected that the true artist, like the honest monk, denied the flesh for the spirit. With Hadley's income dwindling, Ernest began a daily fasting that would last until suppertime. To keep his mind off his hunger—the market streets were filled with irresistible aromas of the best breads and pastries, the finest meats and cheeses in the world—Ernest spent hours in the Luxembourg Museum. He made himself believe that the hunger sharpened his perception, that he could see more in the Cezannes, in the sharpness and clarity of the landscapes, when he was "belly-empty, hollow-hungry." But Sylvia Beach, at Shakespeare and Company, would accuse him of growing thin and ask what he had had for lunch.

Eventually, Ernest saw the potential for affectation in fasting, for the same sort of posing that made him hate the fakers at the "artists' cafés." One day, in response to Sylvia Beach's remark about his appearance, Ernest went directly to Brasserie Lipp, where he ordered potato salad with oil, a *cervelas*, a heavy, wide frankfurter, split in two, and covered with a heavy mustard sauce, and, to drink very slowly, a *distingué*, a liter mug of beer.

In April 1924, Ernest read the first published letters of Vincent van Gogh. He was overwhelmed. They were, without question, part of a spiritual autobiography without precedent. They revealed the pristine sanity of genius, and a capacity for suffering and sacrifice for the truth that Ernest had never before encountered. Ernest was particularly affected by the relationship van Gogh had with Gauguin. Ernest saw in van Gogh's love for Gauguin, in his yearning for Gauguin's approval, an emotional counterpart to his own feelings for his parents.

Hadley was shocked when Ernest announced he would "make a pilgrimage" to Provence, to van Gogh's pitiful little apartment above the tobacco shop. Ernest told Hadley that Vincent's masterpieces—a father's chair and pipe, a crude and simple bedroom, a worktable with a plate of onions, a candle, a pipe and tobacco, a half-empty bottle of wine, a once-read letter from a friend, a book of home remedies, and, of course, the famous sunflowers, through which, in painting after painting, he expressed his joy at finding a true friend—made that tobacco shop an artists' shrine.

In the letters of van Gogh, Ernest discovered that Paul Gauguin was hardly the man, or the friend, Vincent had hoped for. Small-minded and selfish in the extreme, Gauguin went to Arles only to live off van Gogh until he acquired the money to continue on. Night after night they would argue about aesthetics, Vincent searching for the truth, Gauguin engaged in pedestrian sophistries. Finally, van Gogh wanted to murder Gauguin, and confronted him with scissors at a café on Christmas Eve. Gauguin, however, stood and turned on van Gogh and fixed him with his stare.

Back at their rooms above the tobacconist, Vincent used the scissors on himself, cutting off the lobe of his right ear. Then he staggered off to the whorehouse he and Gauguin spent half their nights in and presented his prize to their favorite whore. Then he staggered home, lay down in bed, and waited to bleed to death. Ernest visited van Gogh's house and the whorehouse, and concluded that Arles was no place for a writer. There was too much power in the Provençal sun.

The trip south lasted six days, and took Ernest, finally, to St. Remy, the asylum where van Gogh had been confined. Which would be worse, Ernest wrote to Hadley, madness or death? Ernest returned to Paris filled with compassion for the long-suffering artist who had wagered his life on his work.

To Ernest, one of his best friends had something in common with Vincent van Gogh. Although Gertrude Stein did not endure the kind of hardships van Gogh had, she knew very well what it meant to work on unappreciated, to be, in some circles, ridiculed and scorned. On his part, Ernest liked Gertrude Stein very much. In some mysterious way she was Paris to him, the one to whom, when he left Canada, he felt he was coming home. While he and Harley were in Toronto, Gertrude had published a review of *Three Stories and Ten Poems* in the Paris edition of the *Chciago Tribune* November 27, 1923. She had sent Ernest her review copy of his book, all "mutilated" because "I have such a strong feeling about the sanctity of the written or typewritten more than I have for the printed but then there is diplomacy." Gertrude's review read:

> Three stories and ten poems is very pleasantly said. So far so good. Further than that, and as far as that, I may say of Ernest Hemingway that as he sticks to poetry and intelligence it is both poetry and intelligent. Rosevelt [sic] is genuinely felt as young as Hemingway and as old as Rosevelt. I should say that Hemingway should stick to poetry and intelligence and eschew the hotter emotions and the more turgid vision. Intelligence and a great deal of it is a good thing to use when you have it, it is all for the best.
>
> Gertrude Stein

During his visits to 27 Rue de Fleurus, Ernest had heard Gertrude read from her magnum opus, a massive, unfinished manuscript, a compendium of Gertrude's experimental writing accomplished over a decade or more. She called it *The Making of Americans*. Ernest saw that it began well, went on that way for a long while, then slipped off into self-parody. Finally, when Gertrude tired of smiling into a mirror, it lost even the power that narcissism gives. Ernest read the first chapters of the manuscript quickly. To be put in shape for publication, *The Making of Americans* clearly required cutting and some line-by-line revision.

Although Ernest needed all his strength and will to get his own work done, he volunteered to edit Gertrude's novel and to see to its serial publication in the *transatlantic review*. He would also champion its cause with Harold Stearns, the continental scout for American publisher Boni and Liveright.

After a few weeks of effort, Ernest said chances for publication in the *transatlantic review* looked good. Boni and Liveright, however, rejected Gertrude's novel out of hand, and Ernest commiserated with her:

I am awfully sorry. It is such a rotten shame to get hopes about anything. I have been feeling awfully badly about it. But there are other
publishers and don't you ever get up any hopes and I will keep on
plugging and it will go sooner or later. . . . I feel sick about it but
don't you feel bad, because you have written it and that is all that
matters a damn. It is up to us, i.e. Alice Toklas, Me, Hadley, John
Hadley Nicanor and other good men to get it published. It will all
come sooner or later the way you want it. This is not Christian Science.

With love,
Hemingway.

Ernest had seen Spain at Gibraltar in 1919, and at Vigo in 1921. But
with Gertrude Stein's rendering of the corrida and her stories of famous matadors, she made Spain come alive for him as it never had before. When she thought he was ready, Gertrude had introduced Ernest
to Picasso, Miró, and Gris—the men and their work. Ernest, at first
sight, liked Miró's work very much, but he thought less of Gris and
Picasso. A certain incident, however, made Picasso an especially sympathetic figure, who, later on, became Ernest's good friend and fellow
critic of Gertrude Stein.

During one of the soirees Gertrude held at 27 Rue de Fleurus,
Picasso arrived early, ready to read his poems. Traditionally, the read-
ings for the evening were given by Gertrude's friends from the lesbian
community: poets Natalie Barney, Robert McAlmon's wife, Bryher, or
Djuna Barnes. As the women read their poems, Ernest noticed how
Alice Toklas burned with jealousy if Gertrude smiled or laughed too
much, or said a work or a reader was especially good. But the real distress was caused by the presence of the black-eyed, intense, wonderfully
built Picasso.

Picasso's poetry was free-verse, an association of images and ideas,
and as loosely written as anything Gertrude had ever done herself.
Picasso's ideas lived for him as images, and in imagistic language they
had undeniable power. But poetry to Picasso was what sign language
is to a man who can speak. Although he read passionately, his performance was met with silence. Gertrude Stein said to him, "Go back
home, Pablo, and paint."

Ernest thought Picasso kind, human, vital, understanding. Picasso
made good jokes with him, Ernest said, as though they were longtime
friends. Ernest and he were "peasants" to the rich, Picasso said. They
both should always accept invitations "with delight," and then never
go. Ernest knew women found Picasso very attractive, "like a little
Spanish bull." Picasso recognized the elemental appeal in Ernest, and
called him "The Savage."

By the time Ernest traveled south with Hadley in July 1924, he felt that Spain was his home. In no other place did he feel, physically, so contented, as if he so much belonged. Spain, like Paris, was old. But Paris was the reign and death of kings. Spain—the medieval village of Algeciras, the dry rolling hills along the Spanish coast, the strange romance of Ronda, the cliff city he'd seen in the moonlight—was pre-historic. In Spain time seemed irrelevant, and moved like a donkey cart along a dusty road. To allow Ernest and Hadley to make the trip comfortably, Gertude Stein said she would take care of Bumby, take him with her to the South of France.

When Ernest found something he loved, something that nourished him and made the most difficult thing in his life, his writing, easier to do, he could not help selling the experience to friends. After his trip to Spain in 1923, Ernest had told "Chink" Dorman-Smith and John Dos Passos how much they'd miss by not going to Spain, and McAlmon and Bird how little they'd managed to get from being there. Spain, Ernest insisted, was the last place left in Europe where the artist could get what he needed: direct contact with the essentials of life, and a sense of his true feelings about them. Naturally this endorsement gave Ernest a certain responsibility, once Chink, Dos Passos, Bob McAlmon, even his skiing friend, young George O'Neil, promised to make the trip. Should Spain not meet their expectations, should the poetry of the land have no effect on them, Ernest must take it upon himself to make Spain come alive.

Each morning, for the free-for-all amateur bullfights, Ernest dressed in white pants (to attract the bull) and wore three sweaters (to offer some protection against the crushing impact of the padded horns). It was as if everything he had said about the value of Spain was mixed up in the value of what he, himself, could do. Dancing, before the bull with his usual big-footed clumsiness, Ernest was beaten in the stomach and chest, lifted and carried on the horns. Full of embarrassment at his lack of skill, his awkwardness and lack of grace, Ernest managed to get his feet on the ground and then, as if it were a small steer, bulldogged the animal.

Don Stewart, Yale graduate and young Boni and Liveright humorist, found Ernest's courage contagious. Ernest was "so God damned brave," Stewart said, that he, Stewart, had to challenge the bulls himself. Unfortunately, Stewart's bull caught him under the arm and tossed him, breaking three of his ribs.

After Stewart's misfortune, everyone's enthusiasm cooled. But Ernest knew he could rekindle it in the stands of the bullring with another performance: his running commentary on the setting of pics, the work of the banderillero, the courage, skill, and aesthetic sense of the matador. Rather than play critic, a role he despised because he felt it made most people arrogant and cruel, Ernest wanted very much to teach his audience how to "see" the bullfight.

It was not, Ernest insisted, a spectator sport. Just as the sun must be very hot and bright for the bullfight to succeed, so the audience must be passionate for success. They must know that the force and veracity of their response affects, intimately and continuously, the performance of the picadors, the matador, even the bull itself. They must discipline themselves to notice everything, and judge nothing, until the rhythm of the ritual makes it time to judge. Then their voice must be profound, and without pity. Each member of the audience must strive to be a true participant. He must bring to the experience all he has, and have the courage to face what it offers. Just what Ernest believed the artist must do.

After the intensity of the bullring, there was for Ernest the Spanish countryside—the most beautiful, he believed, in Europe. As if to compensate the "gang" for what he had demanded at the bullfights, Ernest suggested a trip to the Irati River in the Pyrenees, where he'd found the sort of fishing you only find in dreams. He had discovered the river the summer past, when a Spaniard Ernest had shared a half-dozen bottles of wine with offered to show him the biggest trout in Spain. Ernest had seen the trout—easily a sixteen-pounder—in a hole that the Spaniard professed the fish had lived in for years. The Spaniard said the water was so deep that peasant women, doing their wash on stones on the bank, did not disturb the fish.

Bill and Sally Bird, Bob McAlmon, Don Stewart, Chink Dorman-Smith, George O'Neil, and John Dos Passos left Pamplona before the festival ended, to be off for the country fishing. Drunk on liter earthen jugs of the local wine, everyone boarded the morning bus in the heat, before the blinding white façade of the Hotel San Martin. Bill Bird, in a white rumpled suit, carrying his jug on board, gestured in triumph to Ernest, who took his and Sally's picture. Standing next to them was McAlmon, as slouched and rumpled as Bird.

Ernest told Hadley that despite the wonderful fiesta, he was "terrible depressed." First of all, they were now almost broke. Hadley was surprised at this. Hadn't they brought plenty of money along? Yes, they had, Ernest said. But during the afternoon drunk, he had lent most of it to Chink, Dos Passos, and McAlmon. For God's sake, why? Hadley asked. The men had said they wanted to know the country as Ernest did, and would, after the fishing, hike through the Pyrenees to Andorra. They needed money for food and drink.

Then, too, Ernest said, there had been the insufferable heat in Pamplona, the nonstop drinking, and the pain from three flesh-breaking wounds with the bulls. Finally, there was that awful misfortune on the festival's last day.

Ernest and Hadley had gone down into the crowd that lined the fence from the edge of town to the bullring. The rocket, signaling the start of the running of the bulls, went off, and the crowd started coming on. Two drunks, one who fell on the muddy ground, another who intended to attempt veronicas with a blouse, were dragged away by the police.

But then something unusual happened. A man in the running crowd was singled out by a bull. The bull shot from the herd, caught the man in the back, and lifted him in the air. As the horn went in, Ernest saw the man's head drawn back and his arms go rigid by his sides. It was only after all the bulls had passed and the red door of the bullring was shut that the crowd noticed the man. He lay facedown in the trampled mud.

Later that day, Ernest learned the man's name and something about the family he left. Ernest followed the coffin from the chapel of San Fermin to the train, watched as it was loaded into the baggage car, and watched the train pass down around the edge of the plateau of Pamplona and out into the fields of grain.

When Ernest and Hadley finally got to the Irati River, fifteen miles by foot from Burguete, all of it on mountain roads that Ernest said were steep enough to pass out a mule, he was too exhausted to keep the party going, too exhausted even to try. But soon the ice-cold stream, the virgin forest, the sense of depth the silence gave the woods, revived him. And there was something more. As it was at St. Bernard, a medieval monastery here too embodied the spirit of the terrain. In this monastery, at Roncesvalles, a hero of French national myth had died, the hero of *La Chanson de Roland*.

In the epic poem, which Ernest knew and loved, young Roland is the chivalric ideal: the valiant fighter, the warm and faithful friend, and, above all, the Christian believer. Yet Roland does have a flaw. He personifies too-bold self-reliance. Determined to fight a rear-guard action with nowhere near enough men, he risks the destruction of his army. In the heat of battle, Roland refuses his one hope of salvation, the summoning of his spiritual father, Charlemagne. After watching his comrades die in hopeless combat and being wounded severely himself, Roland does finally blow the alarm. But the strain is too much, and he bursts his temples. Roland is carried to the monastery at Roncesvalles, and there he dies. Yet, according to the poet, Roland is received into Paradise, his excesses sure proof of his merit.

Ernest could not resist going to Mass at the monastery, nor writing Ezra Pound about the experience. He had prayed, he said, "for my kid, for Hadley and for myself and your concert." Ernest had made a fool of himself at the fiesta, he said, because he needed to forget that his life was going to pieces. The critic Burton Rascoe had found *in our time* derivative, an imitation of Ring Lardner and Sherwood Anderson.

What rotten, undeserved luck he had, Ernest said. James Joyce, who was, after all, a "measly and shitty" guy, was having a great success with his art because, with a patroness, he'd had the liberty to do it. But the work Ernest had done on the *transatlantic review* had used up the time and energy he needed for his own writing. Eventually, some son-of-a-bitch would copy everything, and when Ernest finally got a real book done, everyone would call him so-and-so's imitator. Ernest told Ezra that bad news came in clusters. The rest of Hadley's money had now been stolen by George Breaker. "These god damn bastards," Ernest wrote. "Now we haven't got any money anymore I am going to have to quit writing and I never will have a book published."

Nevertheless, when he and Hadley got back to Paris on July 27, Ernest tried his best to keep the *transatlantic* going and to get Gertrude Stein's *The Making of Americans* serialized in it. From August 9 to October 10, the two months that Gertrude Stein and Alice Toklas spent on the Riviera, Ernest wrote them long letters every two weeks, reporting his progress.

In these letters to Gertrude Stein, a new Ernest appears. He is no longer the neophyte, wide-eyed with excitement, charmingly ingenuous. In fact, he writes to Gertrude as if he were her literary agent, capable of appreciating her art, yet ready to function in the cutthroat world of small-time publishing. The "Quarterlys," the "Criterions," the "transatlantics" now seemed silly and self-serving to Ernest, part of a mean-spirited game where bloated egos, insect authority, and the ever-looming patron—part angel, part sucker—prevailed.

It was always best, Ernest had learned, to work hard in the face of despair. Unable to work for himself, he'd try to help Gertrude Stein.

Despite her stature in the Parisian literary community, she was, Ernest knew, still a college sophomore at heart. She said that she especially liked it that Ernest appreciated her work, forgave her her laziness and irresponsibility—as her older brother, Leo, had never done—and now looked out for her interests, too.

Shortly after he returned to Paris, Ernest wrote to Gertrude that, due to the support of one of his Chicago pals, Krebs Friend, who had once been so broke he'd borrowed fifteen dollars from Ernest but was now married to an heiress, the *transatlantic review* was saved. Best of all, there would be "regular and continuous publication" of *The Making of Americans*. Gertrude was overjoyed. She wrote from the Hotel Pernollet in Belley:

> My Dear Hemingway,
> I have had both your letters and I am more pleased than I can say with the good news. I would have been heart-broken if the Transatlantic had stopped and now we will all be printed and we will all be payed [*sic*], both good things, what a wonderful fifteen dollars, bread on waters is nothing to that. We are having a charming time here in the land of your kings, you know there are moments when I almost am going fishing, you drop a line in, and after waiting three hours you pull without any Xertion a large salmon trout out and you can sit down in all between, I mean all in between the pulling out. Alice won't buy me an outfit however until I am sincere, and so I watch the others mostly in the three hours time, a delightful land, we are going to to see where your kings were buried and the other day we went over the collar of the cat and burnt out our brake bands, otherwise everything is serene with us and Gody. I wish you were here because then perhaps I could fish with your line and if it looked as if I could do it again I would have one of my own, perhaps on the whole though it is better just to long.

When Gertrude got her check for the July installment of *The Making of Americans,* she wrote to Ernest again.

> My Dear Hemingway,
> I did as you advised wrote a firm and gentle letter to Ford and the July check has come with Mrs. [Reid or Kreb's] promise of more to come in the very immediate future so I guess you made your effect alright, thanks so much, that little check comes in handy, anything comes in handy particularly when you have gotten used to it and I almost had and now I quite have, I . . . mail often quite a few firm and gentle letters. . . . I am doing something I think will please you. The Brzzilian [*sic*] Admiral's son. I think I have gotten some new tines, a thing much to be desired.

When Ernest and Hadley came to Paris the second time, they had seen enough of the world to know that to succeed one had to be very lucky as well as very good. They never doubted Ernest's talent. Those stories he'd read to Hadley were wonderful; they came from that special part of him, she said, the part that could never lose its shine. Hadley called it his "religiousness," not any set of beliefs, but an instinct for the truth and the talent to tell it in a way that allowed people, comfortably and satisfyingly, to believe. But they were betting their lives on the will of the gods, and they knew it.

Hadley thought that Ernest's "sexual" stories—more penetrating in their analysis of the male and female in America, she said, than anything since Dreiser's *Sister Carrie*—might be the most popular of all. She especially liked "The Doctor and the Doctor's Wife," in which the title characters, modeled on Ernest's parents, Clarence and Grace Hemingway, reveal, in their muted sexual conflict, that the myths American women use to civilize their men make them into spiritual weaklings. Convinced that their passions are somehow wrong and must be repressed and denied, the Clarence Hemingways–Dr. Adamses of this world are boy-men, often impotent, addicted to masturbation, incapable of curing their sexually frustrated wives.

Ernest, of course, had favorite stories of his own. One was about sixteen-year-old Nick Adams, who also feels the tension that grows between a man and a woman when their love goes very wrong. In "The End of Something," Nick has taught his girl, Marjorie, everything he knows about fishing, and about sex. And he has encouraged her to be one of the guys. Marjorie, on her part, is willing, all too willing, to become both his lover and his "pal." Yet love with Marjorie now is not fun anymore. Nick, like the fish they are trolling for, does not bite when Marjorie makes her offer.

"The End of Something" begins with a deserted sawmill and the memory of how, after cutting down and sawing up all the trees, the lumber company, leaving only piles of sawdust, loaded its saw on a boat and sailed quietly away. The story ends with Nick recumbent by the campfire and Marjorie rowing off in their skiff. The symbols of emasculation make the parallel clear. In the final paragraphs, Nick's friend Bill shows up and offers a chance at regression, a move back for Nick to male friendship—a move Nick reluctantly makes in the sequel to "The End of Something," "The Three-Day Blow."

Ernest told Hadley that one of the stories was based on his homecoming after the Great War in January 1919. In "Soldier's Home,"

Nick Adams is now Harold Krebs, named after Ernest's newfound benefactor, Krebs Friend. Now the threat from the female, both mother and wife, is combined in the character of Krebs's mother, the personification of his Oklahoma hometown culture. Mrs. Krebs is selfish and ignorant. She is not intentionally cruel, yet, in her way, she can be infinitely destructive. She offers Krebs the comforts and privileges of home. She'll make him a fine breakfast every morning. He'll be allowed to use the family car. Perhaps he will get a job in the bank, like his father, and date the "nice girls" in town.

What will be the price of this? Nothing less than his soul. Mrs. Krebs's definition of love is the devil's own perversion of it: if you love me, you'll do as I say. Krebs escapes his mother because he has, in the war, developed an aesthetic sense—a sense of proportion. He knows his mother has no conception of what is important in life, and can never have. He would love to make her "see" how things are, but her mind is sealed tight. There is nothing for Krebs to do but leave small-town America for Kansas City, the only wide-open city between the coasts.

Back in Paris, Ernest felt forsaken. There was no money, he said, in helping people, even good people, because it cost too much and things never evened up. Then, out of the blue, he heard from the one man who had been willing to test the Pamplona bulls with him. Don Stewart, home in New York but still in pain from his bull-broken ribs, urged Ernest to get up a manuscript. Include everything good that he had, Stewart said, whether it fit together or not. Stewart would take it to publisher George Doran and make sure that Doran himself gave it a reading.

# 6

## *Mutability*

When Ernest first wrote his fiction for sale in the popular magazine market—on his return from the war in Italy in 1919—he'd had no luck. As the rejections piled up, his Oak Park friend, Lewis Clarahan, had tried to console him. "You've got to find an intelligent editor," Clarahan had said. "At first, all good writers get rejected everywhere."

This had pleased Ernest because he knew Clarahan meant to be kind. But Ernest also knew there was more to it than that. His favorite high school teacher, Fanny Biggs, had told him that the best writing comes from personal experience, and that he must write only of what he knew and felt deeply about. The stories he'd sent to the magazines in 1919—all but one, "Crossroads"—were about what he'd heard, or read, or daydreamed. Because he could not write as a diarist (except in private stories he would never publish), Ernest believed he could never follow Miss Biggs's advice.

By 1923, however, Ernest had learned how to write of what he knew and felt deeply about in "fictional autobiography." The secret was not to simply report his experience, but to report a recreation of it. He explained the process to Hadley this way.

Ernest told his wife that he could never understand a thing, could never write about it, unless he lived it. But "living it" had a special meaning for him. As a boy, he had believed that at night his soul left his body and roamed the oak-lined avenues of his home town. When Ernest sat writing in his room above the sawmill, when he wrote at his window table at the Closerie des Lilas, he also felt his soul leave his body. Ernest said that while he was writing, he was alive only within the story. The act of composition was life itself, lived for a while in another way. That was why a waiter, a passing acquaintance, even Hadley herself, would come and want to speak to him while he worked and suddenly know that he was not really there and that, by their interruption, they would risk breaking a spell.

The stories Ernest wrote in Paris had an intimate purpose. They were written as much for the author as for his reader. Transported into the world of his art, Ernest sought to resolve those personal conflicts that plagued him at the time of composition. The central character in each of his best short stories, in all of his novels, is Ernest himself, trying to work things out.

The story Ernest considered his best, one he was shy about, as he always was about his finest work—so shy that he did not read it even to Hadley—had, in the writing, helped to heal the deepest wounds of Ernest's young life. Ernest called his story "Big Two-Hearted River" because he thought that title poetry, and because it suggested how nature both loves and challenges her own.

Ernest divided "Big Two-Hearted River" into two parts. In Part One, Nick Adams, Ernest's persona, is, in his mind, as fragile as a cracked piece of china. His woundings, by war and love, have left him "sensitized." Life in the city is unbearable. With the slightest stimulation, his emotions go out of control.

To regain his emotional health, Nick reacquaints himself, slowly and carefully, with the world of the senses. He rides a small wilderness train to a small, burned-out town in Upper Michigan. Disembarking, preparing for the hike to come, he adjusts the pack harness and feels with satisfaction the pulling straps tight on his shoulders, the strain of the tump line against his forehead.

As he climbs toward the forest, he sees the burned-out country stop on a range of hills. Ahead of him lies a pine plain and the far blue hills that mark the Lake Superior height of land. Nick keeps his direction by the sun. Once he breaks off some sprigs of heathery sweet fern, and puts them under his pack straps. The chafing crushes the fern, and he smells the scent as he walks.

Before Nick contacts the river, he rests in an island of pines. There he slips off his backpack and sleeps in the shade. When he awakes, stiff and cramped, the sun is almost down. Now the pack is heavy and the straps painful. Nick knows that the river cannot be more than a mile away.

Nick comes down a stump-covered hillside, into a meadow. There is the river. It flows at the edge of the meadow. Nick walks upstream, wetting his trousers in the dew-laden grass. The river flows fast and smooth. It is time to make camp, and to cook supper:

> Nick was hungry. He did not believe he had ever been hungrier. He opened and emptied a can of pork and beans and a can of spaghetti into the frying pan. . . . He started a fire with some chunks of pine he got with the ax from a stump. Over the fire he stuck a wire grill, pushing the four legs down into the ground with his boot. Nick put the frying pan on the grill over the flames. He was hungrier. The beans and spaghetti warmed. Nick stirred them and mixed them together. They began to bubble, making little bubbles that rose with difficulty to the surface. There was a good smell.

When Nick finishes eating, he makes coffee, and lights a cigarette, and then, with the match, extinguishes a loud, buzzing mosquito against the canvas of his tent. Then he falls to sleep.

In his hike to the river, his making camp, his warming and eating supper, Nick has prepared himself, in the old-fashioned way, for healing. He has created a natural, healthy order in his life. He has reestablished his connection with the sensate world. He sleeps in his tent, confident nature will take its course.

In "Big Two-Hearted River: Part Two," Nick Adams tests himself. How far has the healing progressed? First, Nick fishes the river. He employs all his skill; he hooks a trout; he enjoys the wonderful, brief linkage. Although Nick does not land the fish, the effect is profound.

> Nick's hand was shaky. He reeled in slowly. The thrill had been too much. He felt, vaguely, a little sick, as though it would be better to sit down. . . . That was a trout. He had been solidly hooked. Solid as a rock. He felt like a rock, too, before he started off. By God, he was a big one. By God, he was the biggest one I ever heard of.

Nick's fly line is the thin but reliable strand that binds him to the things of this world. It stretches as far as all history: from the creature still of the water, to the evolved creature of the air. And there is "God" in it. Nick has been granted his well-earned epiphany.

Back in Chicago, in 1921, Ernest had seen what happened when a young man, an intimate friend, was put to a test he was not ready for.

In those days, Ernest had lived in a men's domicile. It was run by the brother and sister-in-law of his old fishing friend, William Smith. "Doodles," as the wife was called, couldn't resist the young men boarders. Her excuse was that Kenley, her husband, had tuberculosis, and this had rendered him impotent. Shortly before Ernest's marriage to Hadley, in September, Doodles had said she wanted him. Ernest had turned her down. But he'd made the mistake of telling another boarder, "Dirty" Don Wright, about it, probably because Wright was numbered among Doodles's lovers and had propositioned Hadley a few months before. "Dirty Don" ran to Kenley and Bill with the story. Bill Smith then wrote to Ernest, breaking off their five-year friendship. Eventually, Kenley Smith found a lover of his own, a "hotblooded" Pole named Wanda Elaine Stopa. Miss Stopa tried to murder Doodles, firing three shots at the bed where Doodles lay with her current lover, Henry Manning. As luck would have it, Manning took the bullets. Miss Stopa escaped to Detroit, where she committed suicide the next day.

The innocent victim in all this, at least as Ernest saw it, was his friend, Bill Smith. True, Bill had been unjust to Ernest, but he had acted out of loyalty to his family. Now Bill was coming to Paris, broke and looking for a job. Ernest had heard that Ernest Walsh, the foppish, tubercular Irishman he'd met at Ezra Pound's apartment in 1922, intended, with money from his patroness, Ethel Moorhead, to start a literary magazine. Ernest asked Walsh and Miss Moorhead to give Bill a job. He would be a crackerjack reader of proof, Ernest said. And he honestly needed the work. Walsh considered Ernest presumptuous. He, Ernest Walsh, knew when an increase of staff was in order. Of course, he would refuse.

In the wet Paris fall of 1924, the Hemingways all came down with the "flu." It was the rotten dampness, Ernest said. But there was a way out. An American painter, Bertram Hartman, had told Ernest about a village midway between Zurich and Innsbruck, fifteen hundred meters high in the Austrian Alps. The snow was powder, the air clear. Schruns, as it was called, was a skier's paradise. And a lovely old hotel, the Taube, would cost pennies a day. Ernest told Hadley he could not wait to go. Besides, Dr. Clarence Hemingway was certain the "flu" could not live in dry cold.

The trip from Paris to Schruns worked the same kind of magic on Ernest as his trips from Chicago to northern Michigan had done when he was a boy. Just getting away from the city, just the movement itself, was a tonic to his spirit. The train to Schruns wound through Switzerland, crossed the Austrian frontier, the dollhouse principality of Liechtenstein, and then branched off to run along a small, pebbly river that Ernest said he could feel the trout swimming in. Coming upon Schruns at midday, Ernest saw that it lay in a broad valley, open to the sun. It must be a market town, he thought, with sawmills, stores, and inns for skiers. The most substantial building in town, five stories and faced with white stucco, was the Hotel Taube.

The rooms at the Taube were just what the Hemingways needed. They were the sort of rooms a peasant would prepare for special guests he knew required the comfort of abundant necessities. At the Taube, the big stoves could hold all-night logs, the big windows Ernest could open against the stove's heat, the big beds could accommodate Ernest and Hadley and Bumby, too.

Hadley said she liked the practice ski slope that ran through apple orchards behind the Taube. Ernest liked the slope behind Tchagguns, where, in the late afternoon, he skied from the sun into the darkened valley. After supper, the Hemingways drank at the inn amid a splendid collection of chamois horns on the walls of the drinking rooms.

Ernest and Hadley loved the skiing in Schruns, in part because the skier had to earn the right to do it. There were no lifts, no funiculars. The skier at Schruns had to climb on foot, carrying his skis with him. When the snow got too deep for walking, he must put seal skins on the bottoms of the skies, and walk fishbone up the slopes. There were Alpine club huts, built for the spring skier to rest in and warm himself. If he used the wood and the stove, he must, on his honor, leave payment.

Ernest told Hadley he enjoyed the climbing for a special reason. Ever since he'd learned of his father's heart disease, he had been frightened by twinges in his chest. But up on the slopes above Schruns, with his wife by his side and his baby waiting for him at the inn, he had found that in the deep cold mountain air, the pains, instead of increasing, went away.

Feeling as strong as he'd felt in months, Ernest wrote to his toughest competitor, Harold Loeb. Loeb could box; he could play tennis. But could he ski? Ernest asked Loeb to come to Schruns. It had commenced to snow in the high mountains, Ernest said, and there would be good runs by the time Loeb arrived. The food at the Taube was excellent. There was plenty of red and white wine, and thirty kinds of beer. There was a bowling alley in the hotel, where Ernest bowled the proprietor even. But, of course, Loeb could probably "trim them both." Schruns was "a swell place . . . a wonderful town and the people very God fearing and wonderful drinkers." He told Loeb that if he did not come he was, "not only a low son of a bitch but also ignorant."

When Ernest read this letter to Hadley—he usually read all his letters to Hadley before sending them off—she was irritated, then downright angry. Why had he written such a letter to Loeb, practically pleading with him to "come up"? She was sick and tired of Ernest writing that way to his friends. Did he really want Loeb with them all that much?

In another part of the letter, Ernest had thanked Kitty Cannell, Loeb's mistress, for the hat she had given Hadley. "Kitty's hat is a KO on Hadley," Ernest had written. To Hadley, that was the last straw. Ernest's argument that he was cultivating these people with an eye toward publication had grown old and thin. Look what it had gotten him with Don Stewart, Hadley said. Hadn't that George Doran business come to nothing? Hadn't Doran written that he "couldn't go all the way" with Ernest on "the matter of sex in a book of short stories." Hadn't Doran simply "chickened out"?

But on the other hand, Ernest said, there was Don Stewart's Christmas present, a large check that accompanied Doran's letter of rejection. Couldn't this mean that he was on the right track? Hadley said that Ernest didn't understand the rich. Writing that check had made Don Stewart feel good. Ernest knew that Hadley was right. Don had given the book to Henry Louis Mencken, then editor of *The Smart Set*. Ernest said that he knew Mencken was "at best a shit." But he might recommend the book to Alfred A. Knopf, the American publisher of *Ulysses*. Under Hadley's skeptic gaze, Ernest admitted that that was probably all "horse cock." But Don had also promised that he would show the stories to another friendly publisher, Horace Liveright.


In January 1925, Bumby started teething again, and those beautiful mountain nights of sleeping came to an end. Ernest was astonished at the size of the molars coming through Bumby's gums. No wonder the baby cried. No doubt there would be many sleepless nights ahead. One morning, the mail brought an announcement from Ernest Walsh, soliciting manuscripts for his new magazine, *This Quarter*. Ernest chose "Big Two-Hearted River."

Despite Ernest's friendly invitation, Harold Loeb did not come to

Schruns. He wrote that he must go to New York to check on the progress of his novel, *Doodab*. While at Liveright, his publisher, he would
put in a good word for Ernest. Ernest suspected that Loeb's "Miss
Kitty" had something to do with his refusal to come to Schruns. She
was possessive of Loeb Ernest thought, and she believed that Ernest
would find temptations for Harold because Hadley gave her husband
too free a rein.

Contrary to Hadley and Ernest's expectations, Don Stewart, and even
Harold Loeb, would indeed press Horace Liveright to take Ernest's
*In Our Time*. And Liveright, a small, shy, diabetic man, wanted very
much to accommodate two of his best-selling authors. True, his editorial board, all but one Mrs. Kauffman, had voted to reject *In Our
Time*. They felt sure that, with stories about a dockside seduction, a
homecoming soldier catching gonorrhea, a married couple faced with
impotence, the book would be far too "controversial."

But Horace Liveright had fought, and won, a battle against the
"Clean Books Bill" of 1924, and he said he wasn't about to knuckle
under to timid editors. On February 17, Ernest and Hadley, up in an
Alpine club hut 1,987 meters on the Madlener Haus, got the word in
telegrams from both Harold Loeb and Don Stewart. Liveright would
publish *In Our Time*. Ernest wrote to thank Harold and Don the
next day.

Liveright was Ernest's first chance in big-time publishing, and he
knew it. It was one thing to see your work in Robert McAlmon's Contact Editions and Bill Bird's Three Mountains Press, and quite another
to anticipate national, even international, distribution, and reviews in
the New York papers. True, Harold and Don had been half responsible for Liveright's decision. But, Ernest reasoned, that was the way it
usually worked.

Then came Liveright's letter of acceptance. Horace thought the stories were splendid. But there were one or two things that needed
changing. First of all, "Up in Michigan," Ernest's story of lovemaking
on a dock from the woman's point of view, would have to go. It was,
Horace said, "outspoken." Ernest was amused that this "fighter for
free speech," this defender of the artist's integrity and of the province
of art, would be distressed by something like:

> The water was lapping in the piles and the point was dark across the
> bay. It was cold but Liz was hot all over from being with Jim. They sat
> down in the shelter of the warehouse and Jim pulled Liz close to him.
> She was frightened. One of Jim's hands went inside her dress and

stroked over her breast and the other hand was in her lap. She was very frightened and didn't know how he was going to go about things but she snuggled close to him. Then the hand that felt so big in her lap went away and was on her leg and started to move up it.

"Don't Jim," Liz said. Jim slid the hand further up.

"You mustn't, Jim. You mustn't." Neither Jim nor Jim's big hand paid any attention to her.

The boards were hard. Jim had her dress up and was trying to do something to her. She was frightened but she wanted it. She had to have it but it frightened her.

"Up in Michigan" was the first story Ernest had written in Paris, and he had a special affection for it. He knew the characters—at least the main character, Liz Coates—would seem awfully "simple" to sophisticated readers. But he had known girls up in Michigan, girls with names like "Marjorie Bump," who lived and thought and felt just as Liz Coates did. For a day or two, he considered telling Liveright to take the story or forget the book.

But then, Ernest chose to be practical. To replace "Up in Michigan," he wrote and sent to Liveright a story he at first called "A Great Little Fighting Machine," then later "The Battler." Again, Ernest wrote about the life he knew in northern Michigan. The two characters in the story, besides Ernest's stand-in, young Nick Adams, are the punch-drunk former boxer, Ad Francis—modeled on two club fighters Ernest had known, Ad Wolgast and Bat Nelson—and "Bugs," the black "servant"—modeled on Wolgast's corner man.

"The Battler" takes up the age-old theme of a young man's discovery that, generally speaking, nothing in life is what it seems. Nick Adams, on the bum, is riding the freights. Because he's inexperienced this first time on the road, Nick rides atop the boxcars, instead of down below, on the rods that run between wheel carriages. Soon he is caught by the brakeman. At first, the brakeman is friendly: "Come here, kid, I got something for you." Then, "wham," and Nick, punched off the train, "lit on his hands and knees beside the track." Alone, sore, and hungry, trudging down the track with, he calculates, at least three or four miles of swamp ahead of him, Nick kicks loose a spike from the trestle. When the spike drops into the dark swamp water below, it makes the loneliest sound Nick has ever heard. Then, suddenly, up the track, a fire glows among the trees. Nick had learned from his encounter with the brakeman. He approaches the fire round about, and discovers a little man alone, sitting with his head in his hands. Just then, another

hobo, a black man, comes out of the wood. He's the little man's companion, and he'd gone into the woods at Nick's approach (they had
heard Nick coming on through the dry underbrush) to see what Nick
planned to do. Bugs, the black man, had a blackjack on his hip.

As the story of these two hobos unfolds, Nick learns that the small
man is Ad Francis, the former lightweight boxing champion of the
world. But there'd been some sort of scandal, Nick remembers, and it
had finished Ad's career. Bugs says he had "hooked up" with Ad when
they met in jail. The beatings Ad took in the ring had made him "simple," Bugs says, and he is taking care of him. Ad and Bugs bum on the
money sent by Ad's former wife.

After a while, Nick recalls that Ad Francis was the kind of fighter
who could take it. Despite the pain, Ad would just keep coming in.
He could do this because his heart never beat more than forty times
a minute. That gave him great stamina, great endurance. Nick understands that this endurance had won Ad Francis a world title. And
it was all that sustained him now. But while endurance was the first
requirement for survival, it was obviously not enough. Eventually, the
blows in and out of the ring had destroyed Ad. The beatings made
Ad simple, Bugs tells Nick. What made Ad crazy was the loss of his
wife.

Eventually, Nick remembers that there was a lot in the papers about
the case. Because Ad and his female manager looked alike, the papers
always called them a brother-sister team. Of course, they weren't re-
lated in any way. But when they got married in New York, the papers
made it sound like incest. At first only the public was disturbed by
this. But soon, because of Ad's "simple" condition, he started believing
it, too. It was this, Bugs says, that drove Ad crazy.

By the time Nick leaves the campsite, he's learned a lesson. In fact,
he's learned several. First, it's necessary to be tough, to be able to take
it, to endure. But endurance is not enough. In our time, a man must
also be skeptical, shrewd. Only a child takes appearance for reality, and
when he does, he's punished for his mistake. In Ad Frances, Nick saw
the consequences of growing up a child.

But the most chilling lesson of all, the one embodied in the image
of that single rail spike softly splashing into the dark water below the
bridge, is that the wounded of this world risk spiritual death by yielding to the ministries of those who would "help." No matter what a
man's condition, he is best off acknowledging that he is, finally, alone.

Nick carries this knowledge away from that hobo campfire just as he carries the ham sandwich Bugs wraps for him. He has miles to go before he sleeps in the next town on the line. And the next town is Mancelona.

In the autumn of 1924, Ernest could not help but feel that, despite early promise, his life so far had turned out badly. Like most young men of his time, he had believed wholeheartedly in the war. He had wanted to do his bit, to make the world safe for democracy. But after seeing the slaughter on the Italian Front, and knowing it was worse in France, the idea that young men were destroyed in the name of "national interest," and, more horribly, for "national pride," revolted him.

Then, at nineteen, Ernest had fallen deeply in love with the woman who nursed his wounds in the American Red Cross Hospital in Milan. Back home in Oak Park, he'd worked and lived for the day she would return to the States and they would marry. But Agnes von Kurowsky turned out to be a petty opportunist who threw him over for an Italian duke, who in turn threw her over because his family did not approve. After Agnes, Ernest had felt that his "life," the buoyancy of spirit he had believed to be a part of his physical constitution, was gone. He spoke to his best friend, Bill Horne, of being a ghost, of living in a dream, a nightmare from which he might never awaken.

This sickness of the heart had lasted until Ernest met his wife-to-be, Hadley Richardson. Hadley, at thirty, was a proper young woman from St. Louis, Missouri. Her life had been "tepid," she said. She thought she was bored, but she had only been waiting, waiting for Ernest to bring her to life. Ernest and Hadley had married, had lived in Paris for two difficult years, made worse, finally, by the theft of Hadley's small inheritance. Forced by incipient poverty to return to Canada, to the *Toronto Star,* they felt frustrated and depressed when their baby, John Hadley, was born.

Before the Hemingways left Paris, Ezra Pound had told Hadley that she would be "different" after the baby. He meant that she must redouble her efforts in the marriage in order to remain Ernest's wife. Perhaps because Hadley thought Pound a pretentious fool, she had ignored his advice and had become, first and foremost, Bumby's mother. Though she continued using her baby names for Ernest, Hadley had a new "Wax Puppy."

Ernest also believed he had of late embarrassed himself again and again. In the hope of seeing his work between hard covers, he had "sucked after," as he put it, the expatriate literati—Ezra Pound, Gertrude Stein, Ford Madox Ford. To be published in a magazine, he'd cultivated Margaret Anderson and Jane Heap. For a pitifully thin edition of his work *Three Stories and Ten Poems,* he'd tried to make a friend of the stolid, prosaic Bill Bird. And he'd spent time and patience on the unreliable Edward O'Brien, the aggressive homosexual Robert McAlmon, that silly, arrogant fop Ernest Walsh. Worst of all, Ernest felt, he had toadied to the critics—Burton Rascoe, for one, and Edmund Wilson. After Wilson's lukewarm review of *Three Stories and Ten Poems,* Ernest had sent a letter to Wilson, full of self-deprecation and fulsome expressions of gratitude.

In the weeks just before his trip to Schruns, Ernest had written a story which, he thought, had turned out very well. There was something about this story that touched Ernest deeply, and made him feel a special affinity with the hero.

The hero of "The Undefeated," Manolo (meaning "little man") has sold out, compromised, been defeated, a hundred times. Manolo says he is too young to end his life by his own hand. But what is a luckless bullfighter to do? In "The Undefeated," Ernest discovers an answer. The bullfighter, or, for that matter, the writer, must acknowledge the rule of chance. No matter how hard he tries, no matter what sacrifices he makes, a good man may, in fact, be defeated. But what if the one defeated denies that defeat, refuses to acknowledge it, even in the face of the most reasonable appeals to self-preservation. What then? "The Undefeated" ends this way:

> [The gored bullfighter] inhaled deeply. He felt very tired. He was very, very tired. They took the thing away from his face.
> "I was going good," Manuel said weakly. "I was going great. . . ."
> Manuel opened his eyes and looked at Zurito.
> "Wasn't I going good, Manos?" he asked, for confirmation.
> "Sure," said Zurito. "You were going great."

It was for Ernest a discovery, an insight. For the man who fought against fate, especially if he fought all the way to the end, there would be pity, and compassion, too, from those who, like himself, had never given in. This was the only pity, the only compassion, the only succor that would do any good—the only charity that counted. The hero of "The Battler" would die with a parasite by his side. But Manuel (no longer Manolo, a "little man") died listening to a friend.

When Scofield Thayer, the young Harvard educated editor at the *Dial,* rejected "The Undefeated," Ernest furiously sealed up his story in the same envelope the *Dial* had returned it in, and sent it along to Ernest Walsh.

A few days after Ernest and Hadley came back from Schruns, in early March, Harold Loeb paid them a "welcome home" call. Because he believed Ernest liked and respected him, Harold expected a warm-hearted reception. After all, hadn't he helped push *In Our Time* into Liveright? Loeb was pleased that Hadley answered the door. Gracious as always, she asked him to sit down. She would, she said, see about Ernest.

Ernest was lying on a made bed, wearing a faded sweatshirt, dunga-rees, and sneakers. He had a writing board propped up against his knees and a two-day growth of beard. This surprised Loeb because he knew Ernest prided himself on his wonderfully smooth skin. Loeb was deferential, trespassing as he was, as Ernest made him feel by not look-ing up until he finished the sentence he was writing. Loeb said he didn't want to bother, to take up valuable time. He had come only to invite Ernest to his flat for a party. Actually, Ernest was pleased by Loeb's visit, and happy with the invitation. But now Ernest believed that, to achieve the upper hand, one must never act truly delighted by any offer. Yes, he would be there, Ernest said, and went back to work.

When Ernest and Hadley kept their engagement with Harold and Miss Cannell, they were surprised to find that two young women had been invited, too. After the introductions, Harold told Ernest that Pauline and Virginia Pfeiffer were the very nice, very rich daughters of a man who owned a town in Arkansas. (Piggott, he believed the name was.) The girls were, Loeb said, enamored of "creative people," and they'd been dying to meet Ernest.

Ernest looked over the two women, standing there chatting with Hadley. They were small and dark and well-proportioned. Below their voile "flapper" chemises, in silk stockings, were the best-looking legs Ernest had ever seen. The sisters wore their hair short in the back, like a boy's, with the ears exposed. In Ernest's home town, this style meant girls were "fast." One of the girls, the one a bit taller, Virginia, had coal-black eyes, and she hadn't had them off Ernest since he'd come in. Ernest sidled over to "Jinny," as she at once asked him to call her, and began some stories about how it was to ski in Austria under the threat of avalanche.

Too soon for Ernest, the Pfeiffer sisters announced they would have to be going. Hadley, who had been charmed by Pauline, suggested they all meet again. Harold Loeb helped Pauline into a coat of hundreds of chipmunk skins. Ernest later told Hadley he'd found the coat "exquisite." It was an adjective he'd overheard in her conversation with Pauline.

Within the week, Pauline and Jinny Pfeiffer came to visit the Hemingways again. Ernest remained in the bedroom, "working," he said, and Hadley entertained the women alone. Just before they left, the sisters "looked in" on Ernest. This time Ernest noticed only Pauline, her full lips, dark bangs, and long emerald earrings. In her pleasant, steady-eyed gaze, Ernest sensed the contempt the rich have for those they know have contempt for them.

Although Ernest thought the Pfeiffer girls very attractive, and especially liked the challenge that Pauline apparently presented, he was now in love "romantically" with only one woman, a thirty-two-year-old titled Englishwoman, Lady Duff Twysden.

Lady Duff was built, Ernest said, like the hull of a racing yacht. She had the gray eyes of Agnes von Kurowsky and, like Agnes, long legs and close-cropped chestnut hair. Duff also had a long, and Ernest thought aristocratic, neck. In this way, at least, she reminded him of the praying mantis he'd caught in the Luxembourg Gardens and now kept in a large jar as his "small green friend." But for Ernest, Duff's fascination came most from her effortless indifference to almost everything. She was somehow disengaged, and could comfortably remain that way, and be charming still.

No doubt Duff's lineage added to her allure. Her Christian name was Mary Duff Stirling Byron, and she had been married to Sir Roger Thomas Twysden, tenth baronet. Duff and Sir Roger had had a child, Anthony. He was being reared by the Twysden family. Duff wore no makeup, and she affected a masculine style, with tweed suits and a felt hat. But "delicate as a cameo" was how the heiress Nancy Cunard, herself a blunt-faced, peasant-looking woman, described her.

Although recreational drugs—cocaine, hashish, marijuana—were a part of the Paris 1922–23 scene, everyone considered Duff a true addict. Her drug of choice was opium. It gave just the high she said she needed. After smoking her Turkish water pipe, she felt at peace with the world. If she did not bathe, Duff wore the scent of opium like a perfume.

Ernest wanted Duff the first time he saw her. And Hadley knew this. During their courtship, she had watched Ernest struggle with his desire for a girl named Rita, and then, more hurtfully, for her best friend, Kate Smith. But this time, Hadley was confident nothing would come of the infatuation. Yes, Duff wanted Ernest. But, more than sex, she needed a source of money for her habit. And Duff knew that Ernest was, for the most part, broke.

Nevertheless, Ernest was crazy for Duff. He would leave the flat early in the morning, so early that the shopkeepers were still hosing down the sidewalks, and he would have to walk in the street. Ernest would stand outside Duff's flat, where he knew she was sleeping with a rich bisexual, Pat Guthrie. Duff would come out early, too, clothed, it seemed to Ernest, in secrets, and she would want to plot with Ernest the conduct of their romance. Back home, Ernest secretly recorded what he wished to remember of the lovers' conversation:

> [Duff:] "You must make fantastic statements to cover things. It is like living with fourteen men so no one will know there is someone you love."
> [Ernest:] "We can't do it. You can't hurt people. It's what we believe in in place of God."
> [Duff:] "I have to have it and I can't have what I want with you so I'm going to take this other thing. . . ."
> [Ernest:] "And I looked at you and I thought I wouldn't be able to stand it."
> [Duff:] "What a shame he put the top thing down just as we came up."
> [Ernest:] "What are you so merry about. What were you so merry about the other day."

Ernest and Duff met often at the Dingo Bar on Rue Delambre, not far from the Tuileries Gardens. The Dingo was dark and somber, all maroon and brown, but very welcoming—so intimate compared with the high ceilings and white-tiled floors of La Rotunde, Le Select, Le Dome. Most often their rendezvous was late in the afternoon, when the bar was empty, and Ernest and Duff sat before the bronze beer taps with their shiny porcelain handles.

One afternoon in May, as Ernest sat with Duff at the bar, Scott Fitzgerald tapped him on the shoulder, introduced both himself and the tall, pleasant man who accompanied him. This was Dunc Chaplin, formerly a star pitcher at Princeton.

Just before he'd signed with Liveright, Ernest had gotten a letter from Fitzgerald's editor at Scribner's, Maxwell Perkins. Perkins said he'd heard from Scott that Ernest was a wonderful writer and, perhaps, he had a manuscript to sell. For one reason and another, Ernest had not written to Scott at the time, and then he'd let it go too long.

Ernest believed in first impressions. He always chose his friends that

way. In this regard, Scott was a disappointment. Years later Ernest remembered, "Scott was a man then who looked like a boy with a face
between handsome and pretty. He had very fair wavy hair, a high forehead, excited and friendly eyes and a delicate long-lipped Irish mouth
that, on a girl, would have been the mouth of a beauty. His chin was
well built and he had good ears and a handsome, almost beautiful, un-
marked nose." A notion that Scott was a homosexual had crossed
Ernest's mind.

Because Scott was a successful and respected writer, Ernest was, at
first, happy with Scott's attention. Scott gave an impromptu critique
of Ernest's work—he had read *Three Stories and Ten Poems*—and declared it all wonderful. Fitzgerald said that Ernest had the talent to
tell the "simple" truth about things and get it believed. Ernest could
do this because he had the true humility of the artist. Ernest's work
was pristine, Scott said, because Ernest had managed to keep "opin-
ions"—his and anyone else's—out of the writing. The reader did not
feel "instructed," and therefore condescended to. "I have found something beautiful," was what Ernest's work said. "Come share it with
me." As for Ernest's style, Scott said it was on a par with "Let there
be light." Reality itself was expressed in Ernest's prose.

Duff seemed uncomfortable, Ernest thought, hearing all this praise.
Then, with not so much as a squeeze of the hand, she excused herself.
Ernest wanted to follow Duff out of the Dingo. But he was thrilled by
Scott's assessment of his work. Before he had a chance to do some ap-
propriate self-deprecating, Scott was on a new tack:

> ". . . Tell me, did you and your wife sleep together before you were
> married?"
>   "I don't know."
>   "What do you mean you don't know?"
>   "I don't remember."
>   "But how can you not remember something of such importance?"
>   "I don't know," I said. "It is odd, isn't it?"

After just having seen Duff, having heard her voice, always weighted
with sexual innuendo, having yearned for those beautiful upturned
breasts to which her sweater clung, Ernest was loath to talk or even
to think about Hadley. Yet Scott would ask these outrageous questions
and wait, desperate, for Ernest's reply.

Then, suddenly, something happened to Scott. "As he sat there at
the bar holding the glass of champagne, the skin seemed to tighten

over his face until all the puffiness was gone and then it drew tighter until the face was like a death's head. The eyes sank and began to look dead and the lips were drawn tight and the color left the face so that it was the color of used candle wax." Then Scott passed out, flat on the table. Ernest was terrified. For a moment, he thought Scott had died.

A few days later, Ernest ran into Scott at the Closerie des Lilas, on the corner of St.-Michel and Montparnasse. They sat at a wide table in the shade of the awnings, across from a bronze statue under the new-leafed chestnut trees. Ernest had come to consider the statue—of Napoleon's infamous Marshal Ney—a friend. When Scott asked Ernest why he liked this café, Ernest told him that Marshal Ney, after fighting personally with the rear guard in Napoleon's retreat from Moscow (while Napoleon had ridden away in a coach with Caulaincourt), had disgraced himself with one blunder after another at Waterloo. Then Ernest and Scott just sat there, Ernest liking the place, Scott trying to.

At this meeting, Ernest found Scott "cynical and funny and very jolly and charming and endearing," though Ernest knew he should always be cautious with people who seemed "endearing." What actually attracted Ernest to Scott was the good taste Scott showed by speaking "slightingly but without bitterness of everything he had written." Ernest knew that for Scott to speak this way, his recent book, *The Great Gatsby,* must be very good. There was also in Scott that shyness "that all non-conceited writers have when they have done something very fine. . . ."

Yet all was not well between Ernest and Scott. Ernest was troubled by what he considered Scott's mercenary attitude toward writing. Scott maintained that an artist, like a politician, must first of all survive. The writer must be able to put bread on the table and a roof over the heads of those he loved. Scott insisted that a writer could divide things up. He could write the kind of stories that would appeal to the masses, stories that satisfied their desire for comfortable—that meant predictable—romance. He believed there was nothing wrong with giving his good and simple audience the assurance that life was quite pleasant after all. That sort of writing made money, Scott said. And it was a form of charity, too.

The real stuff, all Scott really believed in, could come in the novels. Of course he knew that *Gatsby* wouldn't sell, at least not the way *This Side of Paradise* had. But that was all right. *Gatsby* would last, and would be testimony to his talent, and a valuable book for the best of readers. There were no more patrons, Scott told Ernest. Certainly the publishers were not. And that included Scribner's. Novels had to make some money. And, most often, good novels did not cover the author's advance. Writing magazine stories was no worse than doing catchy, slice-of-life pieces for newspapers. And *The Saturday Evening Post* paid a lot more than any newspaper.

Ernest was stunned. How could Scott prostitute himself in that way, how could he take such risks with his talent? Ernest said that if a writer did not write his best, always his best, if he took the easy way out on a story, and allowed himself to fall into the smooth, acceptable, sweet-sounding lie, little by little he would lose the artist's one essential gift: an instinct for the truth.

Despite their disagreement on artistic integrity, Ernest was so attracted to Scott this time that he agreed to go on a trip with him. Scott, of course, promised to pay all their expenses. He said that he just wanted Ernest along. The reason for the trip was that Zelda, Scott's wife, had had to abandon their little Citroen in Lyon because of bad weather. Scott said that Zelda could not abide cars with tops, and, to please her, he'd had a body man cut through the posts with an acetylene torch. There had been a downpour in Lyon, however, and Zelda, and the interior of the Citroen, had been drenched. Nevertheless, the car was in running condition again, and Scott proposed that he and Ernest take the train to Lyon, pick up the car, and drive it back to Paris. Despite his reluctance to be anybody's paid-for guest, Ernest said he would be happy to go.

Because Ernest believed in the sacredness of arrangements made, he could not accept it that Scott would intentionally miss their train. When he did not find Scott at the station, Ernest bought the ticket himself and boarded the train. He was sure he'd find Scott somewhere, drunk, perhaps passed out, in the long line of cars. But Scott was not on the train, and Ernest sent a wire to Paris. Zelda replied immediately. Scott had indeed left Paris for Lyon, but on another train. He had not told her where he would be staying.

Ernest had dinner his first night in Lyon with a "man who ate fire for a living and who also bent coins which he held in his toothless jaws with his thumb and forefinger." Upon discovering that Ernest was a writer of short stories, the man proposed that they travel together to North Africa, where he would take Ernest to the country of the Blue Sultan. There, he said, Ernest could get stories such as no man had ever heard. When the night wore thin, Ernest thanked the fire-eater for his company and his invitation, paid for the dinner, and went back to the hotel to check on Scott.

The next morning, while Ernest was shaving, the desk called. A gentleman had asked to see him. Naturally, it was Scott. But why, Ernest thought, hadn't he given his name? Ernest told the desk to suggest the gentleman come up. After a moment's delay, the desk informed Ernest that the gentleman had declined.

Scott was embarrassed by his irresponsibility. And he tried to cover it with the sort of denials of fact he'd used at the Closerie des Lilas. It was Ernest, not he, who had missed the agreed-on train. It was Ernest who was acting odd, by disappearing as he had into this obscure hotel. Scott said he'd had to hunt "all over town for you."

Ernest let all this go. The sooner they got into the trip, the better. But Scott wanted to continue the illusion that he, and not Ernest, was in control. First of all, he would make what to eat for breakfast, and where, a significant decision:

> "Let's get some breakfast and find the car and roll," [Ernest said].
> "That's fine. Should we have breakfast here?"
> "It would be quicker in a café."
> "But we're sure to get a good breakfast here."
> "All right."

Ernest reminded himself that he had accepted Scott's invitation because he valued being in the company of an older and successful and truly wonderful writer, especially since Scott seemed anxious to talk about writing. But before too long, the deepest feelings of both men began to emerge. Although Scott was indeed an established, successful author, and Ernest had only just received his first advance—$250 from Horace Liveright for *In Our Time*—each saw in the other the stuff of immortality. Ernest had read McAlmon and Stein and Pound and Dos Passos and Ford Madox Ford. And he valued some of the work of each. But none of them "threatened" him with their talent. Ernest loved reading the dead: Chekhov, Flaubert, Mark Twain. The genius of such writers was an inspiration to him. They were his heroes. But living writers were a different matter. So few were really good that one could waste a lifetime reading junk. But Ernest saw in Fitzgerald a competitor for the laurels of their generation. And he was certain Scott felt the same way.

On this trip, Ernest and Scott induced in each other the role each always wished to play. Scott was the selfish little aristocrat, to be indulged and pampered. To Ernest, it was fine that Scott insisted on having the hotel pack a "picnic lunch" at four times the cost of such a thing at a local café. Then, after a drenching rainstorm, endured in Zelda's topless sedan, Scott insisted he had contracted "congestion of the lungs." All this gave Ernest the chance to be the strong-willed father-doctor to Scott, the embodiment of self-control, common sense. At the hotel, Ernest felt Scott's brow for fever, mixed lemonade and whiskey—a specific, he told Scott, for lung congestion—and gave Scott two aspirins to swallow. As Scott lay on his bed, looking "like a little dead crusader," Ernest took his pulse, unbuttoned his pajama tops, and put a big bath thermometer under Scott's arm.

This performance by both men created an imaginative environment suitable for self-revelation. Ernest told Scott of his first love, Agnes von Kurowsky, of how she had jilted him, and how that heartbreak had brought him to the discovery of his own voice, and his writing "style." Ernest spoke of his mother, Grace, of how he hated her for all she'd done to him and to his father. "If you love me, you'll do as I say" had been Grace's motto. And Ernest felt this was the archetypal emotional crime. Yet, at twenty-six, given the chance, Ernest admitted he still could not help trying to earn his mother's love.

Then, Ernest talked to Scott about Hadley, the wife he was sure had been too good for him from the start. Hadley was a serious woman. She had been beautiful before the child, and she loved Ernest unreservedly. She was the only person Ernest knew who could have meant it when she'd said, "For better or for worse, in sickness and in health, till death do us part."

Scott had a story of his own to tell. And he was certain Ernest would agree it was a tragic one. The year before, when he and Zelda had summered at St.-Raphael, Zelda had fallen in love with a French naval aviator. The Frenchman had been dark and slender, composed of rope-like muscles, thick black hair, and brilliant teeth. He had spoken with an urbane fluency. He was "skeptical, scoffing." And "his manners were formal, even perfunctory." Zelda said he had made her feel no guilt, by conceding she had "white crook's eyes." It was, Zelda said, her nature to be unfaithful. But the actual sex had been onanistic. During the intercourse, she had thought of nothing but herself.

Scott hurt Ernest with this story. It was so sad, especially the way Scott made Ernest see so clearly "the single seater seaplane buzzing the diving raft [Scott and Zelda lay on] and the color of the sea and the shape of the pontoons and the shadow that they cast."

A week after Ernest and Scott got back to Paris, Ernest and Hadley visited the Fitzgeralds in their posh apartment on Rue de Tilsitt. This was the first time Ernest had seen Zelda. From the way Scott had spoken of her, Ernest expected a beauty. But as Zelda welcomed her guests in an enhanced Southern American accent, Ernest saw only a red-headed woman with wide-spaced jet-black eyes, a tiny, thin-lipped mouth, an aquiline nose. She reminded him of a hawk, a pigeon hawk.

As the evening got under way, Zelda seemed convinced of her own genius and jealous of the success Scott had had. She wanted to drink like the whores Ernest had known on the west side of Kansas City, when he'd been a reporter for the *Kansas City Star*. Drinking was like animal combat to Zelda; she threatened that in drinking bouts the male left standing could claim the harem, even if only a harem of one. Zelda knew that Scott would take her to all the parties, and drink with her, because he dared not let her go alone.

Christian Gauss, a professor of French at Princeton, and his wife, Alice, made the third couple at this party. To get his sort of conversation started, Gauss brought up the question of literary "influence." What did Ernest and Scott think of Robert Louis Stevenson's advice to young writers—that they should imitate established writers until they developed a style of their own? Scott admitted that in his first novel, *This Side of Paradise,* there was some Joyce and some Compton Mackenzie. Gauss then pressed Ernest. Hadn't Ernest, as Gauss's fellow Princetonian Edmund Wilson had said, imitated Sherwood Anderson?

Ernest was furious. People like Gauss were exactly why he detested academics. Unable to say something useful, something that would open up a work for readers, they insisted on setting themselves above the artist, making his work the subject of their "interest." They would ignore the obvious and seize instead the insignificant, the abstruse, the arcane. Literary "influence" was a favorite subject, since it allowed the scholar to cast his net over a half-dozen writers at a time. The scholar pretended that individual talent meant far less than the tradition, which, after all, the scholar could best explain. In this way, the scholar put the artist in his place.

Ernest knew what Gauss was doing. So did Scott. But Scott felt the Princeton ties hold, and remained polite. Ernest, however, launched into "the dangers of influence." He said that the help a young writer got from imitation was safe only when it came from writers he loved but knew he could surpass. It was a kind of cannibalism. Reading these writers was a ritual, to be performed again and again. By devouring these writers, ingesting their art, the young writer acquired their "virtues" and enhanced himself. A writer would destroy himself by imitating Shakespeare, or Homer, or even St. Luke—whose story of Christ Ernest cherished. The wiry little Gauss, sardonic, quick-witted, had nothing to say.

# 7

# *No Swan So Fine*

In the late spring of 1925, when the cold rains that ended the winter had come and gone and the warmth of the sun increased each day, Ernest loved to take his son in the stroller, "a cheap, very light, folding carriage, down the street to the Closerie des Lilas." They would each have brioche and café au lait, Ernest pouring some of the hot coffee into the saucer to cool it, and to let Bumby dip his brioche before eating. Ernest would read the papers, now and then looking up to see his son attentive to everything that passed on the boulevard. After breakfast, Ernest would wheel Bumby across the street from the café and past the Place de l'Observatoire. Bumby loved to see the bronze horses rearing in the fountain spray that made the June air smell so clean.

While Ernest and Hadley prepared for the annual pilgrimage to Pamplona, Hadley wondered secretly why, again this year, they had to go. Ernest had seemed happy to come home from Schruns. He liked the skiing and the dry, healthy cold, but she knew he missed city life. This year, however, Pamplona lured Ernest with more than the bull-fight.

As he had for the festival of 1924, Ernest made arrangements for his friends to accompany him. For 1925, it would again be Bill Smith, carrying among his other burdens the affliction of impotence, which he felt the bullfight might somehow cure, and Don Stewart, to whom Ernest thought he owed the publication of *In Our Time*. Then there were the others: Duff Twysden, Pat Guthrie, and Harold Loeb. Hadley feared these newcomers would turn the festival into a tragedy for the Hemingways. She knew that Loeb was in love with Lady Duff. But sadly, she admitted to herself, so was Ernest.

Ever since she'd first met Ernest in Chicago, at the Smiths' party in 1920, Hadley had recognized his need for romantic stimulation. She knew he wanted and needed the serious love, the emotional security, of a wife. But, at the same time, he yearned to be infatuated always with some "lovely young thing." Duff Twysden was hardly young, Hadley reasoned, but with her small-bosomed, slender body, her tantalizing ennui, with her air of naive expectancy, she did have the quality of youth.

No doubt Duff was attracted to Ernest, too. But she had other considerations. Despite her title, there was no family money. And Duff's addictions—opium and alcohol—were expensive. The only money in the crowd on its way to Pamplona lay with Don Stewart and Harold Loeb. Stewart seemed inclined to men, or at least indifferent to women. Loeb, on the other hand, was passionately sexual.

On Thursday morning, June 25, Ernest and Hadley finished packing for their third trip to Pamplona. The night before, James Joyce had sent Ernest word that a section of his "work in progress" (*Finnegans Wake*) would be finished "in ten days." Joyce was worried that Ernest Walsh had lost patience with him, and the work would not be enthusiastically received at *This Quarter*. Despite his poor opinion of Joyce, the man, Ernest believed in the talent "absolutely," and took care to tell Walsh exactly how he could, and, by implication, should, get in touch with Joyce: through Sylvia Beach at Shakespeare and Company.

Just before they left for Pamplona, Ernest felt strangely moved by the look of the early-morning sun on the cobblestone courtyard. M. Chautard, the artisan, had not yet started his saw. The cat, F. Puss, yawned at his milk bowl, unaware that his people were going away.

This year, Ernest suggested to his friends a "preliminary" to the Spanish festival. Wouldn't it be wonderful, he said, to spend a few days fishing the Irati River. Don Stewart and Bill Smith were all for the Irati. But Harold Loeb and Lady Duff were tentative. Ernest knew that fishing was an unlikely diversion for Duff, and Hadley said she doubted Duff could make the climb from Burguete. Loeb, meanwhile, behaved strangely. Each time Ernest pressed him for a commitment or tried to evoke an enthusiastic response with his stories of the Irati's pristine beauty, Harold hinted there'd be reasons why he and Duff might not go.

Long after the 1925 festival, Ernest learned that the morning he and Hadley left Paris, Harold Loeb had called Duff. He had told her he knew of a perfect spot for an assignation: St. Jean-de-Luz, just over the border from Spain, only sixty kilometers from Pamplona. Harold said they could be comfortable at an *auberge* "poised on the side of a hill." Harold spoke of how the mountains "fell away" to reveal a "small triangle of sea bounded by two green hills and the fragile blue of the sky." Beneath their windows would be Japanese iris and a flagstone terrace. "Man and Nature had combined to do their best," Harold said. He was delighted when Duff said yes.

At Ascain, a small town just north of St. Jean-de-Luz, Harold tried his best to create the ambience of romance. He took Duff for long walks down dusty lanes; he insisted she drink only champagne; he doted on her. Unfortunately, Harold also unintentionally embarrassed Duff at dinner one night by remarking, in front of the waiter, on her wearing the same shabby stole three nights in a row. (Harold, in fact, considered the "minor variations" Duff had made in the stole the epitome of style.) After dinner and drinks, Harold took Duff's hand and said, "You are beautiful, darling; more beautiful tonight than last night even."

After the first week, Harold became restless. He told Duff, "I don't do anything but look at you, and I don't entirely approve of that." He wanted to be "back at work," he said. Did she know how hard he'd worked at his book shop, his magazine, and then his novel? He was used to working, Harold said. He was worried. He felt far too contented.

At one point, Harold thought he'd inquire of Duff if she were "the jealous type." He explained that he had known women who would cause a scene "if one so much as mentioned another female." He saw Duff grimace above her glass at this. He took her expression to mean that she was distressed at the possibility of his interest in another woman. Harold told Duff, "Love comes and goes and there is little you can do about it. But there are other things that we can do." He meant having his career, fulfilling a destiny. The two meant the same to him.

After a fortnight with Loeb on the Riviera, Duff offered a toast: "In Scotland when the Black Watch drink a toast, they throw their glasses against the wall so that no one will ever drink from them again. . . . To us! May we see each other always as we do tonight." Harold considered this a declaration of love.

When Duff had agreed to go away with Harold Loeb, Pat Guthrie was broke. Since Guthrie's mother held the family purse strings, he'd returned to Scotland, to his ancestral home. He had promised to be back in two weeks.

Ernest loved a train ride through beautiful country, and part of the pleasure of Pamplona was the getting there. In late June the fields he saw from the Pullman windows were all ripening grain, poppies, and pasture. The pastureland was still pale green compared to the darker hues of the copses. There were fire gaps cut through the pines and chateaux off in the trees. Sometimes the tracks lay beside fishing rivers, and Ernest told Hadley how much he wished to stop and unpack his flies and his jointed bamboo pole. The train stopped at Bayonne at nine o'clock. Ernest and Hadley and Bill and Don got off, carrying their rod cases, and went through the dark station and out to the line of cabs and hotel buses.

Bayonne had a cool, fresh, early-morning smell, and it was pleasant sitting for breakfast in the café. A breeze started to blow, and Ernest could feel that the air came from the sea. There were pigeons snuffling the dust out in the square, and the houses were a yellow, sun-baked color.

The next morning, the streets of Bayonne were already baking hot when Ernest and his entourage boarded the bus for Burguete. It was a two-tiered bus, and riding high up in the second tier, close under the trees, Ernest felt happy. The bus was loaded with Basques, and with them they had their wine skins. By the time the bus got to Burguete, Ernest, Hadley, Bill, and Don were drunk and exhausted. The houses in Burguete, all whitewashed stone, lay along both sides of the main road. Families sat in doorways, watching the arrival. Hadley said she yearned for whatever comfort the inn at Burguete would provide.

While Ernest was being welcomed by the fat female Basque who ran the inn, he heard someone say that these English were fools to come for the fishing. Hadn't they heard that the Irati had been ruined by loggers months before? Ernest was stunned, and he asked the madame if this were true. Yes, she said, it was true. All winter and spring the loggers had been working in the beech and pine forests, and running logs down the river. All the pools were cleaned out, dams broken down, the trout killed.

That night in their room at the inn, Ernest told Hadley he hated to go up to the river, even just to take a look. What a terrible way to start the fiesta, he said. Hadley agreed. And besides, she said, their room was none too pleasant. There were two hard beds, a washstand, a clothes chest, and a big, framed steel engraving of Our Lady of Roncesvalles. The room was on the north side of the inn. She could hear the wind against the shutters.

After unpacking quickly, Ernest and Hadley washed and went downstairs to the dining room. It was oak-paneled, with a low ceiling and a stone floor. While they waited for supper, Ernest noticed that if he breathed out deep and hard, he could see his breath.

There was a piano in the far corner of the dining room, and Hadley went over to play. She had to keep warm, she said. Ernest ordered a bowl of hot rum punch. But it was weak and thin. Ernest saw a bottle of rum in the cupboard, and he poured a tumblerful into the pitcher. Later, the young daughter of the innkeeper brought in hot vegetable soup, fried trout, and a big bowl of wild strawberries. Weren't the Spaniards odd, Hadley said. She'd looked in opened doors, and all the rooms at the inn had only beds for one.

At first, Ernest and Bill Smith worked hard at fishing the trash-filled Irati. They tried flies: McGintys, Royal Coachmans, Yellow Sallys. The next day, Ernest woke early, when the sun had not yet dried the dew, and dug with a mattock from the damp ground two tobacco tins of worms. Ernest wanted to try some of the smaller streams where one might slip a worm just under the bank and, with a strike, simply "horse" the trout out. But it was no use. In four mornings, neither Bill nor Ernest took a single fish.

On July 1, Ernest wrote a long letter to Scott Fitzgerald. He did not mention the pollution of the Irati, nor the deep disappointment and anger he'd felt at the destruction of the fish. Instead, he congratulated himself on drinking nothing but wine since he'd left Paris, and kidded Scott about his lack of interest in "country."

Then Ernest launched into a fanciful comparison of what his and Scott's heaven would be like. Scott would be happy in a "beautiful vacuum filled with wealthy monogamists, all powerful and members of the best families all drinking themselves to death." But for Ernest,

heaven would be a big bull ring with me holding two barrera seats and a trout stream outside that no one else was allowed to fish in and two lovely houses in the town; one where I would have my wife and children and be monogamous and love them truly and well and the other where I would have my nine beautiful mistresses on 9 different floors and one house would be fitted up with special copies of the Dial printed on soft tissue and kept in the toilets on every floor and in the other house we would use the American Mercury and the New Republic. Then there would be a fine church like in Pamplona where I could go and be confessed on the way from one house to the other and I would get on my horse and ride out with my son to my bull ranch named Hacienda Hadley and toss coins to all my illegitimate children that lived [along] the road. I would write out at the Hacienda and send my son in to lock the chastity belts onto my mistresses because someone had just galloped up with the news that a notorious monogamist named Fitzgerald had been seen riding toward town at the head of a company of strolling drinkers.

Scott must have recognized the mock parallels with one of Ernest's favorite romances, Spenser's *The Faerie Queen,* and been amused at Ernest's casting himself in the role of the quester for truth, the Red Cross Knight. But he probably saw too that Ernest realized what was coming in Pamplona. Ernest had ended the letter with sadness and resignation: "Well anyway we're going into town tomorrow early in the morning. Write me at the / Hotel Quintana, Pamplona, Spain. Or don't you like to write letters. I do because it's such a swell way to keep from working and yet feel you've done something."

Ernest, Hadley, Don, and Bill took the bus from Burguete into Pamplona. They were all sleepy from the altitude, and watched the long brown mountains pass in silence. The road down was always white, and the bus passed an old castle with a field of grain growing right up to the walls and shifting in the wind. Twice the bus swerved, slowly, the driver laughing with his riders at a donkey and its owner sleeping in the road. Before long, the plateau of Pamplona appeared, then, closer, the broken skyline of churches. Finally, the bus pulled into Pamplona's square and stopped in front of the Hotel Quintana. Ernest told Hadley he couldn't wait to get out of the sun. Hadley, her freckles spread all over her face, said neither could she.

Juanito Quintana, the proprietor of the hotel, thought Ernest a man of rare sensibilities. Of all the Americans Quintana had known and seen at the bullfight and talked to afterward, Ernest seemed the only one with "afición"—that meant not interest in, or curiosity about, the bullfight, but rather a genuine appetite for it. For Quintana, this quality made Ernest an instant, special friend. Their "afición" for bullfighting was a secret between them, not to be exposed to others who would not understand. The sign of recognition would always be some touching of the shoulder or the arm—always with some embarrassment.

Just after their meeting, Quintana told Ernest that his other friends had already arrived.

Ernest had a talent for making people feel that any pretension toward an appetite of life must be backed up with a healthy appetite for food, and he encouraged Quintana and his kitchen to produce a bountiful meal. There were hors d'oeuvres, an egg course, two meat courses, vegetables, salad, and dessert and fruit. Ernest told Harold and Pat they'd better drink plenty of wine to get it all down.

Fairly drunk, and "stuffed to the gills," Ernest and Hadley, Pat and Duff, Harold Loeb, Don Stewart, with Bill Smith "bringing up the rear" as he liked to say he did—and Hadley going back to "fetch him up"—all strolled down to the railroad yards to watch the bulls unloaded. They "walked along, past the Ayuntamiento with the banners hung from the balcony, down past the market and down past the steep street that led to the bridge across the Arga." There they passed a wine shop. The sign in the window read, "Good Wine 30 Centimes A Litre." Duff said to Ernest, "That's where we'll go when funds get low." Duff wore a felt fedora, a jacket shirt and tie. The woman standing in the doorway of the wine shop "called to someone in the house and three girls came to the windows and stared" at Duff.

The bulls, from a breeding ranch in Castile, were in big gray-painted cages, one to each. Everyone found a place on the wall where they could look down into the corral. First, a mule dragged one of the cages against the gate in the corral wall. Then, at the other end of the corral, two steers came in. There was a great noise in the arena. Then the bull charged into the corral, "skidding with his forefeet in the straw as he stopped, his head up, the great hump of muscle on his neck swollen tight, his body muscles quivering as he looked up at the crowd on the stone walls." Ernest told Duff to watch the bull carefully—he had a "left and a right," just like a boxer. When the second bull hit a steer and killed him, Duff coolly told Ernest that she had seen the bull shift from his left to his right horn.

On the way back to the hotel, everyone wanted to stop at the café. Hadley took the occasion to sit between Ernest and Duff. Hadley and Duff were the same age. They'd both had children, had studied the piano, had always enjoyed the attention of men. To her surprise, Hadley found she admired Duff. Ernest had called Duff's special quality "the courage to be." Hadley knew that Duff was addicted to drugs. But it had become part of her charm, part of her statement about life. Hadley knew, too, that Duff had experienced the lesbian world of

Paris, a world Hadley had heard about from Renata Borgatti. (The English tea room, Renata had mentioned, above a book shop on the Rue de Rivoli.) And Duff had everything: a cameo neck, legs that made her five-feet nine, a figure Ernest loved. But she didn't have Ernest yet, and Hadley was determined she would not get him.

Hadley believed that the way to fight fire was with fire. If Ernest would hurt her with Duff, she would hurt him with the most attractive man she could find. For two days, ever since Ernest and Hadley had met him at the hotel—the introduction arranged by Quintana—Hadley had spoken of Cayetano Ordoñez. He was young and confident, sincere, strong, and reverential toward his profession. And he was, Hadley said, "just beautiful."

The next day, in the plaza, the festival spirit burst forth like the fireworks the night before. Everyone drank heavily, mostly from "botas," flasks of hide that held a sweet muscatel. The sun was strong, the heat dry, the dominant colors red and sand.

Ernest had taken six seats for all the fights: three "barreras," the first row at the ringside; three "sobrepuertos," seats with wooden backs, halfway up the amphitheater. Pat Guthrie wanted Duff to sit high up, for her first time, he said. Harold Loeb suggested that he sit with them, so Pat and Duff wouldn't miss the subtleties of the spectacle.

Bill Smith had seen a novillada, a bullfight for those in training to be matadors, and had gotten sick over it. Although he recognized the "comedic nature" of the poorly trained, overexposed toreros, jabbing hopelessly at bloodied masses of animal, with ridicule rolling down from the seats, Bill said it had all made him vomit. But Bill said the "cervida corrida, as the Spanish refer to them, had to be great." They were certainly "worth risking another large Spanish lunch over."

On the avenue to the bullring were the customary horrors: the professional cripples who follow the fairs of Spain. They wagged stumps at everyone, exposed sores, waved monstrosities, and held out their caps, "in their mouths when they have nothing left to hold them with." To Ernest, the path to the bullring was an emotional gauntlet, lined with agonies beyond anything he'd see inside.

Duff sat in the sobrepuertos with Guthrie and Loeb; Hadley sat with Ernest and Bill in the barreras. Just before Duff left for her seat, she told Ernest she was a bit apprehensive. The goring of the horses might be too much for her. She should not look at the horses after they had been hit by the bull, Ernest said. She must wait until the horse was dead to look again. Hadley heard all this and thought how disgustingly solicitous Ernest could be.

Cayetano Ordoñez had poor bulls to work with in the ring that day. But, just the same, he was splendid. Ernest thought his cape work wonderful. He told Hadley he had never seen "such suave, slow, perfectly timed cape work." Ernest said Ordoñez's work with the muleta was "merely intelligent," but he did kill "quickly and well." His talent lay in his ability to make the difficult easy, simple, and unhurried. Hadley said she was "enthralled."

That night, after dinner and many bottles of wine, Duff and Harold Loeb excused themselves. As they walked off—Duff long-legged, graceful, Loeb rolling with an athlete's rhythmic stride—Ernest excused himself, too. Hadley believed she caught something about his wanting to "protect" Duff. But she was too drunk, and too angry, to protest.

After they left the table, Duff and Harold went up to a second-floor apartment, overlooking the square. In the corner of the living room stood a piano. Duff wanted to play. But an older man with a monocle brushed her gently aside and began some Gershwin. Then came Duff's turn, and she played French songs and, in a low voice, sang them, too. Soon there were many men around the piano. When Harold approached Duff, said it was late, and asked her to leave, she was singing requests and drinking champagne. She told Harold to go away. She said that she had slept with other men before, but they had not been of Harold's race and had not afterward come on parties. On the way out, Harold passed Ernest coming in.

The next day, Duff came to lunch with a black eye and a bruise on her forehead. Loeb asked Duff about it. Ernest answered for her. She'd fallen against a railing, he said.

The situation, all of it, enraged the drunken Guthrie. He did not blame Ernest for what had happened. Had he, Guthrie, not been "blind" the night before, he might have beaten Duff himself. Instead, he started in on Loeb:

"Do you think you amount to something Harold? Do you think you belong here among us? People who are out to have a good time. For God's sake don't be so noisy Harold."

"Oh, cut it out, Pat," Harold answered. He was in love with Duff and she had slept with him while Pat was away in Scotland and told Pat about it and it had not seemed to make any difference but now whenever he got drunk he kept coming back to it. . . .

"Do you think Duff wants you here? Do you think you add to the party? Why don't you say something?"

"I said all I had to say the other night, Pat."

There had been one of those barnyard scenes about two o'clock in the morning three nights before.

"I'm not one of you literary chaps." Pat stood wobbly. "I'm not clever. But I do know when I'm not wanted. Why don't you see you're not wanted, Loeb. Go away. Go away for God's sake. Don't you think I'm right?"

He looked at us.

"Sure," I said. "Let's all go over to the café."

"No, not joking. Don't you think I'm right? I love that woman."

"Oh don't start that again. Do shut up Patrick," Duff said.

"Don't you think I'm right, Ernest?"

Loeb just sat there. He never had enough sense to go away. He seemed to enjoy it. Someway it was pleasant, all a form of connecting him up with Duff. He sat there looking through his spectacles, taking it all seriously. His affair with a lady of title.

"Ernest," Pat said. He was almost crying. "You know I'm right."

"Listen you," he turned to Loeb, "go away. Go away now."

Loeb turned to Duff. He asked, did she want him to leave. Ernest was desperate to fight Loeb, and this was his chance. He called Loeb a "lousy bastard" for "running to a woman." He called Loeb a "kike" and a coward, and said that the two amounted to the same thing. Harold had no choice. He got to his feet and asked Ernest to "step outside."

Ernest could see that Loeb was scared. But there was no panic in his fear. As Harold took off his steel-rimmed glasses and put them carefully into the side pocket of his jacket, he seemed sad. Ernest knew that he outweighed Loeb by forty pounds. He saw Harold standing there, squinting, bravely waiting to have his face smashed in. At that moment, Harold Loeb, ready to do battle for Duff, seemed to Ernest so much like himself at nineteen, when he would have fought anyone for his own perfidious love. In the dim street light, there in the alley behind the café, Ernest decided Harold Loeb was worth more than a drunken nymphomaniac.

The next morning Ernest wrote to Harold:

I was terribly tight and nasty to you last night and I dont want you to go away with that nasty insulting lousiness as the last thing of the fiestas. I wish I could wipe out all the mean-ness and I suppose I cant but this is to let you know that I'm thoroly ashamed of the way I acted and the stinking, unjust uncalled for things I said.

So long and good luck to you and I hope we'll see you soon and well. Yours, Ernest.

In the twelve days at Pamplona, Ernest got over Lady Duff. He decided that, from the start, it had been nothing more than an infatuation. But while he was playing Duff's game in fiesta, something terrible had happened close to home. Now it seemed to Ernest that every other remark Hadley made was about Cayetano Ordoñez. How "lovely" he was, what style he had for one so young, and what bravery. Hadley begged Ernest to follow Ordoñez on his circuit. The first stop was Madrid.

Ernest believed that one had to pay for everything in life. One of the swell things you could count on, he was fond of saying, was that the bill always came due. Coming to Pamplona, he had been in love with Duff Twysden. He knew Hadley was tortured with the knowledge of this, and he was sorry, but he believed it was all out of his hands. Now, leaving Pamplona, Ernest found himself suffering the gnawing pangs of jealousy himself. Duff was gone, and he didn't care. But now Hadley might be in love. And with a young man Ernest was fond of and deeply admired.

Ordoñez, fighting under the name "Niño de la Palma," performed in a "Corrida de la Prensa" the afternoon of July 15. He challenged, "mano a mano," the aging legend Belmonte. "Niño," Ernest believed, "did everything Belmonte did and did it better—kidding him—all the adornos [decorations] and the desplantes [poor stances] and all. Then he stepped out all by himself without any tricks—suave, templando with the cape, smooth and slow, splendid with the banderillos—and began with 5 Naturales with the muleta—a beautiful complete faena all linked up, and then killed perfectly."

The morning of the fight, "Niño" had taken Hadley to the Prado. That afternoon, he gave her his cape to hold, and dedicated a bull to her. Hadley said she was no longer shocked or horrified by what happened to the horses. It was part of a great spectacle, she said. When Ernest brought up Bumby, that he would be lonely without his mother, Hadley said she had great faith in Marie Rohrbach, the nursemaid. Surprisingly, Ernest turned to Gertrude Stein for advice.

Gertrude had always insisted that art was therapy for life. It could be used by the artist for his own good. What should Ernest make of all that had happened in Pamplona? Gertrude suggested a novel.

In Ernest's fictional world, there were only two "real" people: himself and the woman he loved. Everyone else was shaped, modified, distorted. Everyone else played a role, or rather had one created for them. Ernest claimed that, as an artist, he did not think, he noticed—that he was objective, clinical in his observation. But everything Ernest wrote was autobiography in colossal cipher. In *The Sun Also Rises,* Ernest is most himself in Jake Barnes, the reporter with a war wound that, according to his decoration, had cost him, "more than life itself." Barnes had lost his penis in combat, but he still had his testicles. He was the quintessential twentieth-century man—alive, sensate, but without the capacity to act. Although Ernest had not been sexually mutilated in the war, he'd been rendered impotent in Pamplona. In love with Duff, passionately desirous of her, Ernest was repelled by what he saw as her vulgarities with Loeb. Yes, she was a dope addict, and needed money for her habit, money Ernest could not hope to supply. But she had acquiesced to all Loeb was, had played the romantic whore for him.

For the heroine of his novel, Ernest would use Duff. He would call her Brett Ashley, and make her a "Lady." She would have Duff's appearance and attitude, her habits and vices. There would be no mention of Duff's drug addiction—just the suggestion of a vague ennui and the mysterious need to bathe.

Ironically, Duff, in the novel, is herself an addiction—for the men she seduces. Robert Cohn calls her Circe because, he felt, she turned men into swine. Jake Barnes is "hard-boiled" with everyone, even himself, when he fights his own weakness for self-pity. But, as Robert Cohn says, Jake will play the pimp for Lady Brett. When Brett drops the bullfighter, and is alone and broke in Madrid, Jake wires he'll take the Sud Express that very night. Then he reflects: "Send a girl off with one man. Introduce her to another to go off with him. Now go and bring her back. And sign the wire with love. That was it all right. I went to lunch."

But Lady Brett Ashley is not all Duff. After reading *The Sun Also Rises,* Duff told Ernest he had "got" her pretty well, except that she hadn't "slept with the bloody bullfighter." And she hadn't. Lady Brett in *The Sun Also Rises* sleeps with the handsome young matador, Pedro Romero, because Ernest suspected Hadley wanted to make love, and perhaps had, with Cayetano Ordoñez.

Don Stewart, who shared the role of Bill Gordon in *The Sun Also Rises* with Bill Smith, told Hadley that the evil in their 1925 Pamplona was the "devil sex." Ernest thought so, too. In the novel, the fishing on the Irati is the wonder it was in 1924. The river is clear-flowing and pure, the trout plentiful, the forest intact. But the Irati is the abode of the male, for him to enjoy in his innocence with comrades as innocent as he. For Ernest, innocence was not synonymous with ignorance. It was not the absence of experience. Innocence was a state of mind, hard to achieve. It was what he had worked so hard to acquire in both his life and his writing. It was what he now felt he had lost.

In an autobiographical short story he would never publish, Ernest, at twenty-one, had written of the first flush of his love for Hadley: "Those days to me were wonderful for I was awakening from a sleep which I thought was everlasting." Throughout their courtship, Ernest and Hadley did their best to convince each other that they had come to each other with hearts as pure, as new, as children. It was a useful fiction. In their first years Ernest had written his testament to innocence, *In Our Time*.

But Ernest had a double standard. He believed that it was inevitable that he, as a man, should fall prey to desires of the flesh. During their courtship, Ernest had made love to Kate Smith, Hadley's best friend. And while he was away on his trips to Turkey for the *Toronto Star*, Ernest had indulged himself with an Armenian whore. In one of his private recollections of 1925, Ernest wrote that he had been unfaithful to Hadley "$\cancel{3}$, $\cancel{4}$, $\cancel{5}$, 6 times." These, however, were not "spiritual" affairs. To Ernest, a man could make love with only his body. A woman made love heart and soul. Therefore, Hadley must never be unfaithful to Ernest. In deed or even in desire. If she were, she would break their bond of innocence. Hadley, in her attempt to "fight fire with fire," to make Ernest as jealous of her desire for Ordoñez as she had been of his for Duff, had, Ernest felt, broken the bond. In the novel, Brett allows Jake to use, when needed, a cherished illusion of Ernest's youth—he is her "one and only love." It is an illusion Jake denies at the end, but only temporarily. Jake Barnes and Lady Brett, the reader understands, will go on and on. But Ernest and Hadley would not.

When Ernest got back to Paris in late August, he wrote to his father not about the ordeal at Pamplona but about the fishing trip to Burguete: "We had no luck fishing this summer. The wonderful stream we got so many out of last summer was ruined by logging. Fish killed, pools destroyed, dams broken down. Made me feel sick." Ernest believed that something beautiful had gone out of his life, and he wanted to tell the one member of his family he truly loved, in a way his father could understand.

Ernest and Hadley had followed Ordoñez from Pamplona to Madrid, from Madrid to Valencia, from Valencia back to Madrid. It had all became absurd, even to Hadley. She saw that Ernest was now living in the world of his fiction. She felt he was going to decide something momentous, and she was afraid. Hadley announced, on August 12, that she would return to Paris alone. She had the dreadful feeling that Ernest was glad to be rid of her.

# 8

# *Life's Parallels*

On September 21, back in Paris at the apartment above the cabinet maker, Chautard, and his relentless band saw, Ernest finished his story of Pamplona, 1925. He had often used the metaphor of distance running to describe his philosophy of composition. A writer, Ernest would say, must train for the novels by building up to them with progressively longer and more demanding work. The vignettes had been wind sprints, the short stories of *In Our Time,* the mile, the novel he must eventually write, a marathon.

But the metaphor changed when Ernest had actually written a novel. Now it was boxing. The writer's opponent was chaotic reality—a swarmer, a two-fisted liar. In this battle, the writer had to be willing to take it as well as dish it out. Ernest felt that the distress he endured after finishing his book—sleeplessness, constipation, excessive drinking, "white nights" filled with nightmares that lingered on after waking, even the physical deterioration he saw in his face (pasty white, puffy) every morning he shaved—was inevitable when "a guy went fifteen rounds."

Ernest was struggling after a title for his novel. So far he had called it *Fiesta.* But, he told Hadley, he didn't want to use a foreign word. Then there was a phrase he'd heard from Gertrude Stein that sounded like a title. Ernest was part of "The Lost Generation," she'd said. But when he remembered how well, how valiantly, boys his age had fought at the Piave River in 1918 and, against this, put Gertrude's egotism and her mental laziness, he dismissed that title, too. Ernest finally decided on lines from Ecclesiastes, suggestive of the cyclic quality of life.

> One generation passeth away, and another generation cometh; but the earth abideth forever. . . . The sun also ariseth, and the sun goeth down, and hasteth to the place where he arose. . . . The wind goeth toward the south, and turneth about unto the north; it whirleth about continually, and the wind returneth again according to his circuits. . . . All the rivers run into the sea; yet the sea is not full; unto the place from whence the rivers come, thither they return again.

Pamplona, 1925, had given Ernest his first novel, but it had also fouled much of his life. He had made a fool of himself over an alcoholic nymphomaniac who, he felt, had betrayed him with a "kike" for the price of her drugs. His wife, hurt and humiliated by Ernest's passion for Lady Duff, had fallen in love, she said, with a handsome bullfighter half her age. Ernest had always found in Spain the quintessence of all he admired. Now everything—the fishing on the Irati, the camaraderie at the festival of San Fermin, even the bullfight itself—was polluted.

Because Ernest had paid so dearly for his novel, he did not want to see it undervalued. His publisher, Horace Liveright, had, under considerable pressure, brought out Ernest's short story collection *In Our Time,* and Ernest was committed to him for a second book. But Liveright had spent little money on advertising *In Our Time,* and less on distribution. Most of the one thousand copies printed had stayed in New York. Even after a strong review in the *New York Times*—the stories had a "lean, pleasing, tough resilience," the reviewer had said—Liveright had refused to push.

Ernest said he was furious about the lack of advertising. But even worse was the careless production of the cover. Liveright had used blurbs from Sherwood Anderson, John Dos Passos, Edward J. O'Brien, Waldo Frank, Gilbert Seldes. But they had been grouped together in what appeared an attempt to defend the actual publication.

Then there was the conflict over the inclusion of "Up in Michigan." Liveright enjoyed the reputation of a "progressive" publisher. But in Ernest's eyes, his rejection of "Up in Michigan" proved him a hypocrite. Then came the rumor, brought to Paris by Liveright representative, Mrs. George Kauffman, that "Indian Camp" would have to be cut. My God, Ernest thought, it was the best story in the book. He had pleaded with John Dos Passos, Horace Liveright's friend, "Don't let them cut it. Tell Liveright not to be a damn fool."

1. Gertrude Stein (right) and her lover and companion, Alice B. Toklas, attend to Bumby, their godchild. Paris, spring 1924. (The Hemingway Foundation)

2. Ernest at the Irati River, before loggers polluted the stream and destroyed the best trout fishing Ernest had ever known. Burguete, Spain, 1924. (The Hemingway Foundation)

3. "Chink" Dorman-Smith, in a skier's pose, without the skis. Schruns, Austria, 1924. (The Hemingway Foundation)

4. Gerald and Sara Murphy, Pauline Pfeiffer, Ernest, and Hadley. Pamplona, July 1926. Pauline looks to see if Ernest and Hadley are holding hands, as they had been for a photo taken seconds before. (The Hemingway Foundation)

Ernest and Hadley after the flight in the biplane, before the encounter with the Germans. chwarzwald, August 1922. (The Hemingway Foundation)

6. The Irati, summer 1924. Hadley felt miserable over the pregnancy weight she couldn't lose. Ernest said the poplars made him feel he was back in Michigan, fishing the inlets of Lake Charlevoix. (The Hemingway Foundation)

7. Ernest at Gstaad, Switzerland, February 1927. His wedding to Pauline had been postponed until May. (The Hemingway Foundation)

8. Ernest and Pauline. Gstaad, February 1927. (The Hemingway Foundation)

9. Hadley in the Black Forest, 1922. Ernest has composed her portrait with symbols of his first loves: Nature—the "sensitive" ferns in Hadley's hair; Agnes von Kurowsky—the "uniform" of a World War I Red Cross nurse. (The Hemingway Foundation)

o. Robert McAlmon and Ernest fter the incident of the dog. Ma-rid, summer 1923. (The Hem-ngway Foundation)

11. Ernest flanked by Gerald Murphy and John Dos Passos. Schruns, 1926. Ernest later called Dos Passos a "pilot fish" for the rich, guiding them to the naive and creative. (The Hemingway Foundation)

12. Pauline Pfeiffer. (The He ingway Foundation)

13. Ford Madox Ford. (The Hemingway Foundation)

14. Ernest, the distressed lover; Duff Twysden, in an opiate haze; Hadley, brave-faced; Pat Guthrie (in beret), insouciant, bisexual. Pamplona, July 1925. (The Hemingway Foundation)

15. Ernest's grandfather and Civil War veteran, Anson Hemingway, with Ernest's father, Dr. Clarence Hemingway, outside the doctor's Oak Park, Illinois, home shortly before Anson's death. (The Hemingway Foundation)

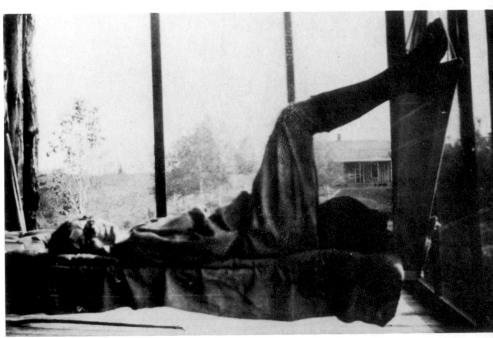

16. Hadley, on a pine-filled mattress, moved to a screened-in porch. Black Forest, 1922. (The Hemingway Foundation)

17. Ernest, in white pants and three sweaters, coaxing the bull to charge. Bullring at Pamplona, 1925. (The Hemingway Foundation)

18. Hadley and Ernest. Schruns, 1926. Both know the marriage is coming to an end. (The Hemingway Foundation)

19. Hadley and Pauline Pfeiffer. Schruns, 1926. (The Hemingway Foundation)

20. Hadley and her "advisors." Paris, 1926. (The Hemingway Foundation)

21. Hadley and Ernest, four months after their wedding, on their trip to Chamby, Switzerland, 1922. (The Hemingway Foundation)

22. Pauline and Ernest. Schruns, 1926. Hadley took the picture. (The Hemingway Foundation)

23. Jinny Pfeiffer, Pauline's lesbia sister. Paris, fall 1926. (Ayleen Spence)

24. Duff Twysden. A passport photograph.

25. Harold Loeb, in his "Barrymore" pose.

26. Ernest on his solo visit home to Oak Park, Illinois. With "kid brother" Leicester. Just before Christmas, 1923. (The Hemingway Foundation)

27. F. Scott Fitzgerald with his wife, Zelda. (Princeton University Library)

28. Ernest Walsh, editor of *This Quarter*. He would die of tuberculosis within a year. (Princeton University Library)

29. Ezra Pound at Sylvia Beach's bookshop, Shakespeare and Company. Paris, 1923. (Princeton University Library)

30. Sylvia Beach. Paris, 1923. (Princeton University Library)

31. Maxwell E. Perkins, 1925.

Just after Ernest had signed with Boni and Liveright in early 1925, Scott Fitzgerald had told Maxwell Perkins of Charles Scribner's that Ernest was "the real thing." Scott had said that one day Ernest would dominate American fiction. At Scott's urging, Perkins had written Ernest an invitation to submit his work.

Ernest had been sorely tempted. After all, Scott was an honest friend, Perkins had a fine reputation, and Scribner's was a first-class house. But Ernest had the Liveright contract in hand, and he was well aware that an honest-to-God contract was worth any amount of talk. Nevertheless, he told Perkins that, while Liveright had an option on his next three books, he must agree to publish the second book to keep that option alive. In June, Ernest had received a gift from Perkins, a copy of Bill Bird's nearly extinct publication of Ernest's vignettes, *in our time*.

Ernest had always felt it bad luck that Boni and Liveright also published Sherwood Anderson. There was something gothic about Anderson's work. In fact, without the incipient madness, Anderson was the new century's Edgar Allen Poe. Like Poe, Anderson acknowledged a futility to life, a sense that some mysterious fate had ultimate control. Ernest hated it that *In Our Time* should be compared to Anderson's *Winesburg, Ohio*. In Ernest's stories, Nick Adams is wounded by life every bit as much as, for example, Anderson's Wing Biddlebaum. Yet Nick does not yield to fate's ultimatums.

Sherwood Anderson, by breaking free of a suffocating marriage to a dimwitted woman, and by rejecting the "pillar of the community" status he had achieved in Cleveland, was living proof that a man of spiritual courage, no matter how bound he was to the common life, could break away to freedom. But Anderson's latest novel, *Dark Laughter*, like *Many Marriages* before it, was, in Ernest's eyes, a desecration of the heroic choice Anderson had made. Anderson had been the willing victim, Ernest believed, of New York intellectuals who had praised his work for its "primitive quality." Ernest regarded such praise as condescending nonsense. There was nothing primitive about Anderson's characters. These simple people were subtly, exquisitely complex. Unfortunately, Anderson had believed the critics and now wrote stories celebrating "primitive" races.

There was something else, too. Sherwood Anderson had been Ernest's hero. He had turned his back on the matriarchal culture of Midwest America, as Clarence Hemingway, Ernest's father, had steadfastly re-

fused to do. For Anderson now to regress, to replace one set of lies
with another, was more than Ernest could stand.

With his feelings against Anderson and Liveright running so strong,
Ernest began the strangest book he would ever write. He took the title,
*The Torrents of Spring*, from Turgenev, whose *Fathers and Sons* he
had loved, and the epigraph from Henry Fielding's mockery of the
sentimental effusions of Samuel Richardson in his *Pamela:* "The only
source of the truly ridiculous is affectation."

Ernest claimed that he wrote *The Torrents of Spring* in six days. He
also wrote to Horace Liveright that it was a satire of Anderson's *Dark
Laughter*. In fact, Ernest does make a pass in *Torrents* at Anderson's
simple-minded portrayal of the dark-skinned people as keepers of racial memory, of primitive emotions forgotten by the white man. But
Ernest's Michigan Indians, his noble savages, are much more intelligent, more socially sophisticated than the white man they deflate
through ironic reverence.

In *Torrents* Ernest's real intention is twofold. First, in Ralph Waldo
Emerson's words, he would "study to utter our painful secret." The
central character, Yogi, falls in love at first with an old woman. This
woman supports him, loves him, caters to his every whim. But soon, all
too soon, Yogi grows tired of her, and all her trying to regain his love
only makes her more repulsive to him. Eventually, Yogi falls in love
with a young waitress named Mandy. He knows she is insubstantial,
"cheap," but her youth makes up for all that. Besides, she is well-read
and aware of current literary fashion. She knows how to interest Yogi
with her promises of something new and exciting tomorrow, or the day
after. *The Torrents of Spring* is less Ernest's satire of Anderson than a
confession. Ernest wanted that chic little rich girl who'd been coming
around again.

In late 1925, Pauline Pfeiffer appeared the antithesis of Hadley.
Pauline was small, and thin, and energetic. She had good-sized, flexible
hips, small feet, and a way of walking that emphasized her well-shaped
behind. Ernest liked it that Pauline took it upon herself to defend him
every chance she got. One night, after a dinner she had with Ernest
Walsh, Kay Boyle, and Ethel Moorhead, she told Ernest Walsh that his
current editorial on the qualities in the work of Robert McAlmon was
a piece of tripe. McAlmon was nothing more than a fourth-rate writer,
and a homosexual to boot. He had been spreading false rumors about
Ernest's wife beating because Ernest had told him he didn't desire

"queers." Pauline assured Ernest Walsh that Ernest would "knock McAlmon down" the next time they met. She said that after Ernest had gotten McAlmon a New York publisher—the same publisher Ernest had—McAlmon had told Horace Liveright that Ernest beat Hadley regularly.

Pauline Pfeiffer was not especially young—she was only six years younger than Hadley—but she seemed contemporary. More than that, she was very certain about what was good and evil. If something were good, it worked. She told Ernest that a good religion had pragmatic value, and that it should help one do better, morally and practically, in everyday life. Pauline felt her most valuable asset was her practicality, her "common-sense" approach to everything. She called Ernest a romantic, as all good artists were. Pauline had great respect, even reverence, for artists—she called them "dreamers." But an artist needed someone with him to take care of the nuts and bolts of daily life.

Pauline admired Hadley as well. She thought Ernest's wife a beautiful woman, with exquisite sensibilities, who had sacrificed a career as a concert pianist to support Ernest while he wrote. When Pauline left for Schruns, to join Ernest and Hadley skiing, she was not quite sure whom she most wanted to see.

Ernest's weeks in Schruns the winter of 1925–26 were filled with misery. He arrived with laryngitis, a sore throat, and chest congestion. Fear of pneumonia kept him in bed for five days. When he did finally get out to ski, ice storms had crusted over the packed powder on the best trails. In spite of this, Ernest skied as boldly as ever. But he took some awful spills. After a fall, he would rise up slowly, present his wide-mouthed grin, and start off down the slope again. None but Hadley knew how badly he'd hurt himself. Eventually, he needed her help to get out of bed.

Pauline never got the skiing lessons from Ernest she had claimed to come for. But she did become part of almost everything that Ernest and Hadley did. In fact, in the tiny village of pine trees and green and white plastered houses, Pauline, Ernest, and Hadley were considered a "playful" threesome—as if they were children on holiday, having a good time.

Ernest, of course, knew what was happening. A strange woman was entering his and Hadley's life. Pauline loved him. He was sure of that. But he thought she might love Hadley, too. One of the authors Ernest most admired, D. H. Lawrence, had insisted in his masterpiece, *Women in Love,* that three, not two, was the perfect number in human affairs. And Ernest himself had felt this way for years.

Pauline Pfeiffer was with the Hemingways when the letter rejecting *The Torrents of Spring* arrived from Horace Liveright. Liveright said everyone in the office had agreed that the book was not for them. Nevertheless, he was most anxious for Ernest's Pamplona novel. If it got to New York in the next month or so, it would be published in the fall.

Ernest knew that his six-day self-indulgence with *Torrents* was a "paying back, a getting even." And this was something he desperately wanted to do. If Hadley still loved him, she would appreciate his need to punish Anderson for his cowardice, and to punish Liveright for his lack of appreciation, lack of understanding even, of *In Our Time*. Unfortunately for his marriage, Hadley spoke of loyalty; Pauline spoke of revenge.

Ernest told Hadley there was only one way to handle leaving Liveright. He must go to New York. Ernest said he did not like Horace Liveright personally, and Liveright had done nothing for *In Our Time*. Ernest would be damned if he'd give his novel, which had cost him so much, to such a publisher.

Ernest had recently gotten a couple of letters of inquiry: one from Max Perkins at Scribner's, the other from Alfred Harcourt. Both were forthright—they wanted "to sign him up," they said. In fact, Harcourt said he would advance any reasonable sum if he could secure the rights to Ernest's novel. Harcourt's offer gave Ernest second thoughts. But it did not change his mind. Actually, he had felt "hooked up" with Scribner's ever since Scott Fitzgerald and Max Perkins had said they loved his work.

Ernest cabled Liveright: "Hand over *Torrents* to Don Stewart." Stewart would deliver the manuscript to Max Perkins. It was December 31, 1925, the last day of what had been for Ernest a terrible year.

When Ernest got to Paris the fourth week of January, he did not return to his cold, damp flat in Rue Notre Dame des Champs. Instead, he took rooms at a small, expensive hotel on the Boulevard du Montparnasse. Two weeks earlier, Pauline had returned to her comfortable apartment in the Rue Picot. Although Ernest and Pauline were both "back home" when they met—for a visit to the Louvre, the Jeu du Paume—they felt they were on holiday. Pauline wrote to Hadley that Ernest was a delight, just a splendid companion. Pauline had important assignments offered her—high-fashion openings that her job at

Mainbocher required she attend. But she was willing, even anxious, to give them up, she said, to be with Ernest.

The first few days in Paris, Ernest and Pauline tried to pretend they were "pals." When they met, each would acknowledge all the things the other was compelled, absolutely, to do, and part with a cheerful smile. But the strategy broke down at night. After a day of keeping occupied, Ernest had left only a café supper and an empty hotel bed. He told himself he did not think Pauline beautiful. She looked no different than any other girl, except to someone who loved her. Yet his love for her was so deep and, being unsatisfied, so destructive, that he could no longer write. Loving her, and not having her was to his talent like vinegar to the oyster on the half shell. Pauline did not have to do, or say, anything special. There was something physical, or chemical, or magical between them, and, try as he might, Ernest could not give her up.

At first Ernest and Pauline stayed in his rooms at the Venetia Hotel, then in her flat in Rue Picot. They would go out only for necessities, not wanting to see or be seen by anyone. It was not fear of public censure that kept them reclusive, but rather a profound and mutually acknowledged guilt. Ernest sometimes spoke of their love as if it were a disease. Who was to blame, he asked, for this thing they had contracted, this passion that would prove fatal to his most precious beliefs? How could a man who truly loved one woman fall in love with another? Pauline was wretched, too, about their betrayal of Hadley. How had this all happened? She had not intended it to, and neither had Ernest.

When Pauline pressed Ernest for an explanation, he told her this. He recalled the many times Pauline had come to visit Hadley at the flat over the sawmill. At first, he had thought of Pauline as a most welcome companion for the wife his work made him neglect for most of each day. However, when he finished work, he had two women to greet him. One, his wife, was overweight, shabbily dressed, preoccupied with the care of their child. The other was pert, clever, effervescent. She seemed to want only to entertain him, and to listen to his writing, if only he would read it for her. Her stylish, expensive clothes, her perfume, reminded him she was rich, and anxious to help this artist she believed in. While Hadley sneezed and coughed with maddening regularity, and wore sweaters with a handkerchief stuffed in the sleeve, "the girl," as Ernest called Pauline, even in the miserable Paris winter, never caught a cold.

One night in early spring, when Pauline was about to leave after tea, Ernest had suggested, innocently, that he walk her to a cab. Soon this became a habit, a part of Pauline's visit. Then one night there was no cab at the corner, and Ernest and Pauline walked on, excited by each other. That night, Ernest put his arm around Pauline and drew her to him. He kissed her hard on the lips, and she kissed him back. When a cab finally came along, and he put her in it, Ernest found himself saying, "Good night, darling." And Pauline had said, "Good night, my dear."

During their week together in Paris, Ernest and Pauline promised each other that they would consider Hadley's happiness before their own. Of course, they could not give each other up, no more than they could renounce breathing or make their hearts cease to beat. But Hadley must now be made happy, as happy as they were. In some way, Ernest said, doing this would mitigate their sin.

Ernest had booked passage to New York on the *Mauretania*. He went aboard early, and this gave him the feeling of getting away. The days at sea could be a respite from the complications and the sorrow he had created in his life. Now all he needed were his work and his whiskey. Of course, he could not write. So the drinks would have to do. When the ship started to move, Ernest did not look out the window of the sitting room. Instead he sat in a comfortable chair and read through a pile of papers he had brought on board, and drank Scotch and Perrier. It was only six days to New York, and six days was easy.

Ernest had told Hadley that it would take a week, or less, to clear up things in America. She knew that he hated cities in winter, and New York in January, he said, was like the coast of Labrador. But New York this January of 1926 offered Ernest what he desperately needed: the chance to escape from himself. For nineteen days, he never spent a waking hour alone or drew a sober breath.

The business part of Ernest's stay took little time. The day the *Mauretania* docked, Ernest visited Boni and Liveright at the old brownstone at 61 West 48th Street. His meeting with Horace Liveright was surprisingly cordial, Ernest thought, though he knew quite well that Liveright was probably glad to be rid of him. Nevertheless, Horace played the gentleman, even inviting Ernest to join him for drinks at the publisher's favorite speakeasy.

Next came the meeting with Maxwell Perkins at Scribner's on Fifth Avenue. At first glance, Perkins was the antithesis of Horace Liveright.

While Liveright strained for aristocratic style, to Perkins it came as naturally as the cut of his Brooks Brothers suit, his Harvard accent, his half-handed handshake. Ernest noticed, too, that Maxwell Perkins was quite a salesman. Knowing how much Ernest thought of Scott Fitzgerald, both the man and his work, Perkins called Scott a genius. *The Great Gatsby* was a masterpiece, Perkins said. And the wonder of it was, Scott could do better.

Ernest thanked Perkins again for the gift of *in our time,* and wondered how he'd gotten a copy of so "rare" a book. Ernest said that the promise he'd made when Perkins inquired about the short story collection still held water. Playing the salesman himself, Ernest mentioned that Alfred Harcourt had expressed an interest in publishing his work. In fact, Harcourt had promised that there would always be a place for Ernest with his firm. But, Ernest asked, didn't Harcourt publish, and admire, such third-rate writers as Glenway Wescott? Perkins, who admired Wescott, bit his tongue and changed the subject. *Torrents* was a "grand" book, he said, and he offered Ernest fifteen hundred dollars in advance on both the satire and *The Sun Also Rises.* The royalty rate for both would be the maximum for new authors, fifteen percent.

His business done, Ernest plunged into New York literary society. Because he was handsome, and young, and people who counted had heard of him, Ernest played the toast of the town. Each morning a cluster of the Algonquin Hotel crowd—Broadway producer Marc Connelly; the satirist Dorothy Parker, whose first collection of poems, *Enough Rope,* was about to appear; and Robert Benchley, the drama critic for *Life*—showed up at his door. While Ernest was in New York, he must meet everyone who was anyone, they said. And appointments were made: to Ernest Boyd's at eleven; lunch with Jack Cowles and Ernest's wartime pal and now successful banker, Bobby Rouse. Also, Ernest must visit with Dave O'Neil because Dave had money and influence, and wasn't that what this trip was all about? When Ernest met publisher John Farrar, he told Dorothy Parker that Farrar, though nice enough, "looked exactly like a woman."

Ernest decided there was something to be said for being drunk most of every day. Life became a party that never seemed to end. On a drive back to his hotel, the modest Brevoort down in the Village, he found the writer Elinor Wylie on his lap. She was forty, and not very attractive. But she plied him with literary anecdotes, and Ernest, in a drunken haze, fell in love with her. Ernest's head did not clear until he took the Hoboken ferry and boarded the *Roosevelt* for the voyage home. Bob Benchley and Dorothy Parker boarded with him. Dorothy, after her recent suicide attempt, wanted to rest in the South of France.

The first six days out, however, the case of Scotch Miss Parker had smuggled aboard was consumed. In the midst of his drinking, Ernest managed to forget again the troubles to which he now returned. His major concern became the recovery of a "grand gold mounted water-man fountain pen, large size" which he had forgotten in his room, number 344 at the Brevoort. (He asked Isabel Simmons to find it for him and to send it along.) As he played whist with Dorothy Parker in the veranda café, Ernest said it was wonderful, this "alchemy of alcohol." But the alcohol could not cure Ernest of his affliction. Back in Paris, wanting with all his heart to catch the first train to Hadley and Bumby in Schruns, Ernest went straight to "the girl."

All of his still-young life, Ernest had awakened happy, he said, without any burden of guilt or regret. He had trained himself to write in the morning because he felt "purest" then. But now, with Pauline in Paris, the two of them all but living in her bedroom in the Rue Picot, making love at all hours of the day and night, eating erratically, sleeping until two or three or four in the afternoon, drinking before and after everything they did, Ernest felt happy in a new way. It wasn't the morning happiness anymore, but rather the joy of constant appetite. Always Ernest was hungry: for food, for sex, for poetry. He looked out the window at a world no longer necessary to him. All he needed was Pauline.

Deep inside Ernest knew that this kind of happiness, wonderful though it was, was "wrenching, killing" something precious and irreplaceable in him. Ernest did not take the second train to Schruns, nor the third. But, finally, like an alcoholic after a binge, he dragged himself to the Gare de l'Est.

Thirty years later Ernest remembered how this train ride ended: "When I saw my wife again standing by the tracks as the train came in by the piled logs at the station, I wished I had died before I ever loved anyone but her. She was smiling, the sun on her lovely face tanned by the snow and sun, beautifully built, her hair red gold in the sun, grown out all winter awkwardly and beautifully, and Mr. Bumby standing with her, blond and chunky and with winter cheeks looking like a good Vorarlberg boy."

"Oh Tatie," Hadley had said, when Ernest held her in his arms, "you're back and you made such a fine successful trip. I love you and we've missed you so."

True, Ernest had been unfaithful to Hadley many times before Pauline. But he had always managed to assuage his guilt with special acts of consideration, and with much lovemaking into which he cheerfully put his heart and soul. To Ernest's surprise, this prescription worked very well again—for himself and for Hadley, too. Alone together in the intimacy of Schruns, husband and wife soon reestablished the pleasant family routine. And again Ernest honestly felt clean and contented.

But fate conspired against him. Without warning, John Dos Passos arrived with "exciting news." Gerald and Sara Murphy—they were the "nicest" Americans in Paris, Dos Passos said—wanted to see Ernest again. They had so enjoyed his reading of *Torrents* to them the past winter in Schruns. They were anxious to hear excerpts from his latest work.

Although Ernest would never admit it, those who knew him best—Hadley, his wartime friend Bill Horne, even Scott Fitzgerald—knew he stood in awe of the "upper class"—people with education, culture, and, most of all, old family money. Ernest disgusted himself by being so impressed, so affected by the practiced grace, the obligatory cordiality, the skill these people had in pretending to delight. Yet he would willingly toady before their charm. Those who loved Ernest knew it was a chink in his armor. But Dos Passos saw it as an opportunity.

In many ways, John Dos Passos was the antithesis of Ernest. He was bald and gangling. He mumbled when, infrequently, he spoke. Chronically ill at ease, he made everyone around him uncomfortable. "Dos," as he liked to be called, blamed the commercial failure of his books on the ignorant masses. He once wrote to Ernest that he was quite sure "one may be better off like the big-nippled black woman with the mind of a buffalo." Lacking a sense of humor, he picked up Pound's epistolary style to use as his own. To Ernest and Hadley in Spain he wrote: "You licky [sic] bastard and bastardina and bastardino.—You're all of you at Pamplona dancing the riau-riau. Well think of the poor heathen in foreign lands." Women, including Hadley, could not endure Dos Passos. Now Ernest was about to become what Dos Passos himself had hoped to be: the darling of the social elite. Dos, this time in Schruns, would expose Ernest as a bounder and a fool.

Gerald and Sara Murphy possessed a "niceness" that Ernest, at first, found irresistible. Gerald was tall, slender, handsome, with a shock of Irish red hair. He had married Sara in 1916, just after she'd made her debut into New York society. A Yale man, urbane, formal, Gerald was the perfect foil for his frank and outspoken wife.

What Ernest most admired about the Murphys was their apparent appetite for living. For them, life was not so much a journey—as it was and always had been for Ernest—but rather a feast, or a series of feasts. The Murphys had, as Ernest called it, a "fiesta concept of life." Invitations to their lovely Villa America at Cap d'Antibes on the Riviera were for the select, the special few possessed of the capacity to enjoy life as they did.

But when Dos Passos and the Murphys arrived in Schruns, the weight of tragedy hung in the air. In December, a party of Germans had forced Herr Lent, the Taube innkeeper, to take them out despite conditions ripe for avalanches. He had taken them to the safest slope, and had skied across it himself. But when the Germans followed, the hillside descended upon them: "Thirteen were dug out and nine of them were dead."

When Gerald and Sara Murphy, John Dos Passos, and Ernest skied together, Ernest and Dos wore long woolens, tucked into their boots. But Gerald wore stylish knickers and an Austrian ski patrol loden coat and cap. Then, back at the Taube, Ernest embarrassed himself by reading for the assembled guests from *The Sun Also Rises*. Of course, the Murphys heartily approved. In fact, they declared it "wonderful." "It's great, Ernest. Truly it's great. You cannot know the thing it has," they said.

That night, in bed with Hadley, Ernest said that by reading his work to the Murphys, by begging for approval, for their appreciation, he'd now sunk as low as a writer could sink. He said his performance for the Murphys made him a bird dog—anxious to please any man with a gun—or a "trained pig in a circus who has finally found someone who loves and appreciates him for himself alone."

In Schruns that January, while Dos and the Murphys were there, Ernest developed a taste for the macabre. He found an ugly witch of a woman, Fraulein Glaser, who loved to fantasize about the best ways to die. She declared that the best death would be to have her heart stop while she was "running straight down in *pulver Schnee*." She told Ernest about an avalanche victim, caught in heavy, wet, old snow. The man had not been found for two days. A trail of blood led rescuers to his body. It appeared that the man, at the first instance of avalanche, had assumed the survival position—head tucked down between arm-encircled knees. He had trapped enough air in this position to have lasted perhaps a few hours. During that time, the rescuers concluded, he had twisted his neck from side to side against the pressure of the snow. The blood had come from his having worn the flesh through to the bone.

Another of Fraulein Glaser's tales struck still more deeply. She told of a peasant named Olz who lived in Paznuntal, toward Innsbruck. His wife, who'd had heart trouble, died suddenly one day in December. Olz had found her lying across the bed. He had notified the commune immediately, but he could not bring his wife's body out until the snow melted. Two months later, when Olz finally brought his wife down, the parish priest saw her face and asked Olz for an explanation:

"I don't know," Olz said.
"You'd better find out," the priest said, and put the blanket back.
Olz didn't say anything. The priest looked at him. Olz looked back at the priest. "You want to know?"
"I must know," the priest said.
. . . "Well," said Olz, "when she died I made the report to the commune and I put her in the shed across the top of the big wood. When I started to use the big wood she was stiff and I put her against the wall. Her mouth was open and when I came into the shed at night to cut up the big wood, I hung the lantern from it."
"Why did you do that?" asked the priest.
"I don't know," said Olz.
"Did you do that many times?"
"Every time I went to work in the shed at night."
"It was very wrong," said the priest. "Did you love your wife?"
"Ja, I loved her," Olz said. "I loved her fine."

Ernest would turn this anecdote into "An Alpine Idyll," and with it mock the romantic conception of "natural man." The theme of his story would be that a man alone, following his instincts, devolves into a beast.

When Ernest and Hadley returned to Paris at the end of March, *The Sun Also Rises* was complete. It pleased Ernest that the manuscript contained more than ninety thousand words. *Three Stories and Ten Poems, in our time,* and *In Our Time,* his three publications thus far, had seemed so brief he had insisted on having blank pages added to bulk them up. Ernest told Hadley, who had typed all his work in the past, that it would cost 1,085 francs to have the novel done professionally. It would be money well spent, she said.

Although they could still joke with each other, liked each other's company, and were pals, Ernest and Hadley knew they were no longer heart to heart. As she had before the time in Schruns, Pauline began coming around to the Hemingways' flat again. Ostensibly, she was still Hadley's friend, still an admirer of the loving couple who produced together, she insisted, such wonderful art.

# 9

# *Ménage à Trois*

Ernest was in love with Pauline Pfeiffer. He could not help it. But he knew that he would never be able to tell Hadley this truth. Did Hadley know that he loved Pauline? Did she know that he and Pauline had made love? Ernest was certain she did. But he believed that knowing and the declaration of that knowledge were two different things.

In observing such masters of diplomacy as David Lloyd George of Britain and the Russian Tchitcherin at the Genoa Conference in 1922, Ernest had learned that the ebb and flow of human emotions need not be specifically reported. The best decisions were often made on the basis of mutual interest and were rigorously logical. Passion had no place in diplomatic affairs. Harmony and social progress were the ideal. Perhaps between husband and wife it should, at times of great stress, be the same. Desiring another person, even the consummation of that desire, should not end a marriage. Only the confirmation in words could make it real, "a treaty violation" that must be acted upon, something to change one's life.

Pauline feared that Ernest would never tell Hadley the truth, never break her heart, that he would allow their love affair to go on until he could define and dismiss it as an infatuation. With this in mind, Pauline and her sister, Jinny, devised a plan. They would invite Hadley on a quiet "all girl" automobile trip along the Loire. They would break the news when Hadley felt trusting and at ease.

Pauline and Jinny had chosen well. The Loire was the most beautiful of all the rivers of France. Along its banks lay a twelfth-century abbey, standing amid walls and fields and tumbled gates. Just to the east, "near Sainte-Maure, was the chalk plateau on which in 732 Charles Martel turned back the overwhelming Arab wave that had swept across Spain and might have drowned all of Europe." The three women visited a house with deep window embrasures with names from centuries past inscribed into the soft stone. In the forest of St. Benoit, they walked ancient paths, talking loudly and sometimes singing in order to frighten away the indigenous snake—tiny, no bigger than a pencil, but poisonous, Pauline explained, and terrified of noise. Jinny suggested they swim in the wide, slow-flowing Loire. But Hadley preferred browsing an open market where artichokes were big as melons and wine was nearly given away. Occasionally, Pauline was charmingly loquacious, full of the wry humor Hadley so admired her for. But then she would drift into a melancholy silence and snap when Hadley said anything at all. Alone with Jinny for a moment, Hadley asked if she thought Pauline was "falling for" Ernest. Jinny replied, "I think that they are very fond of each other."

When Hadley got home, she was frightened and confused. She had known for some time that Pauline and Ernest were in love. Her question to Jinny served only to get it said. Now she must get it said to Ernest. She knew that Ernest truly suffered from the state he was in. Hadley was certain he still loved her, but he had indeed fallen hard for Pauline. Ernest was filled with remorse, but, Hadley knew, he could not help himself.

Finally, Hadley spoke to Ernest about the affair. He confessed, "very stumbly," that it was so. Suddenly, his confusion turned to rage. He berated Hadley for ever mentioning it between them. He told her that they could have gone on if she hadn't broken the spell. Now that it was out in the open, he wouldn't be able to live without Pauline.

Desperate for something to say, anything to calm Ernest, to prevent his "forcing a decision," Hadley cried out that Bumby was ill. It had begun with only a runny nose, dry cough, a slight fever. She had been sure it was nothing more than a cold. But the past few days it had gotten worse. Nose drops did nothing; the bouts of coughing lasted a minute or more. Sometimes Bumby's face would turn deep red after the coughing, and then he would vomit. Distracted by concern for his son, Ernest calmly told Hadley that Bumby had whooping cough, and that, strong boy that he was, it would probably not kill him, but that he would be sick for more than a month. Hadley, of course, would have to remain with their son while Ernest went on to Spain this summer himself. With Pauline? Hadley asked. No, Ernest said. She had left for Italy with her aunt and uncle.

Ernest had found that work could cure his spirit of almost any malaise. In Madrid, alone, he would see again if this was so. With his marriage falling apart—all of his own doing, he said—Ernest needed some good work to justify himself. Fortunately, that May, Madrid was a good place to write in—dry and unseasonably cold, with a high, early-winter sky. And there were no distractions. The bullfights were poor: small bulls, sick bulls—and for matadors, a boy from Seville with a "dose of the clapp" and "Fortuna," "one of the lousiest bull fighters on Earth."

Ernest had with him rough drafts of stories he wanted very much to finish. In his heatless room at the Pensión Aquilar, swathed in a rough woolen blanket, he worked in bed on the story of his first experience of sexual intercourse.

The girl was an Indian, Prudence Boulton, the daughter of a half-breed who lived at the Indian camp not two miles from the Hemingway cottage on Walloon Lake. Nick Adams is perhaps eleven or twelve years old, and he has been to a Fourth of July celebration in Petoskey with the Garner family. Driving the wagon toward home in the dusk, the father of the family encounters, one by one, nine Indians lying drunk in the road. "Them Indians," his wife says. Carl, one of the family boys, begins to ridicule Nick. "You got an Indian girl," he says. He compares the smell of an Indian girl to a skunk. But then the father cuts his own son down. "Carl ain't no good with girls," he says.

When Nick gets back home, his own father has cold chicken and milk waiting for him in the icebox. "There's some pie too," his father says. It is huckleberry pie. His father sat watching Nick eat the pie. Then he told him that he had seen his friend, Prudence Boulton, "threshing around" in the woods with Frank Washburn. "Were they—were they—" Nick begins. "Were they what?" his father asks. "Were they happy?" "I guess so," his father replies.

In his room that night Nick thought, "My heart's broken. . . . If I feel this way my heart must be broken." But after a while, Nick heard his father blow out the lamp and go into his own room. Then Nick heard the wind come up in the trees and "felt it come in cool through the screen." But "in the morning there was a big wind blowing and the waves were running high up on the beach and he [Nick] was awake a long time before he remembered that his heart was broken."

Under the pressure of guilt, Ernest had transferred his ideals to Had-

ley. Now she was his "Nick," and he had become the faithless Prudence
Boulton, "threshing around." With this story, Ernest resolved that
Hadley would in time, and with the change of seasons, recover. And
he knew that the real-life Prudence—his persona—had died horribly
in her late teens, and by her own hand.

Ernest was willing to take the consequences of being, as he called
himself, "son of a bitch sans peur et sans reproche." But he would not
apologize for "calling" his friend Sherwood Anderson on the fakery
in *Dark Laughter* with *The Torrents of Spring*. From his room in Madrid, Ernest wrote to Anderson that *Torrents* was a joke and not meant
to be mean, but was "absolutely sincere." He told Anderson: "You see
I feel that if among ourselves we have to pull our punches, if when a
man like yourself who can write very great things writes something
that seems to me, (who have never written anything great but am anyway a fellow craftsman) rotten, I ought to tell you so."

Then Ernest wrote to his father. Ernest knew that in his family
divorce was considered a crime against society, and a moral evil. To
the Hemingways, and to most of the other residents of Oak Park, Illinois, a divorced person was in disgrace. Ernest was not ready to reveal
his situation, but he would, through oblique references, try to suggest
what was going on.

Because he had written to Clarence about Pauline and her Catholi-
cism earlier, Ernest thought these lines might be a gentle introduction
to the coming change in his life: "Pauline Pfeiffer who was down in
Austria with us and is going to Spain this summer lives in Piggott
when she's in the states and is getting us a house there. I heard that
you were upset about my wanting to winter at Windemere so decided
not to bother you on that score. Having been to *mass* this morning, I
am now due at the bull fight this afternoon. Wish you were along."

On May 21, it was cold and raining in Madrid. Ernest was reminded
of Paris springs. Out-of-season weather left him irritated and depressed.
How ridiculous the shops in the Carrera San Jeronimo looked, with
their awnings extended!

But this day Ernest had real cause to worry. Just before noon, a fat
maid, with gray and stiffly oiled hair, had handed Ernest a letter. Hadley, at the invitation of Gerald and Sara Murphy, had decided to take
Bumby with his nurse, Marie Cocotte, south to Juan-les-Pins. Gerald
had met them at the station. And Sara, in bed with a cold, had suggested that the doctor coming to see her should take a look at Bumby.

The doctor had confirmed Ernest's diagnosis of whooping cough, Hadley said.

At this news, the Murphys had decided that they must protect their own children—Honoria, ten years old; Baoth, then eight; and Patrick, six—all weak and unusually susceptible to respiratory disease. Hadley and "Little Jo"—as she was now calling her son—and the nurse, Marie, were to be put up in a local hotel, expenses paid by the Murphys. Sara Murphy had told Hadley that in a couple of days she would be allowed to come back and stay with them. But Bumby would have to stay with Marie at the hotel for at least six weeks, "until the congestion dried right out of his system." Hadley wrote that she would come to Ernest in Madrid as soon as Bumby recovered. She would stay until then only because she did not want, as she put it, to leave the Murphys "responsible for a sick child."

To make Ernest jealous, Hadley mentioned the attention she was getting from a young Russian. Olaf, it seemed, was "coming around a lot." He's "very nice," Hadley said, "with a tragic history." Then she asked if the address Pauline had given her for Italy—"Villa Favorila, Bologna"—would be "tout ce-qu' il faut?" But Hadley said what she wanted most was to be with Ernest. Because of Bumby's illness she could not come to Madrid. Wouldn't Ernest come, as soon as he could, to Juan-les-Pins?

The letter she received from Ernest, by return mail, surprised her. Ernest declared that he himself was ill. The cold and dampness of the rotten Madrid spring had brought out his bad throat again. He hadn't been to the bullfights, and had none of the programs she had asked for. To make matters worse, the hotel did not even have a decent bar.

Hadley answered that he was her "Dearest + well beloved Waxin," "so small + what hard luck has come your way—you poor impoverished Mitten." She assured Ernest that the thing she wanted to do "most in the world" was to leave their son safe and sound and "haste to my Waxin." Unfortunately, there was no one to look after Bumby in quarantine, except Marie, and she, Hadley said, could not be expected to make decisions.

Hadley told Ernest that Bumby's coughing had been severe, and that with every spell now there was vomiting. She was taking "great pains to keep him fairly quiet." Bumby ate well and spent most of his day in the sun, but not on the beach, she assured Ernest, or in the wind. At bedtime, Marie rubbed him with hot lineament, and the doctor had given him drops to be taken three times a day. The vomiting had made Bumby thinner. But he still looked "awfully well and handsome."

Hadley said she was cheered by the recent arrival of Scott Fitzgerald. He claimed to be an expert on lung congestion and had brought a rubber shirt for Bumby, to help him sweat out the cold. Hadley herself had bought a lamp to burn eucalyptus in Bumby's room at night. Anything, she said, to soothe the harsh breathing and the cough.

Hadley added that Marie slept with Bumby in a separate room with single beds, while she, Hadley, slept "in a large bed." "In that bed," Hadley went on, "there is room for a Beauty when he wishes to come to Kitten's side." When Ernest wrote that he would not come south until his throat had cleared up and he felt strong and well again, Hadley was hurt beyond words. She took his refusal to mean that he could not stand even to share her bed, now that he loved Pauline.

But, in fact, Hadley had drawn the wrong conclusion. Ernest would not come to Juan-les-Pins because he was afraid, afraid of catching what his son had, and then dying the way he'd seen an airman die in 1918 in the Red Cross hospital in Milan:

> At one o'clock one morning, Agnes [von Kurowsky] asked Ernest to help her with an influenza patient who appeared to be dying. Ernest, limping with his leg stiff from hours in bed, followed her to a room just down the hall. In a brass bed against the wall, a young man sat bolt upright, soaked with sweat, straining to breathe. There was a small lamp covered by a towel; two girls knelt at the bedside praying; the odor of camphor filled the room. Because the hospital doctor was out of town, Agnes intended to try something desperate with rubber tubes herself. Ernest was to assist. But before she could start, the patient choked and dropped back limp on his pillows. In death, his bowels released and filled the sheets with one final yellow cataract that flowed and dribbled on. After praying with the others, Ernest went back to his room alone, washed his hands and face, and gargled with alcohol and water. When Agnes finally came in, he would not kiss her until she had gargled too.

Unaware of Ernest's true reason for not coming, Hadley continued to promote the attractions of Juan-les-Pins, the Murphys, the lovely accommodations at Villa America. The truth was, she said, that Bumby was very sick and likely to remain so. "Mummy," as Hadley called herself in letters to Ernest, was "small too," and would not be able to come and take care of her "Waxin" in Madrid for a long time. But "Mummy" had an idea. Why not invite Pauline down to Juan-les-Pins? "It would be a swell joke on tout le monde." Hadley signed the letter "Yours longing-to-comfort-a lovely-Wax-Puppy arms-around.

Mummy Kittin." Ernest wrote immediately, in what Hadley called a "love scribble," that he thought it a better idea if Pauline and Hadley came up to him in Madrid.

Now Hadley was frightened. First, she had tried to gain Ernest's sympathy for Bumby's condition. She knew that Ernest would not respond to "crying wolf," so she gave him the details and put a cheerful twist on them. Yes, Bumby's cough sounded worse, but that was only because it was drying up and *"really* better." The Murphys could not take on the care of Bumby while she came north because their "kids had never had the whoops and they are most anxious naturally that they should *not*—they have especially delicate throats."

Then there was the question of accommodations. The Murphys had taken Hadley and Bumby to the Hotel Beau-Site. Hadley and Bumby were "very comfortable" there, but everyone suspected the truth about Bumby and felt that, as Hadley put it, "we should be quietly sent forth to seek our fortunes." It was all quite humorous, Hadley said. In fact, the situation had been desperate until her "knight errant," Scott Fitzgerald, "six-o'clock-in-the-morning-drunk," arrived with the keys to his Villa Paquita. That meant, Hadley said, she and Bumby would have a place to stay until mid-June.

Trying to remain cheerful, Hadley reported that their friends—Ada MacLeish (down with her husband, Archie, a close friend of the Murphys) and Gerald and Scott and Zelda—could not have been nicer. Gerald brought linen, and Scott and Zelda sent chicken, eggs, butter, strawberries and roses. Hadley made a good lunch for everyone. But they all kept their distance "from us poisonous ones."

Ernest wrote again that it sounded as if Bumby's care was assured, and couldn't Hadley come to him in Madrid? But Hadley wrote only that the doctor thought that because Bumby had had the cough for so long, it would "finish fast here." Maybe in a couple of weeks, Hadley said, she might be able to come. But Ernest "mustn't look for me until it's over." Ernest was furious. He wrote that he had intended to take her to the May 30 bullfights.

Hadley was surprised that Pauline answered her letters with a warmth and concern that suggested she was Hadley's closest friend. To the invitation that she join "the crowd" at Juan-les-Pins, Pauline sent an enthusiastic "Yes." Whooping cough meant nothing to her, Pauline said. She had had "whoops" as a child and was therefore immune.

In the midst of Hadley's wretchedness, Bumby started the violent coughing again. His physician, a Dr. Jenner, announced that he was now sure the genuine whoops had just begun, and that Bumby could not go back to the Murphys' home for at least two months. Hadley told Ernest she suspected the doctor's caution had something to do with the Murphys secretly paying his bills.

Hadley said that her plans were "(1) To stay until the tenth (2) to fumigate (3) to install Marie and Bumby in a 'chambre menblie' (4) to stay a couple of days in a hotel or pension to see all goes well, then (5) if Bumby *is much better* as doctor says he should be by that time, leave with Pauline for Madrid + a Waxin." But Hadley added that if Ernest did feel he'd like to come down, they could "swim + drink their heads off in great comfort" and with much less expense than in Spain. Just as Hadley finished her letter, the Murphys' chauffeur came to the door with "4 beautiful lettuce + some little teensy baby carrots for us all." Because Ernest had not written for two days, nor had he answered her telegram, Hadley wrote: "If I don't get a gram from you by 4 this afternoon I shall gram you again for fear you didn't get mine of yesterday." She told Ernest that his passport had just arrived, and now she awaited his decision.

The next morning Hadley got more bad news. Scott Fitzgerald came over with a letter he'd gotten from Ernest. Ernest claimed in the letter that Hadley was down south, having a good time, and that she obviously didn't mind being away from him, and that she was not wretched at the thought of being separated for so long. Hadley was stunned. How could Ernest misconstrue everything in this way? For God's sake, what should she do?

Scott suggested that Hadley indulge Ernest, tell him what he wanted to hear. Hadley knew that Scott meant, "Don't let Ernest create an excuse for turning to Pauline." Choking back her anger, Hadley wrote: "Poor Lambskins, can't I just get these arms around you and hug and warm you and tell you how lonely I am—*only* staying because it's the only thing to do." Then Hadley suggested something extraordinary to Ernest: Pauline would be there in two days. If Ernest should not use the passport, mailed to him that very day, Pauline could come to him and make Madrid a "place of pleasure instead of the awful place it's been for you alone."

Worst of all for Hadley, Ernest, in his letter to Scott, had accused her of being "in the hands" of Scott and Zelda, and of assuming their "party" attitude toward life. Hadley wrote that this was not so. She and Bumby were using their villa, and that was all. Then Hadley went on to defend her behavior: "I am using [Scott and Zelda's] at *no* (they are giving it) and being heartily supplied with food wither by Gerald + Sara who are worried about one inconvenient upset. Bumby is a *little* better. I don't even spend money on drink, however bad I feel—until yesterday + then I had the curse and got so low I went downtown and spent 8 frcs. on whiskey + and felt repentent. I don't talk to a soul except Marie all day. . . . It's comfortable + the best of luck under the circumstances but not exactly a *joy-life.* You ask under what category I am staying here? Well, shall I call it business or duty or what—necessity perhaps." Hadley worried that, when she and Marie and Bumby were forced to leave the villa, she would have to bear the cost of rooms herself. She was considering, she said, putting her girl-friends—Letticia and Renata—"out of the flat at 113, and take Bumby back there."

Then Hadley played her trump card: "Wouldn't it make a difference to you if Pfeiffer or some other friend turned up [here] to mill around with?" Ernest should not worry about her, Hadley said. She was only a "hurried, worried Kittin." Hadley wrote: "I'm living here the cheapest possible and *not* being a bad. I've got a headache and a heartache, and I want for the common good and am sorrier than I can say I haven't been able to expend myself more on you and not so much on the smaller shad."

Knowing how begging disgusted Ernest, Hadley tried very hard not to plead with him. But occasionally she broke down: "I'm small and I am a tired cat but I could get so well here if not so worried and unhappy about a Waxin." Because her hand shook when she wrote these lines, Hadley's penmanship was hardly legible. Ernest wired her twelve hundred francs and took the train for Antibes. Pauline would meet him there, he said, the first week of June.

Juan-les-Pins lay in a curl of the Mediterranean, between Cap d'Antibes and Cannes. The bright tan beach sloped to the shallow, tepid water. In clear view across the water rose "the distant image of Cannes, the pink and cream of old fortifications, the purple Alp that bounded Italy." At the town's back lay the mile-deep forest of pine that gave the town its name. To Ernest, the coast embodied the word *serene,* except that each morning a harsh wind drove down from the gray and purple mountains. Juan-les-Pines was now a summer resort for rich and fashionable Americans, and the Murphys were well established there.

The Murphys' Villa America was just what Ernest expected. The

Murphys had the money, and the time because of the money, to create the illusion of gentile life, and to keep that illusion alive. The Villa America was indeed grand—white stucco, two stories, fourteen rooms, a lush garden, a shaded terrace, a beautiful view. It was the second largest estate on the cape, surpassed only by the property, near the lighthouse, of the Aga Khan.

But Gerald had modeled the life lived at the Villa America upon what he knew of the Renaissance courts of Italy. The rule of life at the Villa was proportion. Neither too much nor too little of anything. Just enough to make everyone comfortable, to put them at ease. Gerald's passion, he said, was his hundred-foot schooner, *Weatherbird,* which he had named after a Louis Armstrong recording and on which he took great pleasure in introducing people like Hadley to sailing. Ernest told Hadley that the Murphys were indeed considerate and generous hosts. And they truly intended to create a lovely atmosphere for their guests. It was clear they took this as a duty.

Nevertheless, Ernest said, the summer of 1926 must have been a failure at the Villa America. Sara Murphy, ill with a summer flu, had spent most of each day in her room. Gerald, instead of sailing his *Weatherbird,* ran grocery errands for his guests. Scott had told Ernest that Zelda was "sick" again—meaning she had lapsed into the madness Ernest had seen flashes of in France. And Scott was drinking gin again, after having forsworn it in Paris.

But, Ernest said, Hadley and Bumby seemed worst of all. Pale and fat, with dark circles of sleeplessness under her eyes, Hadley had insisted on holding Bumby during her reunion hug with Ernest. "Can't he walk?" Ernest asked. "Of course he can," Hadley replied, and she put their son down for a few tottering steps. God, the boy looked thin, Ernest thought. And Hadley's usually tight-skinned face had the puffiness that comes from too much drinking.

At first, Ernest was furious with Hadley. Why was the boy so run down? "The doctor said the disease is very debilitating, and it takes a long time," Hadley replied. What she had said in her letters—all about Dr. Jenner's contentions that Bumby had come into the true "whoop" after a month of illness—was, Ernest said, utter nonsense. And Dr. Jenner was a quack.

What had Bumby been eating? Ernest asked. Provençal with the rest of them, Hadley said. Ernest could have struck her. His father, Clarence, had taught him that a healthy diet was the best defense against disease. The spicy, garlic-ridden southern food would be indigestible to a boy in Bumby's condition. And to hell with the miserable lettuce from the Murphys' garden. From now on, Bumby would eat eggs, solf-boiled, three times a day. He would eat fish, and drink plenty of whatever milk they could get. The only French food he'd eat would be the bread. And, Ernest said, they'd have to move out of the converted donkey stable that the Murphys had made their guest house. Of course, it was lovely now, and picturesque. But the donkeys could have left disease behind.

Then, too, a hard fact remained. Ernest was ashamed of himself. He had not come to his son, and to Hadley, when he knew, despite the strained cheerfulness of her letters, that they needed him. Afraid of catching Bumby's disease, he had been, again, as much of a coward as in that hospital in Milan when, in fear of catching the flu, he'd refused to kiss Agnes.

Pauline Pfeiffer arrived in Antibes the day after Ernest. Fresh from her weeks in Italy, she was eager to be the Hemingways' helpmate and "best of all" friend. She insisted it should be the Hemingways plus one for the next weeks on the Riviera. Pauline brought confidence and a badly needed energy to Ernest and Hadley. And she treated Bumby like the dearest nephew. When Fitzgerald's lease was up at the Villa Paquita, Pauline rented two rooms at the Hotel de la Pinede in Juan-les-Pins, and asked Ernest and Hadley to be her guests.

Ernest insisted that they all take up physical conditioning. That meant bicycling through the pine-scented countryside every morning to build their legs and wind, and then swimming and sunning at a special cove he had found. Ernest believed strongly in the curative power of routine. The day should be planned, hour by hour. The purpose, however, was not simply to get things done, but rather to achieve what Henry Thoreau called "economy"—a husbanding of spiritual resources, a spending of them on only that which enhances life. If the spirit is well, Ernest believed, the body functions well. One can eat without indigestion, defecate with regularity, sleep the night through without soporific. To achieve such "economy," everything, even the mundane acts of daily life, must be performed deliberately—in a measured, attentive way. At first, Ernest drove Pauline, and Hadley, too, crazy with his insistence on making a ritual out of the simple act of having breakfast, or of going to the beach. But in time the women caught Ernest's rhythm. And they reveled in it.

A day for the Hemingways and Pauline began, most often, in Ernest and Hadley's bedroom. Pauline, an early riser, who woke quickly, she said, would knock and come into the Hemingways' room dressed in her morning robe, covering her tomboy pajamas. At first, Hadley was distressed by this. She and Ernest wore only pajama tops to bed, and Pauline, "without her bottoms," would soon be in bed with them. But Pauline was affectionate to both Ernest and Hadley, and sexually spontaneous in a way that made all they did seem like fun, like three children at play.

Next came breakfast, which Ernest would order with the care of a good doctor prescribing. A favorite combination was brioche and red raspberry preserve, with a cup of two soft-boiled eggs, still steaming hot, cleanly shelled and white against the melted pat of butter. Ernest would grind the pepper for each of them—pepper cleansed the morning stomach, he believed—and pour the hot coffee for the café au lait.

After checking on Bumby, now exclusively in the care of Marie, Ernest and his two girls, as he called them and they called themselves, drove to their special, secret cove. They all loved this cove, with its gentle breeze and scent of the stone pines, and the sea so dark and blue as they came down to it. To induce an appetite, Ernest brought along, wrapped in a Turkish towel, a small block of ice, and the makings—Gordon's gin and Noilly Prat vermouth—for his best martini.

Pauline soon suggested they all might enjoy swimming naked. It was, after all, the custom along the coast. Ernest, who had swum "in the buff" with his sisters, diving off the dock at the family summer cottage on Walloon Lake in the moonlight when they were all in their teens, was all for it. But Hadley was embarrassed. It wasn't fair, Hadley thought. Pauline seemed made for the sea and the sun. Ernest called her a seal, and he was right. Small, thin, compact, with an olive skin that turned golden tan in the sun, she would wade out until the water came over her belly and touched her breasts, and then break into a beautiful crawl. Hadley was fair and freckled, and still held the weight she'd gained carrying Bumby. While Ernest and Pauline showed off for each other—Pauline floating, back arched, breasts lapped gently by the movement the light breeze gave the sea; Ernest, from a high rock, diving close enough to Pauline to make her a partner in the thrill—Hadley lay slathered in oil, baking in midi sun.

But Ernest did not accompany his girls to the beach every day. Sometimes he would spend his morning reading the "mixed reviews," as Maxwell Perkins called them, of *The Torrents of Spring,* and writing letters in defense of his book—nasty letters to reviewers, letters that he knew he would not send.

One morning, on an impulse, Ernest showed a carbon copy of *The Sun Also Rises* to Scott Fitzgerald. Embarrassed that he had not yet followed *Gatsby* with anything worthwhile and inclined to believe that Ernest had become Perkins's favorite, Scott was poised to be critical. And critical he could be:

> Dear Ernest:
>
> Nowadays when almost everyone is a genius, at least for awhile, the temptation for the bogus to profit is no greater than the temptation for the good man to relax (in one mysterious way or another)—not realizing the transitory quality of his glory because he forgets that it rests on the frail shoulders of professional enthusiasts. This should frighten all of us into a lust for anything honest that people have to say about our work. I've taken what proved to be excellent advice (On The B. + Damned) from Bunny Wilson who never wrote a novel (on Gatsby—change of many thousand wds) from Max Perkins who never considered writing one, and on T. S. of Paradise from Katherine Tighe (you don't know her) who had probably never read a novel before.
>
> [This is beginning to sound like my own current work which resolves itself into laborious + sententious preliminaries].
>
> Anyhow I think parts of *Sun Also* are careless + ineffectual.

Scott went on to present a detailed analysis—page numbers and quotations included—of what he called Ernest's "elephantine facetiousness." His criticism centered on the tone of the first thirty pages, which he considered sneering, superior, "nose-thumbings-at-nothing." In general, just the kind of "horseshit" Ernest would himself ridicule. There was plenty to praise in the book, Scott said. And he noted a place that he'd "happened on" and not "picked out." But he concluded, "I go crazy when people aren't always at their best."

Although Ernest often said that only an amateur can't take serious criticism, Scott's remarks put him in a fury that lasted half a day. He felt as if he wanted to kill someone. Not Scott, especially, but someone. Then he became ill. But the next morning, Ernest told Hadley that Scott was probably right, that he, Ernest, had written "smart-ass" and Scott had called him on it. Scott had suggested cutting the whole first part, Ernest said. The tone was offensive, and the information emerged later on anyway. Why not make the cuts and see what Perkins had to say?

Hadley listened quietly to Ernest argue with himself, asking questions or making comments just often enough to show she was attentive. When Ernest finished, she told him she had her own decision to make, and it was an important one, too.

During one of her beach afternoons with Pauline, when they swam together at the cove, Pauline had declared she was as much in love with Hadley as with Ernest. At first, Hadley said, she thought it part of the "acolyte" strategy Pauline had employed since they'd first met. But Pauline made it clear that those mornings in bed—the three of them together—was the way she hoped it could always be. Desperate to save her marriage, Hadley wondered, might Ernest accept such an arrangement?

To Hadley's surprise, Ernest declined. Hadley must remember, he said, that Pauline had been brought up, by and large, in a convent. There the girls, so he'd been told by Kate Smith, engage in quite intimate displays of affection. But this means little to them—only a substitute until the "real thing"—that is, the love of a man—comes along. Hadley said nothing more on the subject. Instead she suggested they go on to Pamplona. (She knew that Ernest was never so in touch with himself as when he absorbed the performance of a matador.) Ernest said they all needed a change of scene.

It did not take Ernest long to assume his role in Pamplona: that of apologist for the bullfight. And he was happy to have three new students. Yes, Pauline and the Murphys had seen bullfights before. But seeing one with Ernest, Hadley told them, was an altogether new experience.

Although he usually denied it, Ernest judged people in large part by their ability to enjoy life. And he believed no experience placed more demands on one's capacity for enjoyment than the bullfight. The spectator-student must possess courage, and emotional integrity, intelligence, and imagination. Those who turned away from the goring of the horses lacked courage. Those who pretended to feel nothing, or worse, to be bored by the spectacle, were hypocrites. Those who could not appreciate the aesthetics were insensitive and stupid.

Despite Dos Passos's adulatory characterization of Gerald and Sara Murphy at Antibes, Ernest had been distinctly underwhelmed. Just what had this rich and happy couple done with the opportunities their wealth and experience had given them? So far as Ernest could discover, the Murphys gave good parties, and that was all. Ernest was particularly repelled by what he took as Gerald's affectation of a world-wise–world-weary melancholy, and by Sara's frankness, which often managed to hurt the feelings of people who would willingly take an insult from her.

Yet much of this attitude changed when Ernest watched the Murphys at the bullfight. Gerald, though deeply affected by the mutilation of the horses—he had ridden extensively in the army—nevertheless truly enjoyed himself. And Gerald had an instinct, Ernest believed, for judging the cape work of the matadors. When some Spaniards sitting nearby hooted down a matador Gerald thought superb, he threatened them with his fists. Later, in the running of the bulls, Gerald, standing his ground before a charging bull, managed what Ernest considered a "perfect veronica" with his top coat. Although Sara could not match Gerald's courage about the horses, she dressed for the bullfight as she did for church, and tried hard, and succeeded, in having a good time.

Pauline, who had ridden horses as a child and had owned her own pony, was unaffected by the brutality. Once she understood the fight, Pauline enjoyed it more than anything, she said.

Hadley, of course, had seen Ernest's bullring performance before. And his analysis of people who were now their friends bored her. Besides, Hadley was sick and tired of Pauline. Wherever they walked, wherever they sat, usually at a crowded table, harassed by bootblacks and sellers of souvenirs, Pauline managed to get hold of one of Ernest's arms.

Although he was proud of himself at Pamplona, the way he'd initiated the Murphys and Pauline into the secrets of aficionados, there was something about Ernest's current predicament that filled him with self-loathing. When he thought of the way he was abusing two women—hurting both because he could not control himself, using both for support he had not earned—Ernest saw in himself traits of his former publisher at *This Quarter*, Ernest Walsh.

During the weeks in Antibes, Ernest had gotten three letters from Walsh, and he had replied, assiduously, to each one. Ernest knew that the tubercular Walsh was running now, running from death as he had always ran from creditors. And Walsh was dragging his two women with him: the mistress of long standing, Ethel Moorhead, who paid all the bills; and a young, beautifully built aspiring novelist, Kay Boyle, who was pregnant by Walsh.

As a critic, Walsh revolted Ernest—he once compared McAlmon favorably to Mark Twain. And one of Walsh's published poems, about masturbating into his pants, actually made Ernest sick. But worst of all, Ernest Walsh was a fraud. Yes, Walsh would die of tuberculosis, and die soon. But did he have to take so much of Ethel Moorhead and Kay Boyle with him? "A son-of-a-bitch living is a son-of-a-bitch dying," Ernest said to himself. And yet he could not help but see how much like Ernest Walsh he had become.

Ernest and Hadley took the train back to Paris on a stifling August weekend. A middle-aged woman with whom the Hemingways shared a compartment told them that she had just left the Continent with her daughter. She insisted on telling Hadley their story:

> "I'm so glad you're Americans. American men make the best husbands," the American lady was saying. "That was why we left the Continent, you know. My daughter fell in love with a man in Vevey." She stopped. "They were simply madly in love." She stopped again. "I took her away, of course."
> "Did she get over it?" asked my wife.
> "I don't think so," said the American lady. "She wouldn't eat anything and she wouldn't sleep at all. I've tried so very hard, but she doesn't seem to take an interest in anything. She doesn't care about things. I couldn't have her marrying a foreigner." She paused. "Some one, a very good friend, told me once, 'No foreigner can make an American girl a good husband.' . . . Americans make the best husbands," the American lady said to my wife. I was getting down the bags. "American men are the only men in the world to marry."

The "American lady," of course, had no idea that Ernest and Hadley were about to separate, that Ernest had asked for a divorce.

# 🔟 10 🔟

# *A Diminished Thing*

On the trip from Cap d'Antibes, eleven hours by train, the Hemingways drank, Ernest claimed, a vintage. They argued, viciously; then, because it was late and close to home, they made up. In Paris, Ernest wanted to spend the night with his wife at the studio Gerald Murphy had lent him for the separation, in Rue Froidevaux. The high-ceilinged apartment was cool, Ernest said, and, in the morning, the whitewashed skylight gave the room a wintery glow. Did this mean they might get back together? Hadley asked. No, Ernest said. But they both had a right to a little relief.

The next morning, Ernest left the studio before Hadley awakened. Before she left, too, she wrote him a note:

at 69 rue Froidevaux, 8:30 A.M., Aug. 20, 1926.
Dearest Chickie
    Such is ALCOHOL! and my hand is still trembly from same, is yours? My mind as I recall things I said in that damn taxi, was positively senile. I think however that I have forgotten most of what it was that caused our bitterness and I hope you can too darling. You *were really* sweet and held yourself in *noblige*. In a word you are a true love-bird and Mummy's Paltie.
    "Say yes Paltie!"
    Will not look for you until I see you but will go to Lavignis this noon and out to dinner tonight with Bernadine + Elgo—in case you want to get in touch.

Tell me when I'm to come housekeeping at your studio. I'd better
bring my sewing kit tho not much of a sewing
Kat
Your loving Mummy.

Ernest did not accept Hadley's invitation to do "housekeeping" at
his studio. Nor did her "Paltie say yes" to her. Instead he cordially
assisted her in finding a room at the Hotel Beauvoir.

Distraught and feeling alone in Paris, Hadley sought advice from
those she considered loyal friends—Dorothea and John Moore, Don
and Beatrice Stewart, Ada and Archibald MacLeish. Each of them told
her that she'd be a fool to fight for Ernest. Money, not love, made him
desire Pauline. And there was no weapon strong enough for that.

Putting it all in terms of economics eased Hadley's pain, and she
wrote to Ernest that it would be best if they did not see each other at
all, but rather conducted "their affairs," as she put it, through the
mail. When they were lonely for each other, she said, it would be best
if they saw other people, "or something." She declined Ernest's invitation to go bicycle riding. But she would leave his address lying about
her new apartment at 35 Rue de Fleurus, a stone's throw from Gertrude Stein, just in case "anything should happen" to her and Ernest
had to assume the care of Bumby.

Hadley also wrote that she was worried sick about what she had said,
in fatigue and anger, when they'd first gotten back to Paris. Of course,
she hadn't really meant it when she'd told Ernest that his romance
with Pauline had almost killed her love for Bumby. If Ernest had not
yet told Pauline about this remark, Hadley pleaded that he not do so.
Pauline was clever and quick, Hadley said, and she might somehow
manage to get the boy, too. Didn't Ernest remember that Pauline,
when they all kissed goodbye at Pamplona, had promised "to teach me
a lesson"?

Hadley expected a response to this letter by return mail. But she did
not hear from Ernest for more than a week. During that time, he said,
he had accompanied Pauline on the boat train to Boulogne, to wish
her bon voyage. Hadley assumed that Pauline's return to her parents'
home in Piggott, Arkansas, was in response to a condition Hadley had
imposed as part of the divorce. Writing a kind of contract one drunken
evening—on foolscap and in pencil—Hadley had declared that Ernest
and Pauline must stay apart one hundred days. Then, if they still
wanted each other—not "loved," but "wanted"—Hadley said she would
give Ernest his divorce. The morning after, Hadley was ashamed of

having written such a thing. How arrogant, and foolish, she had been. And yet, to her surprise, Ernest and Pauline had acquiesced.

But Pauline and Ernest had their own reasons for agreeing to Hadley's conditions. Pauline had told Ernest that her parents were dead set against him. They were rigid on the subject of divorce, she said, as only Catholics could be. Ironically, they did not so much blame her for the situation. They believed the man to be responsible in matters of love. Pauline's father would not even discuss the issue. She'd heard it could not even be mentioned in his presence. Pauline's mother was more tolerant, but only because she believed, Pauline said, in the words of the Lord's Prayer: "Forgive us our trespasses, as we forgive those who trespass against us." Pauline believed she would not be allowed to marry Ernest unless there was some way his marriage to Hadley, since it had occurred "outside the Church," could be declared null and void. Nevertheless, at "home," Pauline felt she could soften her parents' hearts.

Then there were the practical concerns. Ernest had assigned all his royalties from *The Sun Also Rises,* in perpetuity, to Hadley and to their son. This meant that Ernest, except for the occasional hundred dollars he could make selling his stories to magazines, had no source of income. Pauline and Ernest, once married, would have to live on a special trust fund she had, and on a dole from her relatives. Actually, this was just the sort of arrangement Pauline wished for. She would be Ernest's patroness, she said, and his Svengali. Ernest was secretly mortified. But mortification seemed a just reward to him in the late fall of 1926—a penance he should willingly endure.

The studio Gerald Murphy lent Ernest was at the end of a courtyard closed with an iron gate. The gate was locked every night at dark. All those who lived in the studio on the court had keys to lock or unlock the gate. During the daytime, the gate was open and the concierge, from her window at the end of the block of studios, watched who went in and out. There were four studios together on a courtyard, bounded on the farther side by a brick wall. Beyond was the traffic of Rue Froidevaux.

As soon as he moved in, Ernest made an arrangement with the concierge. She would sweep out the studio and make his bed every morning, and do his mending and washing. The concierge was grateful to Ernest. Her husband, a taxi driver, was usually out of work. She told Ernest her husband was not worthless. But he was not worth much.

Ernest liked the concierge. She was small and, he thought, delicately built, with dark short hair and bright, lively eyes. Ernest found her cheerful but not humorous. She reminded him a little of Sylvia Beach. Although he gave her the courtesy due a true concierge, the woman was only the caretaker of the place. The owner of the apartments, in order to avoid taxes and police supervision, had registered the property as working studios, not to be occupied at night.

One of Ernest's neighbors, a woman painter, used the studio only during the day. Every time Ernest looked in as he passed, the woman was at work. In the next studio lived a painter who hardly worked at all. Yet he seemed healthy and cheerful to Ernest, and was off for hours on his bicycle every day.

Ernest's most interesting neighbor, with whom he had nothing at all to do, was an old man who taught painting, sculpture, and design at a Paris art school. Ernest had heard from the concierge that the old man lived with a girl of twenty. When Ernest saw the girl pass off to morning errands, he admired her lovely breasts. The partition between the old man's studio and the one Ernest occupied was very thin. Ernest could hear the old man's coughing far into the night. But he never heard the old man and his young mistress quarrel.

Gerald's studio made Ernest feel like a monk. There was a cement floor, the skylight, a wooden model stand, and a sleeping alcove reached by a ladder of wooden stairs. A window by the bed opened onto the courtyard. The floor of the alcove was the roof of the bedroom shared by the old instructor of painting and his young mistress.

The damp Paris winter kept the studio miserable most of the day. Only in late morning, in the thin winter light, when the cast-iron stove grew red hot and drafts circulated the heat, could Ernest attempt to work. But try as he might—every morning on the plain wooden table by the bed, and every evening, at this same table, now in the harsh light of a white gas lantern—he could not write.

Perhaps because he could not now write, Ernest characterized his early work, at least to himself, as fantastical and rather delicate. It was certainly well done and had given him great pleasure to do. Readers who shared his delicacy of perception and taste had enjoyed it, he thought. But now he considered his early work "unreal," little more than a conspiracy between writer and reader, a pretense of trust and confidence enjoyed by the most attractive children.

Now all that had happened to him—the bad luck of falling in love with Pauline, the bad luck of Hadley's needing a showdown, the bad luck of Bumby's illness, the bad luck of having friends who would be happy with his and Hadley's divorce, and, worst of all, the bad luck of having this all happen so suddenly—had, Ernest believed, "burned him out."

Each day that Ernest lived alone he felt the loss of his defenses. Once he'd had a wall of protective beliefs: in the sanctity of art; in the sanctity of love. Now that wall had fallen. He had prided himself on his ability to create small daily happinesses—from his eating and drinking, from his making love. But now he had only an "unreal" existence, engendered by chastity, and by eating and sleeping without routine.

To counteract the effects of his monastic life, Ernest slept as late as he could—he could get sound sleep only after sunrise—and he read. He was especially fond of *Old Calabria* by Norman Douglas, and, to save it, he would read only a little of it each day. The books he cared for most were *Alice in Wonderland*, George Moore's *Hail and Farewell*, *Huckleberry Finn*, and *Far Away and Long Ago* by W. H. Hudson. He felt that he could reread all of these books. But he was not sure that he would be able to reread *Old Calabria*, so he read it slowly.

In time, Ernest carefully dovetailed his days toward the ritual of going to supper at a new and therefore private café. Against the cold winter rain, Ernest would bundle up with toque, double woolen sweater, and woolen muffler, turn out the gas reading lamp, and go downstairs and out the door. He would make a point to say good evening to the concierge, and she would say good evening to him.

His route to the café took Ernest along the Avenue de Maine. For the months he spent at the studio there seemed always to be a carnival on the avenue, and, on his way to the café, he walked between rows of gaslighted wooden stalls with wheels of fortune. They were rudely made—no more than a wagon wheel with heavy nails pounded into the rim and a thick piece of leather to flap with resistance against the spinning wheel and eventually catch the winning number. The prizes were various forms of colored sugar candy, worth nothing at all. But each night there were plenty of players. From the merry-go-round, steam music blared, and on the revolving stage were "rising and falling circles of cows with gilded horns, miniature engines, autobuses, taxicabs, and air-planes." On the street farther down, Ernest looked into the windows of clothing stores with wax models of unbelievable handsomeness, their arms stretched out, blank looks of expectancy on their faces. Then he encountered a bicycle supply store, a cheap jewelry store with a brightly lighted window, a cleaners and dryers.

The Three Musketeers café sat on one corner of a square. Ernest had chosen this place because the name reminded him of his high school years, when the only clique he'd ever belonged to named him "Prothro," for the largest, most gregarious of the Dumas heroes. In this café, there were paintings on three of the walls of the Musketeers, all in plumed hats and high boots. By the zinc bar were leather-covered benches and small tables. Off in the corner by the ladies' toilet were two telephone booths that women were always waiting to use.

Ernest would walk into the café slowly, self-consciously, and select a table close to the windows. He felt calmed by the knowledge that he would meet no one he knew in this café. Ernest would usually order a vermouth cassis, and when the waiter would bring it, Ernest would squirt "charged water into the glass so that the vivid color paled and the glass filled." Ernest would taste his drink, and, before he ordered his food, look out the window for a while. Under the drink was a saucer with the price of the drink as part of the design. Each cassis cost Ernest two francs—little enough for a "ticket that entitled him to stay as long as he wished in the warmth of the café."

In this state of mind, Ernest could not help but recall a story he'd heard of an old man, a man in his eighties, who had lost his wife. The Valencian paper had said that Valentin Magarza climbed the Miguelete tower, jumped, and was destroyed on the pavement. Ernest imagined himself as that old man, sitting in a café, barely holding on to life in a clean, well-lighted place.

But Ernest would not think about suicide for himself, at least not directly. He had been frightened instead by his response to a minor problem. After walking home in the rain and getting his shoes soaked, Ernest became distraught. There must be, he said to himself, a way to prevent this from happening ever again. So, while his shoes dried tipped up on their sides, against the stove, he set about cutting out a pair of inner soles from the back cardboard of a drawing pad. He knew, of course, that this would not work. Even in a light rain, the cardboard would be sodden in a block or two. But, suddenly, he was obsessed with keeping his feet dry. All that night, in insomnia, Ernest felt something advancing on him, looming in the dark recesses of the studio, beyond the gaslight. He had felt it each night, ever since he knew he would, against all justice and probably against all reason, too, leave Hadley for Pauline. It was what came to a man, he thought, when faith in what he had once considered sacred was gone.

Before Ernest and Pauline had parted at Boulogne, Ernest had extracted from Pauline a promise to write every day. Letters, he said, could keep people intimate, providing they were from heart, soul, and glands. James Joyce had been away from his wife for months at a time. His solution to this had not been infidelity, but rather the writing of obscene letters, with an end toward masturbation. Pauline reminded Ernest that she'd been a journalism student at Missouri. She was confident she could give him all he wanted.

Letters from Pauline arrived at Ernest's studio almost every day. They were placed by the concierge on the smooth, tight-fitting covers of Ernest's bed. Pauline had gotten home to Piggott, she told Ernest, at exactly four-thirty A.M. the thirteenth of October. Her mother had met her at the station. Her father, Paul, would have been there, but business had taken him to Memphis. Something about boosting the price of cotton.

That first night home, as they sat talking calmly in her room, Pauline had told her Irish mother, Mary Downey Pfeiffer, all about Ernest. Mother felt terrible, Pauline said, because she was "awfully intelligent, awfully simple, awfully unworldly, awfully good." She'd kept asking Pauline, "How does she [meaning Hadley] feel?" Mary Pfeiffer said she would try to change Pauline's mind. When Pauline told her this was impossible, her mother declared she would not speak of the issue again. Then, as Mary left the room, she asked Pauline not to tell "Papa" Pfeiffer.

On the boat from France, Pauline had compiled a list of improvements she knew Ernest expected her to make while they were apart. First of all, she must gain weight. Yes, she was naturally much smaller than Hadley, Ernest told her—and Pauline knew that meant in the breast—but something could be done. Ernest said she must drink two quarts of milk a day, and be at least one hundred and twenty pounds when he saw her again. There were other orders, too. Ernest expected Pauline to keep good muscle tone by bicycling a few miles each day. And, because he loved Spain and intended to spend much of his life there, she must learn Spanish. There must be, he said, some instruction available at the University of Arkansas. Ernest also wanted Pauline to pay less attention than she did to contemporary style. Once she was his wife, he told her, he would not permit her to shave her legs, or to shave under her arms. Finally, Pauline must not complain of worry, because worry was self-indulgent. She must learn to sleep under stress, must learn how to move her bowels no matter how distressed or frightened she was. Pauline wrote that she would try her best to please Ernest, be Galatea to his Pygmalion.

On October 22, Ernest found on his bed, along with a note from Pauline, a letter from his father. Before Ernest opened it, he knew what it would say. Anson Hemingway, Ernest's paternal grandfather, a genuine Civil War hero and a kindly benefactor during Ernest's hospitalization in Milan in 1918, was dead. Ernest had never been close to his grandfather. The old man, for all his good intentions, had been what Ernest called a "YMCA type." Yet Ernest knew his father to be very much a boy at heart. The loss of Anson would be devastating to him. It would change Clarence's world. As Ernest read over the only typewritten letter he had ever received from his father—Ernest correcting the errors as he went along—he could not help but be moved by his father's awkward formality and his simple heart:

Oct. 7th, 1926

My dear Ernest and Hadley and John Hadley,

I have been very anxious to hear from you, but so far no word. The sad news must at last come and now I tell you that my dear father died this morning at Seven O'Clock.

He died with no suffering, slept away. The day before he had written several letters and paid up all his bills. The funeral will be Saturday afternoon, Oct. 9th. He was Eighty two years and one month and eleven days. His birthday was August 26th, 1844.

He always asked about you and was so anxious to see your boy. There were three Great grandchildren when he died.

Although we were prepared for this to happen, it has caused us all grief and sorrow. We like to think of the happy union of Mother and Father and brother Tyler. Please let us hear from you as to your plans. The home has not yet been sold and we are still hoping to get to Florida this winter. We are all well here at home.

Much love to you all. Dad CEH.

Ernest answered his father's letter the same day he received it. He wrote that he was dreadfully sorry to hear that his grandfather had died, but glad that he'd died so happy and peaceful. Ernest said he would not be able to come to the States for some time. He thanked Clarence for birthday letters sent six months before. Ernest said he could not remember whether or not he had answered these letters. Ernest's penmanship was barely legible.

In part to keep his thinking straight, Ernest began writing to Maxwell Perkins at Scribner's in New York. There were, of course, matters to discuss about the sale of *The Torrents of Spring* and the publication of *The Sun Also Rises*. Yet, although Ernest wrote to Perkins as often as he did to Pauline, he did not give Perkins his "secret" address on Rue Froidevaux. All of Perkins's letters came through Guaranty Trust Company, 1 Rue des Italiens.

For all his "cooperativeness," Ernest felt there was something about Perkins he could not trust. It wasn't so much that Perkins was dishonest. But he seemed always to want to create a sense of obligation in Ernest. "I've been good to you" was the underlying theme. "If you don't want to hurt me, you'll do as I say." Hadn't he published *The Torrents of Spring* to help Ernest out of his contract with Liveright? Hadn't he sent out dummies of *The Sun* with his salesmen even before he'd had the manuscript in hand? Hadn't he sent Ernest two, three, four, five, even six hundred dollars, each time Ernest asked? Somehow Perkins got the weight of these obligations into every letter he sent.

On May 18, 1926, Perkins gave Ernest his first impression of *The Sun*. It was, Perkins said, an extraordinary performance. He had never read a book with more "life" in it. All the scenes, he said, particularly when Jake and Bill cross the Pyrenees and come into Spain on that bus, and then fish in the cold river, or when the bulls are sent in with the steers, then fought in the arena, were like "actual experience."

Perkins yearned to use the popular critical phrase "pity and irony." He wanted, he said, to note the "pity and irony" of the book. But Ernest had abolished that cliché in the river conversation between Jake and Bill:

> "What's all this irony and pity?"
> "What? Don't you know about Irony and Pity?"
> "No. Who got it up?"
> "Everybody. They're mad about it in New York."

The book, "as a work of art," astonished Perkins. How could Ernest have brought together in what Perkins thought the most "skillful manner" that "extraordinary range of experiences and emotions" (after his secretary had typed the letter, Perkins made the plurals)?

Then Perkins got to his objection. And, he said, it was a "hard one." Perkins said he did not see how the "speech" about Henry James could be printed:

> [Speaking of Jake's loss of his penis to a wartime injury] Bill says, "Never mention that. . . . That's the sort of thing that can't be spoken

of. That's what you ought to work up into a mystery. Like Henry
James's bicycle."

In this passage, Ernest had referred to what James himself had called
a "horrid even if an obscure hurt," "a single vast visitation," "an injury suffered while jammed into a corner formed by two fences in a
Newport field, working a small hand-engine, with others, to put out
a 'shabby conflagration.'" Did James suffer permanent injury to his
genitals? Was he impotent as a result? Ernest told Perkins there was
reason to wonder about this.

The truth was, Ernest said, that James wrote like a "maiden aunt,"
and that, late in life, in England, he had turned "queer." Perkins replied
that none of that mattered. Rumors about James were not printed while
he was alive for fear of a lawsuit, "and in a way it seems almost worse to
print it after he is dead." Beyond that, Scribner's had been James's publisher in the United States. For Perkins, the matter ended there.

True to her word, Pauline continued to write to Ernest from Piggott, Arkansas, almost every day. She reported that the night of October 14, she had had the "horrors," from two to three A.M. She thought
at the time that she must leave for New York and the boat to Paris the
next day. But her anxiety passed, and she went to sleep.

The next day Pauline started a "regime." She would have a good
breakfast, and then milk at ten-thirty, then study Spanish until lunch.
Then she would write a letter to Ernest. When the sun cooled in the
afternoon, Pauline would walk for an hour and a half to two hours.
At four o'clock she would have another pint of milk. Then there
would be dinner. And milk again before bed. Also, she had been doing
"lots of reading," French and English especially. And she did her calis-
thenics morning and night.

Pauline happily told Ernest that there was a chance an oil well on
the Pfeiffer property, one in which she had invested five dollars for
each of them, would come in before she returned to him. That ten
dollars would mean at least five thousand more, she said. And because
the cotton crop had been poor, the town was desperate for the oil.

To make good letters for Ernest, Pauline would "interest herself" in
town life, and report to Ernest "interesting things" upon which he
might base a story. She found fascinating the idea that one Mrs. Jones
painted landscapes and then hung them in the cells of the county jail.
Perhaps in a few days, Pauline said, she would be able to introduce
some humor into her letters. She felt awfully "solid" about Ernest and

his "Pfeiffe." Ernest was "perfect." He was her "Dear, Dear Ernest," and she "loved him so."

On November 17, Pauline wrote that she now "folds up the days like sheets and puts them away." Time seems so *"useless* now. . . . But it really isn't, because I'm having a fine routine." Pauline promised that there would be letters waiting for him on his bed when he returned from his brief trip to Spain, for the bullfights in Zaragoza, with Archie MacLeish. And she had a remedy to offer for his insomnia. He should get cock-eyed tired. That was what she did, and it worked.

Pauline said she knew that her letters weren't much, and she was sorry. But she sent along a reading list, given to a friend of hers in a night-school course at the University of Arkansas. Perhaps Ernest would find some good, diverting reading there. The first name on the list was "Sherwood Anderson."

When Pauline had been home a week, she had herself weighed by her doctor. She was happy to report some progress. Although she had on a heavier dress than usual, she did weigh "110," and "no dress could weigh three pounds, do you think?" Ernest should never worry about his girl leaving him again, Pauline said. And, contrary to his accusation of neglect, she had only missed writing him two or three days. She had been following his orders about the bicycling. "Today 35 min. Tomorrow," she hoped, "40." Pauline said that she still got very tired after any exercise at all. Nevertheless, this all must be "making her stronger."

Pauline wrote that she felt badly about not cabling Ernest at the publication of *The Sun Also Rises.* But her father had been in the telegraph office, and she had not yet told him about Ernest. The photo Ernest had sent her of himself Pauline kept in the top drawer of the dresser near her bedroom door, where she could look at it, she said, each time she came into her room. Pauline said she would read anything Ernest told her to. She was "useless without him."

Ernest found Pauline's letters disappointing. They were short. "That was the principal thing. They were short and they were not intimate." Because these letters were the substitute he had for a wife and a home and the comfort of home, and what he considered his lost honor, they should have been very good. Yet they weren't. Nevertheless, Ernest bound each five or six with a rubber band, and then put the little stack under his pillow. During the long hours of night, Ernest would cherish his cache of letters, and carefully take them out and read them each over again.

In mid-November, when life in Paris slowed under the gray, misty weather that would last till May, Ernest and Hadley met, quite by accident, at the Closerie des Lilas. As soon as he came in, Ernest saw Hadley at a table against the wall. She had looked up just then, and so there was no possibility of avoiding her, and, as he thought about it for a moment, no reason to.

The first thing Hadley asked about was breakfast. Had Ernest had any? Ernest told her he had, and a long while ago. Hadley took the opening. Since he was alone he must get up very early. Ernest countered with, I always got up early. And, in fact, he had. Then they both decided to stop it. Hadley looked so handsome, Ernest thought. He could think of nothing to say.

Suddenly, Hadley accused Ernest of being a fool. Ernest agreed that this was true. Then Hadley suggested they call off the whole thing. Ernest said he couldn't. Hadley insisted that Pauline didn't even love him. How could she have gone off and left him that way? Ernest said that going back home had meant an awful lot to Pauline. That was nonsense, Hadley said. Pauline had no right to treat him like this.

When Hadley asked Ernest what he'd been doing with his time, he replied, Painting. Hadley told him he was a writer, and the best one she knew. Ernest said he was through with writing. It's all finished, he said. Hadley told him not to be silly, that of course he would write again. How could he expect to be able to write with all this going on? Ernest said he didn't want to talk to Hadley about any of it, that if he'd had any idea she was in the café he wouldn't have come in.

But Hadley was angry, and she wanted to talk. In fact, she declared it her right. Ernest should write to Pauline and tell her it was over. Hadley would promise never to devil him about the affair. Hadley said she understood the reasons for it. Why couldn't she and Ernest go on a good trip together somewhere, to some of the places they'd always planned to go? Hadley was terribly upset. She called herself a fool. All she had had to do was say to Pauline, No. You can't have my husband. That was it. But down in the South of France they had all acted like silly children. She could not now believe they had entertained such silly ideas.

With the emotional momentum she had achieved, Hadley felt strong enough to bring everything into the open. She asked Ernest just what it was that Pauline could give him that she couldn't. Hadley said she had seen Pauline naked. She was nothing special. Hadley asked about children. Did Ernest want them? (She had always thought he didn't want them around.) Well, Hadley said, she could give him all the children he wanted.

But Ernest said, the hell with children. Bumby was enough. But Hadley said she should have had several children, to hold him with. Still, hadn't she been a proper wife? Ernest agreed there was no better wife than Hadley. Then why, in heaven's name, did he want to change? Why did he have to marry a girl who wouldn't live with him? Why didn't he stop it? Ernest was a fine writer, and she had been a good wife to him. And they had always had a good time. Hadley said she would live anywhere he wanted, do anything he wanted. They could start all over.

But Ernest said no. Then he told Hadley that, although he was in love with Pauline, he still loved Hadley no more, and no less than he had always loved her. Hadley said that that had always been enough for her, and it was enough for her now.

Why couldn't they go on? Hadley wanted to know. Why didn't he just sleep with Pauline? Hadley said. A few times and he'd be sick of it. He only wanted her, Hadley said, because he couldn't get her. Once he'd had enough of her, they could go on.

Because Ernest was a writer, Hadley claimed, Ernest thought he knew everything. Ernest said no, that wasn't true. In fact, he was a goddamn fool. Then why not stop being a fool? Hadley asked. What had Pauline to give him that she, Hadley, couldn't? Except a little newness. Did Pauline know some tricks? Was that what Ernest meant when he said she made him feel wonderful?

Go to hell, Ernest said to Hadley, and he glowered at her across the table. She was not going to get him talking about Pauline in bed. He shuffled back the chair to leave.

Hadley had not intended to go that far. She broke down. She pleaded with Ernest to come back. She took back all the mean things she'd said. She promised not to be jealous. She had learned so much from all this. She promised to be good. Then she asked, Didn't we have fun? That was their special word for the pleasure they gave each other in bed.

Ernest felt he lay upon the rack. He had been celibate for weeks, and he had not masturbated because he considered it an act of cowardice, a waste of an orgasm of which a man has just so many. He knew what Hadley was offering and wanted it more than he could say. Wouldn't he like to come back to the apartment with her? Hadley said. Wouldn't he like to sleep with her?

The bed was the same old bed Ernest and Hadley had bought when they'd returned to Paris the winter of 1923. It was a long bed, wide and low to the floor. It had neither headboard nor footboard, but, as at 113 Notre Dame des Champs, a Persian-figured spread covered the mattress. Hadley, as she had always done, deftly made the head with rolled pillows, and folded the top sheet deep and wide over the blankets.

When they were finished, and lay side by side, Hadley told Ernest he'd been wonderful. Ernest said nothing. But he felt empty and hollow. He was happy, too. He could hear himself laughing. Then he noticed that the drizzling rain had come in through the french doors and had pooled on the bare waxed floor. Hadley was very proud of herself, and of him. How about that! she said, speaking of the wonderful intercourse. But Ernest was fixed on the rain. It won't hurt the floor, he replied.

Ernest said he had gone away during their intercourse. Hadley asked where. Fifty floors above the street, Ernest said, making reference to the old Spaniard who had lost his wife and then committed suicide by jumping from a church steeple. And that was all? Hadley asked. Yes, Ernest said. Except that he must thank her very much.

At this, Hadley slapped Ernest hard across the face. He thanked her very much again. She slapped him hard again. He could keep it up all day if she could, Ernest said. She didn't slap nearly as hard as she thought she did. Then he thanked Hadley again for the pleasant time.

This time Hadley did not slap him. Instead she started to cry. She told him to go away. She said she was sorry. Ernest told her there was nothing to be sorry about. And he said he wanted to stay. Hadley asked, didn't the intercourse feel right to Ernest, the way it used to feel? Ernest said no, but that it made no difference. He told Hadley to take off the Persian-figured spread. She asked him to go into the other room while she made the bed. She said she was happy that he was there.

Ernest left Hadley at five o'clock, cold sober, and hollow with unfaithfulness. And yet he could not deny he felt better than he had in three months. On the way home, he stopped at Lipp's and had a beer and some potato salad. But he was still hungry when he left, and he stopped at a cheap restaurant, ate again, and read the newspaper record of boats arriving.

Back at the studio, there were no letters on his bed. Still, he felt wonderful, and went to bed and slept soundly. It was not until the next morning that the feeling of well-being was replaced by the knowledge that he had done something very wrong.

During his five years of marriage, when Ernest had been unfaithful, he had felt remorse. But each time he had managed to wipe out the remorse by paying more attention to his wife than usual. Ironically, Ernest had found that he loved Hadley more after he had been unfaithful to her. And the remorse at being unfaithful he could "wash away in a bath of sentiment, affections, and good sound intercourse."

The morning after his lovemaking with Hadley, Ernest awoke sick with guilt and remorse. He had broken up both his life and his wife's life because he felt that he and Pauline had something that justified anything they did. Ernest felt that he had sacrificed everything to that precious thing that he and Pauline had. Now, sleeping with Hadley while Pauline was in America, he had been unfaithful to Pauline, and to their love. Yet Pauline was not there in Paris, where he could wipe it all out with her.

Ernest wrote Pauline immediately. He could not be explicit. But he hoped she would get the message nevertheless.

> Dearest Pfife:
> . . . I've felt absolutely done for and gone to pieces Pfife and I might as well write it out now and maybe get rid of it that way. It was certain that your mother would feel badly about your marrying some one who was divorced, about breaking up a home, about getting into a mess—and it is certain too that silent disapproval is the most deadly and something that you can do nothing about. I was sure that part of it would go badly. Your mother naturally could not feel any other way. Jin showed me a letter she wrote, your mother, on November First saying that when you first came back you were looking well and quite happy and that now all that last week—the week during which I didn't hear from you—you were gone to pieces with nerves and in very bad shape. That you were really quite alone in Piggott with your own thoughts and that your own thoughts were *naturally* not pleasant. So it looks as though you were being put through a fairly complete hell—which may—because you are not strong and very run down, break you. And then we're broken and what good did that do. So I have that to think about all day and all night—and the worry is like a band of some sort across the inside of the top of my head—and there isn't anything else. All I can think of is that you that are all I have and that I love more than all there is and have given up everything for and betrayed everything for and killed off everything for are being destroyed and your nerves and your spirit broken all the time day and night and that I can't do anything about it because you won't let me.
> . . . Last fall I said perfectly calmly and not bluffingly and during one of the good times that if this wasn't all cleared up by christmas I would kill myself—because that would mean it wasn't going to clear

up—and I've learned about blowing up from you Pfife and I can't stand it—and evidently all I can do is to remove the sin out of your life and avoid Hadley the necessity of divorce—and compliment Hadley—by killing myself. So then later I promised that I wouldn't do it or think about it under any circumstances until you came back. But now it's getting all out of control again and you have broken your promises and I should think that would let me out. Only nothing ever lets you out. But I'm not a saint, nor built like one, and I'd rather die now while there is still something left of the world than to go on and have every part of it flattened out and destroyed and made hollow before I die. . . .

By the time Pauline read this from Ernest, she had had word from her sister Jinny. Jinny wrote that to everyone's surprise Hadley had fallen in love with someone—name not available due to marital status—that Hadley was going to cancel that hundred days nonsense, and that Ernest's divorce could proceed.

Now, for Pauline at least, the pressure was off. She wired Ernest that she wanted badly to come to him. But it seemed impossible. She would write soon. She signed the cable "love."

Ernest waited ten days for Pauline's letter. He expected it on three different boats, but it did not come. Then, one evening, it was on the bed in the studio when he came in from supper. Ernest saw that Pauline had marked it for the *Mauretania*, the fastest ship across the Atlantic. But apparently she had missed the mailing.

Pauline wrote that she did want so much to come to Ernest, and that she would come if he said, absolutely, that he needed her. But she reminded him that it meant giving up everything they had sacrificed so much for already. In fact, her coming to Paris just then might make things worse. She could not live with him—her father and mother would not stand for that—until the divorce was final and she and Ernest could be married. Ernest could expect her to sail on January 1, right after spending Christmas with her brother in New York.

In the middle of the night, December 2, Ernest, writing in bed, began a letter to Pauline. He wrote that her decision not to come until after Christmastime "seems somehow to make a lot of difference to me." He was, Ernest said, "cock-eyed lonesome" and he felt as badly as when she went away. Ernest said that he had had the "horrors" the night before. He could not write stories that would bring him two hundred dollars each from Scribner's without the tranquillity and freedom from the damned depression of loneliness. All the past week, he said, he would have cabled "hurry," but he knew Pauline must do what she had to do. Ernest said that when Pauline returned, he would begin a play. He could not start it now because of the emotional gauntlets he had to run, which would "bust up" the composition. But it would be terribly exciting to do the play when she, Pauline, was there. He could read it to her, and "find out about it at the time from you." And then he would have someone to feel "swell with" when the day's work was over. This instead of the gradual and regular coming on of evening and despair.

Ernest did not finish this letter, because he had begun to sound angry and disappointed. He would write another, more "understanding" letter the next day. Ernest knew, however, that to understand did not mean to forgive. "She's not coming," he thought. "She's not coming and she won't come." So this was how his strange and mistimed love for Pauline would end. But now that he had ruined Hadley's life, he must not ruin Pauline. He must keep on with Pauline, and accommodate himself to a diminished thing.

The second week of November, Hadley and a new friend, Winifred Mowrer, had taken an auto trip to Chartre. For Hadley it was in part a painful journey. She could not help remembering that it was at Chartre she'd learned Ernest loved Pauline. But this time there would be the company of Winifred's handsome young husband, Paul, then European correspondent for the *Chicago Daily News*. Bumby, still in fragile health, would stay with Ernest, who had promised to move out of his damp and poorly heated studio and into Hadley's comfortable flat in Rue de Fleurus.

A few days after she arrived in Chartre, Hadley wrote to Ernest that she needed her green silk dress and the speckled one that Sara Murphy had given her during Bumby's illness at Juan-les-Pins. These were all in a bundle on the floor of the armoire, and should be taken to the cleaners on Boulevard Raspail, the shop between Rue de Fleurus and the music shop. She asked would Ernest send her the extra pair of pajamas from the middle drawer in her room. Then she added that Winifred's husband, Paul, would be "walking down" Sunday afternoon.

Ernest bundled her things together and sent them along with a touching note. Living as he was in Hadley's flat, sleeping in the bed he knew, eating at the kitchen table, using the dishes and the towels from their place at 113 Notre Dame des Champs, Ernest declared that Hadley could be sure of the love of not only one but "two Bumpsters." Then he was moved to repeat a gesture he'd made with great success while he and Hadley were courting.

Ernest knew that Hadley had always enjoyed pretty handbags. Back in 1921, in St. Louis, he had gotten her a small handbag decorated with glass imitations of semiprecious stones—tiger's eyes, they were called—and Hadley had loved this gift more than anything he'd given her since. Ernest now sent to the Grand Hotel in Chartre another handbag, from "Joe and Little Joe," Hadley's "love names" for himself and Bumby.

Maxwell Perkins, two months after *The Sun Also Rises* had been published and had gotten wonderful reviews—"An absorbing, beautifully and tenderly absurd, heartbreaking narrative," the *New York Times;* "if there is better dialogue being written today, I don't know where to find it," Conrad Aiken in the *New York Herald Tribune*—remained uncomfortable with the novel. After complaining about "dirty" words, libelous references, and the "objective" beginning—which Ernest had made, on Fitzgerald's advice, commence with Robert Cohn—Perkins said that some "tell" should introduce Ernest's "show." For instance, readers should know "right off" that Ernest found nothing glamorous in Brett Ashley. She was, after all, only a "loose woman," Perkins said. Perhaps Ernest had taken aim, in his demonstration of the perils of debauchery, at Michael Arlen's *The Green Hat* and his "glamorous" treatment of Lady Duff Twysden.

My God, Ernest thought, couldn't Perkins see that the narrator of *The Sun Also Rises* was in love with Brett? Could this be the perceptive editor Scott had raved about? "Maxwell E. Perkins," as he could not help sign each letter, sounded here like a narrow-minded prig.

Ernest had suspected for some time that Perkins's enthusiasm for *The Sun Also Rises,* in fact for all of his work, grew more from a corporate than an artistic valuation. He knew that Perkins believed that a Hemingway novel could rock the country, and that Scribner's had slowly become a house of the past. Hemingway, with his "roughhewn realism," would be just the author to attract to Scribner's the lowbrow reader—the book buyer of the future. Then there was Perkins's squeamishness about even the mildest profanity. Even in an informal letter Perkins couldn't bring himself to use the word "balls"—they were "the particular adjunct of the bulls" instead. Finally, Perkins had called him a sensationalist, when Ernest felt he'd tried hard to avoid such a claim.

Secure in Hadley's flat, feeling almost as if he were home again, Ernest mapped out a strategy. First, he would send Perkins the best of the stories he had accumulated over the past two years. He would claim that he was in fact sending them in as soon as they were written. That would keep Perkins sending money. And the weekly mailings would prove that, unlike Fitzgerald, Ernest could produce under stress. All this would make Perkins certain that Ernest had found a home with Scribner's. But Ernest had other ideas.

Just after his return from Toronto, Ernest had begun a novel. It was the story of a boy and his father, and their journey from northern Michigan, to Chicago, and then to New York. Ernest had started with a title. "A New Slain Knight," he would call it: "In which goodbye is said to Old Places in the First Person."

As the story begins, Jimmy Crane and his father are boarding up their lakeside summer cottage, covering the chimney of the fireplace against the nesting of bats, clearing out all the drawers of accumulated summertime possessions that no longer seem important in the early fall. The boy is very fond of the place, and his father is, too. The mother has recently died.

Jimmy and his father leave by motorboat, right from the cottage dock. Jimmy watches attentively as Mr. Crane carefully avoids the treacherous sandbar. By the time Jimmy looks back, the cottage and the dock are gone. As they pass a point just before the open lake, Jimmy sees three crows walking near an old log half covered with sand on the beach.

At the station, Jimmy watches the train coming toward him through the tamarack swamp. Just off the platform, off the piles that support the station, Jimmy sees the clear spring water over the swamp bottom. Through leafless, fire-blackened trees, Jimmy sees the early-morning mist, cold and white. From a drinking spring at the station, clear water poured heavily from a pipe and into an overflowing trough.

Jimmy and his father board the train, sit by the window, and watch Fred Cuthbert, the man his father has hired to take care of the cottage and the boat during the winter, standing on the platform, waving goodbye. Before the train is out of sight, Fred Cuthbert walks away. But Jimmy notices the water, splashing up out of the pipe in the sun and curving in the breeze. Then he sees the ties and rails stretching out and the swamp passing. From a distance, the station looks very small and the lake strangely flat.

In the early chapters, this novel has the elegant voice of youthful observation found in the stories of *In Our Time*. But in Chapter 12 of the twenty-chapter manuscript, the tone suddenly changes. In this chapter, Jimmy and his father are traveling from Chicago to New

York. For some reason, they spend much of their time in the washroom, with its leather seats and smell of disinfectant and cigar smoke.
There are the spittoons, wicker chairs, shiny metal wash bowls, and
the frosted glass door to the toilet. Jimmy notices the abundance of
towels, and at each sink a collapsible cup. Jimmy wants a drink of ice
water from the spigot on the wall, and when Mr. Crane says this is all
right, Jimmy drinks from a collapsible cup. Can he take a towel?
Jimmy asks. Yes, his father says. Jimmy takes one, and a package of
soap, too. It's okay to take the towel, Jimmy's father says. But don't
drink too much ice water. He says that Jimmy is a strange boy, and
that Jimmy's drinking makes him nervous.

Soon, two men come in. They are, Jimmy observes, interested only
in each other. They give a quick look at Jimmy and his father. Then
they begin to talk about something that both agree had been impossible. Jimmy notices that each agrees with everything the other says.
They look happy and excited. The older of the two, the dark-haired
one, says he can't believe they are off.

Mr. Crane begins making fun of the men to Jimmy, mimicking them.
When they hear him, they stop. Not naturally, Jimmy thought, but as
birds do, suddenly.

The older man, about thirty-five, tells Mr. Crane that he is rude. It
is very rude of a man to imitate two other men who happen to be
talking in a pullman washroom, the older man says.

Jimmy's father answers, Well, well.

The two men are homosexuals. And Mr. Crane, in order to provoke
what he considers a comic jealousy, intentionally engages the dark-
haired man in conversation. When the dark-haired man responds to
Mr. Crane's questions, even offering to tell a "frightfully funny" story,
the blond man, his face white with rage, slams out of the washroom.

The remainder of the episode contains scatalogical jokes. When the
dark-haired man offers Mr. Crane a drink, Jimmy's father says, "crapping." The dark-haired man asks doesn't he mean "topping." No,
"crapping," Mr. Crane insists. It is a new one, he says, meaning "no
end of no end." And Mr. Crane, for Jimmy's benefit, relentlessly mocks
and bullies the homosexual pair.

To Ernest, this novel was to be no more a serious work of art than
had been *The Torrents of Spring*. In the short stories "A Simple En-
quiry," "The Sea Change," "Mother of a Queen," and "Che Ti Dice La
Patria?"—all published within two years of this writing—Ernest would
consider male and female homosexuality from an intelligent and sub-

tle, if not quite sympathetic, point of view. But "A New Slain Knight" could, if need be, serve the same purpose as *Torrents* had—to extract Ernest from a publisher, or, better yet, an editor who, he felt, did not genuinely appreciate his work.

Writing almost always made Ernest feel better. A good day's work was his best antidote for depression. But some writings were more efficacious than others. A good, well-crafted story could do wonders. Even good letters to appreciative friends had their effect. But writing satire—not even satire, really, but rather the simple mockery of "A New Slain Knight"—left Ernest more disgusted with himself than his subject.

In December of 1926, Ernest desperately needed to be reassured of his talent and of his essential decency. Unfortunately, Ernest's erstwhile friend John Dos Passos had recently weighed in. A bulky envelope with a black, heavy-handed scrawl contained a long letter from Dos, now in New York, and the review of *The Sun Also Rises* Dos had written for the Communist magazine *The New Masses:*

> Say Hem
> I've just read The sun also rises. the N. Masses sent me over to review. I've written a damn priggish mealy mouthed review of it that makes me sick. The book makes me sick anyway, besides making me very anxious to see you. . . . I never felt so rotten about anything—book I mean. You write so damn well and the books so damn readable and I'd like to get cockeyed on fin a l'eau in your company.
> I'd like to knock yours and Hadley's head together. Hem, please forgive all this rubbish. The trouble with me is that I am expatriate—from Paris. Like hell, ain't we all lil' expatriates from the Garden of Eden? Ain't we.
> I feel thoroughly low about everything. Everything I write seems to be crap and everything everybody I like writes seems to be crap. They're going to kill Sacco and Vanzetti and I saw Harry Wills last fight and everything is inexpressibly shitty.
> Saw Pauline with Gerald and Sara in New York. She's an awfully nice girl. Why don't you get to be a Mormon?
> The Sun Also Rises is just about as bad as streets of night, only its more entertaining and better written. Don Stewart's last Haddock book is lousy. Why can't any of us write. . . . Honestly its pretty damn discouraging for the American Renaissance. The thing is that writing isn't an occupation—it's like raising fancy pigeons or stamp collecting. People who give up all their time to a hobby go sour or crazy or both.
> I'm going down to Mexico—to forget. I'll write you sanely from there. I think I'm getting stomach ulcers like Valintino [sic]. Very probably effect [sic] the brain. Yours Dos.

After reading the letter, Ernest could not bring himself to read the review. Of course, Dos was drunk when he wrote the letter. Maybe he was drunk for the review. Maybe he read the book itself drunk. At any rate, Ernest understood Dos's feelings. Dos, Ernest believed, was "Class A," maybe even "Double A." But he would never reach the majors. Dos was just good enough to dream.

Wasn't it strange, Ernest thought, how alike were John Dos Passos and Ezra Pound? Each assumed a talent he didn't possess. Each blamed the public for his lack of success. For Dos the responsibility lay with government: corrupt, capitalistic, encouraging its people to selfish materialism. For Pound, it was the lowbrow masses, with their invincible vulgarity. Not surprisingly, Ernest thought, Dos became a Communist; Pound, a Fascist.

Thursday morning, just before Christmas, Ernest walked over to Hadley's apartment in Rue de Fleurus. Hadley had been back from Chartre for two weeks. A few days before, he had come to decorate a Christmas tree for Bumby. But this time he needed to see Hadley.

Ernest went up the stairs to the door of the apartment and rang the bell. There was no answer, and so he rang again and waited. When Hadley came to the door, she was wearing a dressing gown. Ernest asked to come in. She was afraid he couldn't, Hadley replied. He just wanted to talk, Ernest said. Hadley told him that he couldn't come in just then. Ernest said he only wanted to talk a little while. Hadley asked him not to make matters worse.

Ernest said he did not want to leave. He had been awake all night, and he was still thinking as he had thought during the night, and he wanted to tell Hadley about it. He could not stop himself from asking Hadley, didn't she love him anymore? That was a lousy thing to ask, Hadley said. Ernest knew she was right. Nevertheless, he persisted. Didn't she? he said. He wanted to know, really. Hadley told Ernest he must go away. If he wanted to talk, she would meet him at a café. When? Ernest asked. How about that afternoon, anytime, Hadley said. Ernest suggested four o'clock.

Hadley came into the café looking beautiful and happy. She sat down with Ernest as if she were in a hurry. Yet, when he suggested she do so, Hadley ordered a drink. As soon as their drinks came, Hadley said she had something to tell Ernest. She had planned on writing him about it, if he hadn't come by. Hadley said that she had fallen in love with another man.

Ernest was disoriented. He did not know what to say. He told Hadley that that was "fine." In fact, it was "grand." He was awfully sorry
he had bothered her that morning. He said that the reason for his visit
was now "all cleared up."

Hadley pressed Ernest. What had he come to see her about? Was it
the divorce? Ernest felt as if he'd been knocked out and, having just
come to, was required to give a deposition.

No, Ernest answered, it really wasn't a thing.

Hadley was surprised. Didn't Ernest even want to know the man's
name?

Of course he did, Ernest said. But he didn't want to ask.

It was Paul Mowrer, Hadley said. Ernest saw the irony in all this.
He knew that Mowrer was married, with two children.

Hadley wanted to know what Ernest had heard from Pauline. Ernest
said that Pauline had written she was all right, but lonely. Hadley said
again that she did not understand how Pauline could stay away from
Ernest, at home in the States. Ernest said that Pauline thought it the
best way for them until they could be married. Hadley said she thought
it was cruel. No, Ernest said. He agreed with Pauline. It was the best
way.

Sitting there in the café, drinking together in the early evening,
hungry for a supper they would not share, Ernest and Hadley went on
and talked for an hour or more. It was the first time since the divorce
was first spoken of that they had talked without quarreling. Ernest
believed that they did not quarrel now because Hadley loved someone
else.

By the time Ernest got back to Rue Froidevaux, he'd decided everything was settled. After all, wasn't the chief ingredient in his and
Pauline's absolution from their sin the certain knowledge that Hadley
would be happy? He cabled Pauline immediately: "Harrison happy."
It was a code he and Pauline had agreed upon to mean they were
morally free. Ernest had picked the code. It was the name of Hadley's
former piano teacher, and first love.

Pauline sailed for France from New York on New Year's Day, 1927.
She thought the date symbolic of the new life she and Ernest would
now have. Ten days later, Ernest would meet the ship at Cherbourg. To
get to Cherbourg, he would rent a Citroen, a two-seater motor car,
from a drive-it-yourself service. He intended the car to be a surprise for
Pauline. It would be wonderful to have a car and drive together back

up through Normandy to Paris. The rental wasn't awfully expensive, and, Ernest felt, it was something good to do—a justifiable extravagance, he told himself. Instead of a miserable meal slapped out in the swaying train, and the need to talk under breath in a crowded compartment, he would have Pauline all to himself. There would be plenty of room for her bags in the spider seat of the Citroen. Of course, the ride to Paris was too long to make without a stop. The best place would be Rouen, for a fine dinner in the fine hotel.

The day before he left for Cherbourg, Ernest bought himself two new suits of pajamas at the Carnaval de Venice. Then he took the morning bus that stopped on the Boulevard St. Germain. As he walked along the boulevard, he passed a gun store. He saw something in the window that caught his eye. There had been two holdups in the papers that week, on the road to Cherbourg. Ernest went inside and bought a pistol and a box of cartridges. The cost was only four American dollars. He had no permit to carry the pistol on his person. But someone whom he believed had told him that carrying a pistol in a motor car was all right. The concierge gave him an overnight bag filled with fresh clothing she'd packed for his trip. The Citroen was in a garage down the street.

At Cherbourg, those who were welcoming disembarking passengers did not go out on a tender. The boats came into the harbor and right up to the quays. But there were cement slips and railroad tracks confusing the scene. Eventually, Ernest found the boat Pauline was on. He was the only one there. Light shined from the portholes; only sailors walked the decks. Ernest could smell the harbor water, the early-morning fog, the dew on the cement, the wet ship's hausers, the bad air and iron smell of the hold. He walked the length of the quay, as far as a fence in one direction and the stern ropes in the other, and waited. The port authorities had not yet gone on, and so no one was allowed aboard.

Just after daylight, the port authorities went on board with a doctor. When they came off, the passengers could be greeted. Ernest was sent to the main dining room. It had been roped off so the passengers would go through in a file and have their passports stamped and get their landing cards. Ernest stood at the exit to the dining room, near the tables where the officials sat. Looking down the line of passengers, he saw Pauline.

The dock at Cherbourg seemed hardly the place for a reunion, and Ernest hurried Pauline along to the waiting Citroen. As soon as Ernest heard Pauline speak he knew he'd made a mistake about the car. The Citroen's gas heater, sparked by a plug, worked like a furnace. But it filled the car with fumes, and Pauline had acquired in New York the worst case of bronchitis Ernest had ever heard.

As they drove along, huddled in moth-eaten blankets they'd found in a box marked "For Emergency" under the bonnet, Ernest and Pauline talked of practical matters. There were decisions to make, and several things, Pauline said, they had to do.

First of all, Pauline could not live with Ernest until the divorce was official. Her parents had insisted on this. But she loved Ernest so much she could not leave him again. There must be a way out of this, Ernest said. They needed to be together now after so long an absence. A trip to Gstaad with the MacLeishes kindly paying the bills would be wonderful for them. How could her parents object, when certified New England Puritans would act as chaperones? Then, Ernest said, he himself would travel for a few weeks with their friend, Guy Hickok. Guy had asked Ernest to show him Italy, the Italy Ernest had known during the war. Pauline said that she would use this time to select and furnish, with Jinny's help, a wonderful apartment where Ernest could work in peace and quiet. And she had Ernest's photo, framed in silver, for her dresser. When they got to Paris, Ernest left Pauline at her sister's flat, then drove on toward Rue Froidevaux.

# Epilogue

Ernest Hemingway's Paris years did not end with the loss of his first wife, Hadley, and his marriage to Pauline, nor with the publication of *The Sun Also Rises,* nor with his move to Key West, Florida. In fact, he often called Paris his home town. And he returned to it again and again, for almost forty years.

In *A Moveable Feast* (1964), Ernest's story of the time he and Hadley, and then their son, Bumby, spent in Paris in the early Twenties, Ernest made Paris the best city to be young in. There the artist could let the world know what a fine young man he was and how what he had to say was worth listening to. Writing of Paris, Ernest remembered himself this way.

But by the late 1920s, Ernest felt his life was in decline, that a premature aging of the spirit had set in, and that the long-awaited success with *The Sun Also Rises* was anticlimactic. Ernest's tone in letters of the time—especially those written to his intimate friend Scott Fitzgerald, and to his parents—is sometimes elegiac, more often quietly sad. To Fitzgerald he would write:

> Summer's a discouraging time to work—You dont [sic] feel death coming on the way it does in the fall when the boys really put pen to paper.
> Everybody loses all the bloom—we're not peaches—that doesn't mean you get rotten—a gun is better worn and with bloom off—So is a saddle—People too by God. You lose everything that is fresh and everything that is easy and it always seems as though you could *never* write. . . .

To his parents, there would be more effort at "explaining," and a gesture of hope:

> I'm sending this letter to both of you because I know you have been worried about me and I am always sorry to cause you worry. But you must not do that—because, although my life may smash up in different ways I will always do all that I can for the people I love (I don't write home a lot because I haven't time and because, writing, I find it very hard to write letters and have to restrict correspondence to the letters I have to write—and my real friends know that I am just as fond of them whether I write or not) that I have never been a drunk nor even a steady drinker (You will hear legends that I am—they are tacked on to everyone that ever wrote about people who drink) and that all I want is tranquility and a chance to write. You may never like any thing I write—and then suddenly you might like something very much. But you must believe that I am sincere in what I write. Dad has always been very loyal and while you, mother, have not been loyal at all, I absolutely understand that it is because you believe you owed it to yourself to correct me in a path which seemed to you disastrous.
>
> So maybe we can drop all that. I am sure that, in the course of my life, you will find much cause to feel that I have disgraced you if you believe everything you hear. On the other hand with a little shot of loyalty as anesthetic you may be able to get through all my obvious disreputability and find, in the end, that I have not disgraced you at all.

In 1927, Ernest published a collection of stories, *Men Without Women*. It was markedly different from his first collection, *In Our Time* (1925). Ernest said that the title, *Men Without Women,* was meant to suggest how life would be without the softening influence of women. But the change was more than that. In *In Our Time* there are many woundings, and plenty of pain—from the trauma of a caesarian section and a suicide in "Indian Camp," to the heart-broken, thrice-wounded veteran of "A Very Short Story," to the doctor who is defeated in "The Doctor and the Doctor's Wife" by both the "savage" at the lake and "civilized" woman at home.

And yet there is also in *In Our Time* the potential for relief from pain, and recovery from its consequences. The last story, "Big Two-Hearted River," presents Hemingway's version of what Ralph Waldo Emerson called a "transcendental experience." Through immersion in nature—trout fishing in Upper Michigan for Ernest—a damaged young veteran of the Great War begins a spiritual cure. *In Our Time* surely suggests that this world offers "less good than ill." But there is a hope in it, that healing will come with effort and time.

In *Men Without Women,* however, all such hope is gone. And a ma-
levolent fate is supreme. In the best stories of this collection—"The Undefeated," "In Another Country," "Hills Like White Elephants," "The
Killers"—there is nothing that can be done about the horrid, oversized
bull, the sudden death of a young wife, the cowardice of a lover who
insists that an abortion is a "simple" operation, the mob's "contract"
on a double-crossing fighter. For Ernest, in the late Twenties, there was
damn little a man could do.

In Ernest's novel *A Farewell to Arms* (1929), fate at work engenders
in the hero first hatred, then contempt. After the gods have taken his
child from Frederick Henry, they take his wife: "It seems she had one
hemorrhage after another. They couldn't stop it. I went into the room
and stayed with Catherine until she died. She was unconscious all the
time, and it did not take her very long to die." Then Frederick Henry
re-collects himself:

> Outside the room, in the hall, I spoke to the doctor, "Is there anything
> I can do to-night?"
>> "No. There is nothing to do. Can I take you to your hotel?"
>> "No, thank you. I am going to stay here a while."
>> "I know there is nothing to say. I cannot tell you—"
>> "No," I said. "There's nothing to say."
>> "Good-night," he said. "I cannot take you to your hotel?"
>> "No, thank you."
>> "It was the only thing to do," he said. "The operation proved—"
>> "I do not want to talk about it," I said.
>> "I would like to take you to your hotel."
>> "No, thank you."
> He went down the hall. I went to the door of the room.
>> "You can't come in now," one of the nurses said.
>> "Yes I can," I said.
>> "You can't come in yet."
>> "You get out," I said. "The other one too."
> But after I had got them out and shut the door and turned off the
> light it wasn't any good. It was like saying good-by to a statue. After a
> while I went out and left the hospital and walked back to the hotel
> in the rain.

Shortly before Ernest finished *A Farewell to Arms* in Key West,
Florida, in January 1929, his father, Dr. Clarence Hemingway, an
obstetrician, committed suicide. Ironically, Dr. Hemingway had long
wanted to retire to Florida but had lost all his retirement money in
land speculation on Sanibel Island. At the time of Clarence Heming-

way's death, Ernest told his editor, Maxwell Perkins, that his father was the only one in the family who meant anything to him. What he did not tell Perkins, what he told no one, was that his father had very much wanted to spend some time with Ernest during the last months of 1928, doing the kind of things they had done when Ernest was a boy:

September 10, 1928

Dear Ernest,
    Please let us know your plans. Would it be possible for you to come down into Smoky Mts. of North Carolina with me about the first week of October! I have hoped you might get in the trip before you went East. [Ernest was in Wyoming, working on *A Farewell to Arms*.]
    [The next day Clarence wrote:] I am anxious to know your plans as to when you may come and visit us on your way East.—Also if you could possibly go to North Carolina Smoky Mts. first week in October? Please let us hear from you soon dear boy.

Your old
"Daddy"

But Ernest replied that he could not take the time for a trip to the Smoky Mountains, that he had to work at his book and at being a new father, too. Clarence replied to his son:

Glad of your statement of facts.—I am now entirely willing to give up the Smoky Mts. trip this Fall—We have had excellent Spring + Summer Vacations and now are ready for Winter's work which has *commenced*. I am sure it is for the best for me not to go away so soon.— No good excuse and obligations here are definite.—

Shortly after Ernest's visit to the family home in Oak Park, Illinois, on his way back from Wyoming with the manuscript of *A Farewell to Arms* in hand, he had received a poem from Clarence. It read:

To My Son
I can't seem to think of a way
To say what I'd like most to say
To my very dear son
Whose book is just done,
Except to give him my love
and "HORRAY"

Six weeks later, Clarence Hemingway was dead.

At his father's wake, Ernest knelt before the casket, blessed himself before his Congregationalist family as a Catholic would, and recited aloud, "In the name of the Father, the Son, and the Holy Ghost." Observing the undertaker's work—covering over the hemorrhagic discoloration of the face caused by the .32 slug Clarence had fired into his head, just behind the left ear—Ernest said, "Poor boy, poor boy."

As the decade of the Twenties closed, Ernest Hemingway believed he had betrayed the two people in the world he truly loved: his father and his first wife. Yet his career was well under way.

# Sources

If you want to read good Ernest Hemingway from the early Twenties, there is no better book than William White's edition of Ernest's *Tomonto Star* dispatches. Entitled *Ernest Hemingway, Dateline: Toronto,* this edition includes every piece Ernest wrote for the paper from 1920 to 1924. The talent that produced his first Hemingway story, "Crossroads," in 1919 and would fulfill itself in *In Our Time* in 1925 is displayed here in abundance.

Long before the "new journalism" of the Sixties, Ernest used techniques of fiction to give his reporting a readability, a flavor of truth, that the "just the facts" school of journalism had never achieved. Beginning with "On Weddynge Gyftes"—the mock archaic spelling intended to suggest the uselessness of "appropriate" gifts—and on through "Living on $1000 a year in Paris," Tuna Fishing in Spain," "Paris Is Full of Russians," "The Luge of Switzerland"; then, later, "Canada's Recognition of Russia," "Tchitcherin Speaks at the Genoa Conference," "Objections to Allied Plan," "Inflation and the German Mark," and "War Medals for Sale," Ernest rejected the notion of "objectivity" and gave his articles the drama of a sharp point of view.

What Ernest valued most in journalism was not so much the writing (journalism was a pale substitute for fiction, the "real thing"), but rather seeing and getting to know the world. Tourist travel, Ernest felt, broadened the ass long before the mind. But travel with a duty to observe and then report that observation gave a wonderful education.

Because Ernest put so much of himself into his articles, they are a treasure for the biographer. Reading his lines, reading between his lines, I discovered intimacies usually found only in diaries.

*A Moveable Feast* was written more than thirty years after the last article Ernest wrote for the *Star.* Ostensibly, it is a direct presentation of Ernest's recollections of his early Paris years, when "we were very poor and very happy." And yet, from the letters of that time, I saw that the Hemingways were neither very poor nor very happy. *A Moveable Feast* is, arguably, as much a work of fiction as a memoir—a part of Ernest's mythmaking, his *Paradise Lost*. But the details presented in this "memoir"—where Ernest slept and ate; what he saw, smelled, and tasted; whom he liked and loved; whom he hated; and most of all how he went about his writing—offer the biographer a chance to give his story of Ernest's life the texture of Ernest's fiction.

In 1985, Jack Hemingway donated to the Ernest Hemingway Collection at the John F. Kennedy Library 457 pages of his mother's correspondence. Almost four hundred of these pages are letters to Ernest. They begin in early October 1923 and end, abruptly, August 3, 1929—when Hadley's second husband, Paul Scott Mowrer, forbade her to write to Ernest again.

Because Hadley was an intelligent and sensitive observer, because she understood Ernest as perhaps no woman ever would again, and because she could write wonderful letters, the biographer has something to set against *A Moveable Feast*, not in the simplistic terms of comparison and contrast, not in pursuit of forensic verification, but rather to create a dialogue, one to reveal more than any single voice could, even Ernest Hemingway's.

But Hadley Hemingway Mowrer's contribution to his biography did not end with the letters her son, Jack, donated to the Hemingway Collection at the Kennedy Library. Three years ago, in the summer of 1986, Jack Hemingway allowed me to listen to almost six hours of tape recordings his mother had made a few years before her death. The inquisitor was Alice Hunt Sokoloff, author of *Hadley: The First Mrs. Hemingway*.

During the interview, Sokoloff seemed in awe of Hadley and approached her gingerly, asking only questions that could not possibly give offense, bringing up only subjects that a gentile woman could comfortably discuss. As a result, Hadley was forced to convey her feelings, her impressions, her long-submerged thoughts inferentially. Yet, because Hadley was a subtle, articulate woman, I heard telling details about Ezra Pound, Gertrude Stein, Ford Maddox Ford, Scott Fitzgerald, even Pauline.

At one point in Hadley's remarks about Pauline, the tape went silent for several minutes. Yet just before and just after this gap, the impression that Pauline was as attracted to Hadley as she was to Ernest is clearly given. Later, what Hadley discloses suggests that much of the Ernest-Hadley-Pauline triangle in *The Garden of Eden* is historical.

On March 29, 1985, I had the privilege of attending the first Ritz-Paris Hemingway Award dinner. My wife, Penelope, and I were Jack Hemingway's guests. For the previous nine days, Penny and I had been living at the tiny Hotel Recamier, on Place St.-Sulpice. Journalist Paul Chutkow had selected this hotel for us because it was in the heart of "Hemingway's Paris."

The Paris weather was cold and dreary when we walked to 74 Rue du Cardinal Lemoine, to the Hotel d'Angleterre, to Le Pre aux Clercs, to the hotel on Rue Descartes. One day we walked half the morning up and down the Rue Mouffetard and into the Place Contrescarpe. One night we found 27 Rue de Fleurus and stood before the facade, trying to imagine.

Another morning, Jack came to our hotel and, after making certain we had our maps, took us on a tour of all the famous Hemingway landmarks. I remember stopping at the tennis courts where Ernest and Ezra Pound used to play, and peering through a space in the iron gate. I remember the Closerie des Lilas, the Luxembourg Gardens, the café and the café creme across from Notre Dame. Then there was Jack's story of how Marie Cocotte, his nurse-maid, would, while he watched, casually relieve herself, pulling up her skirts and settling like a hen on the sidewalk *pissoir*.

No one writing about Ernest Hemingway can ignore the debt owed to the "official" biographer, the late Carlos Baker. Professor Baker's work is a master-piece of diligence, thoroughness, and style. It is the framework for this book, and would be, I suspect, for any biography of Ernest Hemingway.

My one best source for this book was the work of Ernest himself. First there are the *Selected Letters of Ernest Hemingway,* edited by Professor Baker and published by Charles Scribner's Sons in 1981. Malcolm Muggeridge, at the time of publication, called this collection the most important document in American literature since the publication of *In Our Time.* Be that as it may, the more than nine hundred pages of letters selected from those Ernest wrote between 1917 and 1961 constitute an invaluable source for understanding his private life. Many are carefully constructed, heavily detailed—to his family, to the women he loved, to the people who could help him in his career. Some are written in anger or fear, "night letters" Ernest called them, and were never finished or never sent. And there are notes to correct a misunderstanding. Although Ernest called letter writing something to do when you want to avoid working and still get a sense of accomplishment, he often warmed up for his work with a letter or two, then cooled down with a few more after his fiction for the day was done.

For the last, and perhaps most important, chapter of this book, I relied on two of Ernest's still unpublished works. Both untitled pieces, they tell the story of Ernest's life between his first two marriages—the hundred days he lived alone in Paris waiting for his divorce from Hadley and for Pauline to come back to him from the States.

There are minor differences in these stories. In the first, for example, the main character is a writer; in the second, he is a painter. But in both pieces he has separated from his wife, has fallen in love with another woman, lives alone in the same studio. The portraits of Ernest as "Philip Haines" and "James Allen," Hadley as "Harriet" and "Caroline," and Pauline in both stories as "Dorothy Rogers" are drawn almost identically. In both stories there are the letters from America and meetings between husband and wife. Even the dialogue sounds the same. Finally, letters of the time, between Ernest and Hadley and Ernest and Pauline, leave little doubt that this twice-told tale is essentially autobiographical.

Internal evidence suggests that Ernest wrote these pieces some three or four years apart, the first just after the events had occurred (early 1927); the sec-ond some time after the Market Crash (1929 or 1930). The two stories, listed by their first lines in the Hemingway Collection at the John F. Ken-nedy Library in Boston, are "Philip Haines was a writer . . . ," thirty hand-written pages; and "James Allen lived in a studio . . . ," forty-six handwrit-ten pages.

# *Notes*

## Chapter 1

Leopoldina, *appearance and history:* New York Shipbuilding Corporation: *A Record of Ships Built*, 1921, pp. 10–11. *North Atlantic Seaways*, N. R. P. Bonsor, Lancashire [U.K.], 1935, pp. 97, 572.

*Ernest's departure letter:* Ernest to "Dear Folks," Dec. 8, 1921.

*The weather for Dec. 8, 1921: New York Times*, Dec. 7, 1921.

*Boxing story:* Ernest to "Dear Famille," Dec. 20, 1921. Ernest to William B. Smith, Jr., Dec. 20, 1921. Carlos Baker, *Ernest Hemingway: A Life Story*, New York, 1969, p. 83. Hadley's tapes.

*The trip across:* Baker, *Life*, pp. 83–84. *The Nick Adams Stories*, "Night Before Landing," pp. 119–24. Ernest to Bill Smith, Dec. 20, 1921.

*Books Ernest cared for: The Garden of Eden*, pp. 194, 195. "James Allen was a painter . . . ," p. 25.

*Ernest boxing in knitted lavender shorts:* Peter Griffin, *Along with Youth*, New York, p. 194.

*Trip from Le Havre to Paris by train:* Ernest to Sherwood and Tennessee Anderson, Dec. 23, 1921.

*First days in Paris:* Ernest to Sherwood and Tennessee Anderson, Dec. 23, 1921.

*"The good restaurant":* William White, *Ernest Hemingway, Dateline: Toronto*, New York, 1985, pp. 88–89, 425–26.

*The Russians of Paris: Dateline: Toronto*, p. 98.

*Louis Galantiere:* Baker, *Life*, p. 84.

*Life at 74 Rue Cardinal Lemoine:* Alice Sokoloff, *Hadley: The First Mrs. Hemingway*, p. 15. "The Snows of Kilimanjaro," p. 70. *A Moveable Feast*, pp. 3–4. Baker, *Life*, p. 84. Hadley to Baker, answering questionnaire, Dec. 1962.

*Paris:* Author's trip to Paris for the Ritz-Paris Hemingway Award, 1985. Robert E. Gajdusek, *Hemingway's Paris,* New York, 1978.

*Where and how Ernest worked: A Moveable Feast,* pp. 11–13. Baker, *Life,* p. 85. Sokoloff, *Hadley,* pp. 48–49.

*Chamby sur Montreux:* Baker, *Life,* p. 85. Ernest to "Dear Dad," May 24, 1922. *A Farewell to Arms,* pp. 289–92. White, *Dateline: Toronto,* p. 110.

*Ernest meets Ezra Pound:* Baker, *Life,* p. 86. *A Moveable Feast,* pp. 107–12. Ernest to Sherwood Anderson, March 9, 1922. Hadley to Baker, Dec. 1962.

*Ernest and Gertrude Stein:* Baker, *Life,* pp. 86–87. *A Moveable Feast,* pp. 9–31.

*Ernest and Sylvia Beach:* Baker, *Life,* p. 87. *A Moveable Feast,* pp. 33–38. Kenneth Lynn, *Hemingway,* New York, 1987, pp. 154–55, 162.

*Ernest's review of* Batouala: White, *Dateline: Toronto,* p. 112.

*Ernest at the book stalls: A Moveable Feast,* pp. 41–45.

*Kate Smith:* Ernest to Kate Smith, asking for money she held for him, Feb. 13, 1922.

*Ernest in Genoa:* Baker, *Life,* pp. 88–89. Ernest to "Dear Dad," May 2, 1922. White, *Dateline: Toronto,* pp. 138–61.

## Chapter 2

*Ernest's illness on his return from Genoa:* Baker, *Life,* p. 67. Griffin, *Along with Youth,* pp. 156, 212.

*Ernest and Hadley hike with Eric Dorman-Smith in Switzerland:* Baker, *Life,* pp. 91–92. Griffin, *Along with Youth,* pp. 95, 100. Ernest to "Dear Dad," May 24, 1922. Ernest to "Dear Miss Stein and Miss Toklas," June 11, 1922.

*Ernest fishing the Rhone Canal:* White, *Dateline: Toronto,* p. 169.

*Ernest to Italy:* Baker, *Life,* pp. 93–94. White, *Dateline: Toronto,* pp. 172–80.

*Ernest on Italy:* Ernest to Bill Horne, July 17–18, 1923.

*Ernest and Hadley back in Paris:* White, *Dateline: Toronto,* pp. 182–84.

*Ernest and Bill Bird:* Baker, *Life,* pp. 95–96. White, *Dateline: Toronto,* pp. 205–7.

*Ernest in Germany:* White, *Dateline: Toronto,* pp. 194–215.

*Ernest to "Dear Folks" from Germany:* August 25, 1922.

*Ernest to Constantinople:* Baker, *Life,* pp. 97–99. White, *Dateline: Toronto,* pp. 217–33.

*Ernest's return:* Baker, *Life,* p. 99. White, *Dateline: Toronto,* p. 249.

*Ernest's poetry:* From Nicholas Gerogiannis, ed., *Ernest Hemingway: Complete Poems,* Lincoln, Neb., 1979, pp. 46, 42, 43, 49, 61.

*Ernest and Ford Maddox Ford:* Baker, *Life,* p. 101. *A Moveable Feast,* pp. 83–88.

*Ernest on Dave O'Neil:* Ernest to Ezra Pound, Jan. 29, 1923.

*Ernest and Ernest Walsh:* Baker, *Life,* p. 101. *A Moveable Feast,* pp. 119–27.

*Ernest in Lausanne:* Baker, *Life,* pp. 99–105. Ernest to Hadley, Nov. 28, 1922.

Ernest to Isabel Simmons, Dec. 1, 1922. *White, Dateline: Toronto,* pp. 253–59.

*Hadley's loss of Ernest's Manuscripts:* Baker, *Life,* p. 103. *A Moveable Feast,* pp. 73–74. *The Garden of Eden,* pp. 218–24.

*Ernest's response to Hadley's pregnancy: The Short Stories of Ernest Hemingway,* New York, 1938, p. 187. Jeffrey Meyers, *Hemingway,* New York, 1985, pp. 119–21.

*Ernest's letter to Agnes von Kurowsky:* Baker, *Life,* p. 100.

*Ernest's retrieving of George O'Neil's ski:* Baker, *Life,* p. 104.

*Ernest's glands inoperative:* Ernest to Ezra Pound, Jan. 29, 1923.

## Chapter 3

*Ernest with Ezra Pound in Italy:* Baker, *Life,* pp. 105–7. Ernest to Gertrude Stein, Feb. 18, 1923. Author correspondence with James Wilhelm, May–July 1986.

*Portrait of Robert McAlmon:* Robert McAlmon and Kay Boyle, *Being Geniuses Together 1920–1930,* San Francisco, 1984.

*"The Lady Poets With Foot Notes":* Gerogiannis, *Complete Poems,* pp. 76–77.

*"Cat in the Rain": Short Stories,* pp. 167–70.

*Hadley and Renata Borgatti:* Baker, *Life,* p. 108. Hadley tapes. Hadley to Ernest from Cortina, March 1923 ("3:30 Thursday"). Author's conversation with Laura Huxley, Aug. 16, 1987.

*Ernest in Germany again:* Baker, *Life,* pp. 108–9. Ernest to "Dear Dad," March 26, 1923. White, *Dateline: Toronto,* pp. 260–92.

*Ernest's first day in Spain:* Ernest to James Gamble, March 3, 1919. Author's conversations with Angel Capalan, Fall 1978.

*Ernest's opinion of Picasso:* Unpublished portion of *The Garden of Eden,* chap. 38.

*Ernest's first broken heart:* Griffin, *Along with Youth,* p. 113.

*Ernest to Spain with Robert McAlmon and Bill Bird:* Baker, *Life,* pp. 109–11. Ernest to Bill Horne, July 17–18, 1923. McAlmon and Boyle, *Being Geniuses Together,* p. 160.

*McAlmon at the bullfight: Death in the Afternoon,* p. 498.

*McAlmon on Anderson:* McAlmon and Boyle, *Being Geniuses Together,* p. 158.

*Money worries:* Ernest and Hadley to George Breaker, Oct. 15, 1923. Two cables to Breaker: "Brevity due cable cost month's rent" and ". . . would prefer immediate deposit of all funds Mercantile as *originally* requested November." Ernest and Hadley to George and Helen Breaker, Aug. 27, 29, 1924. Hadley's tapes indicate the trust fund had been dwindling for some time, but the Hemingways were reluctant to question George Breaker because Helen was Hadley's friend.

*Ernest and Hadley to Spain:* Baker, *Life,* p. 112. Ernest to Bill Horne, July 17–18, 1923.

*Ernest and Hadley to Canada:* Baker, *Life,* p. 113. Ernest to Ezra Pound,
    Aug. 5, 1923.
*Ernest on bullfight: Death in the Afternoon,* pp. 1–15.
Three Stories and Ten Poems: Ernest to Robert McAlmon, Aug. 5, 1923.
    Baker, *Life,* p. 114.


## Chapter 4

*Ernest arrives in Toronto:* Ernest to Ezra Pound, Sept. 6, 1923. Gerogiannis,
    *Complete Poems,* p. 68.
*Ernest and Hadley's apartment:* Baker, *Life,* p. 115.
*Ernest's condition in Canada:* Ernest to Ezra Pound, Oct. 13, 1923. Ernest to
    "Dear Dad," Nov. 7, 1923. Ernest to Gertrude Stein and Alice B.
    Toklas, Nov. 9, 1923.
*Ernest and Harry Hindmarsh:* Baker, *Life,* p. 116. Hadley tapes. Ernest to
    John Bone, Dec. 26, 1923; Dec. 27, 1923.
*Ernest asks Oak Park friend for help in New York:* Baker, *Life,* pp. 116–17.
    White, *Dateline: Toronto,* p. 329.
*Lloyd George in Canada:* White, *Dateline: Toronto,* pp. 319–28.
*Ernest in New York:* Baker, *Life,* p. 116. Ernest to Ezra Pound, Oct. 6, 13,
    1923. Ernest to Gertrude Stein and Alice B. Toklas, Oct. 11, 1923.
*Birth of John Hemingway:* Baker, *Life,* p. 117. Ernest to Ezra Pound, Oct. 13,
    1923. Ernest to Sylvia Beach, Nov. 6, 1923. Ernest to "Dear Dad,"
    Nov. 7, 1923.
*Ernest home to Oak Park:* Baker, *Life,* p. 121. Ernest to "Dear Dad," Dec. 18,
    1923. Marcelline Hemingway, *At the Hemingways,* Boston, 1962,
    pp. 215–17.
*Ernest's break with Star:* White, *Dateline: Toronto,* p. 336. Baker, *Life,* pp.
    121–22. Ernest to Ezra Pound, Oct. 13, 1923. Ernest to John Bone,
    Dec. 26, 27, 1923.
*Grace Hemingway compares Ernest to her father, Ernest Hall:* Grace to Ernest,
    Dec. 23, 1923.
*Ernest sends Edmund Wilson* Three Stories and Ten Poems: Baker, *Life,*
    p. 118. Ernest to Edmund Wilson, Nov. 11, 25, 1923.
*Edward J. O'Brien to publish "My Old Man" and dedicate the volume to
    Ernest:* Ernest to Edward O'Brien, Nov. 20, 1923.
*Ernest and Jim Gamble:* Ernest to "Dear Jim," Dec. 12, 1923.


## Chapter 5

*Ernest in New York:* Baker, *Life,* p. 122. Ernest to "Dear Jim," Dec. 12, 1923.
*The trip across: Islands in the Stream,* p. 263.
*Ernest and Hadley's apartment:* Ernest to Ezra Pound, Feb. 10, 1924. Baker,
    *Life,* p. 123.
*Ernest meets Ford Maddox Ford:* Ernest to Ezra Pound, March 17, 1924.
    Baker, *Life,* pp. 123–24. *A Moveable Feast,* pp. 79–88. Hadley tapes.
*Excerpted portion of "Indian Camp": The Nick Adams Stories,* pp. 3–5.

*Ford Maddox Ford's opinion of Ernest:* Baker, *Life,* p. 126.

*The baptism of Ernest's son:* Author's conversations with Bill Horne, July 1983.

*Harold Loeb:* Bertram D. Sarason, *Hemingway and the Sun Set,* Washington, D.C., 1972.

*Ernest's boxing in Paris:* Baker, *Life,* p. 126. Ernest to Bill Smith, Dec. 6, 1924. Ernest to Howell Jenkins, Feb. 2, 1925.

*The gardening barman at Closerie des Lilas: A Moveable Feast,* pp. 137–38.

*Ernest writing in room at home:* Hadley tapes.

*The Luxembourg Gardens: A Moveable Feast,* pp. 69–70. Gajdusek, *Hemingway's Paris,* pp. 88–93. *Islands in the Stream,* p. 56.

*Ernest and hunger: A Moveable Feast,* pp. 69–73.

*Ernest writing "Big Two-Hearted River": A Moveable Feast,* p. 76.

*Ernest and Vincent Van Gogh:* Ernest to Ezra Pound, May 2, 1924. *The Garden of Eden,* p. 4.

*Ernest and Gertrude Stein's* The Making of Americans: Baker, *Life,* pp. 124, 128. Ernest to Gertrude Stein and Alice B. Toklas, Nov. 9, 1923. Ernest to Gertrude Stein, Feb. 17, 1924. Ernest to Gertrude Stein, May 5, 1924. Ernest to Gertrude Stein and Alice B. Toklas, Aug. 9, 1924. Ernest to Gertrude Stein and Alice B. Toklas, Aug. 15, 1924. Ernest to Gertrude Stein and Alice B. Toklas, Oct. 10, 1924.

*Picasso and Gertrude Stein:* Author's conversation with Jack Hemingway. April 12, 1986.

*Gertrude takes care of Bumby:* Gertrude Stein to Ernest, Aug. 3, 17, 1924.

*Ernest in Spain, 1924:* Baker, *Life,* pp. 128–30.

*Ernest on bullfight: Death in the Afternoon,* pp. 1–15.

*Ernest's last days in Pamplona:* Ernest to Ezra Pound, July 19, 1924.

*The running of the bulls: The Sun Also Rises,* pp. 196–98.

*Ernest to mass at the monastery at Roncesvalles:* Ernest to Ezra Pound, July 19, 1924.

*Ernest on Joyce:* Ernest to Ezra Pound, July 19, 1924.

*Ernest on quitting writing:* Ernest to Ezra Pound, July 19, 1924.

*Ernest on* transatlantic: Ernest to Gertrude Stein and Alice B. Toklas, Aug. 9, 15, 1924.

*Gertrude Stein to Ernest:* August 17, 1924. Sept. 18, 1924.

*Ernest's hope with Doran:* Baker, *Life,* pp. 138–39.

## Chapter 6

*Lewis Clarahan encourages Ernest to write:* Author's conversations with Clarahan, Summer 1984.

*Ernest and Fanny Biggs:* Griffin, *Along with Youth,* pp. 24–25, 26, 30

*Ernest remembering his soul leaving his body: A Farewell to Arms,* pp. 54–55. Ernest Hemingway, unpublished novel, "A New Slain Knight," Chapter 11.

*Art as life itself, lived another way: The Garden of Eden,* pp. 179, 193, 197 ff.

*The Smith family tragedy:* Carlos Baker, ed., *Ernest Hemingway: Selected Letters, 1917–1961,* New York, 1981, p. 132n.

*Ernest introduced to Schruns:* Baker, *Life,* p. 137.

*Ernest and Hadley in Schruns: A Moveable Feast,* pp. 195–204.

*Ernest asks Harold Loeb to Schruns:* Ernest to Harold Loeb, Dec. 29, 1924.

*Money from Don Stewart:* Baker, *Life,* p. 139. Ernest to Harold Loeb, Jan. 5, 1925.

*Liveright accepts* In Our Time: Baker, *Life,* pp. 140–41. Ernest to Harold Loeb, Feb. 27, 1925.

*Liveright as fighter against censorship:* Baker, *Letters,* p. 151n.

*Ernest's response to* Dial *rejection of "The Undefeated":* Baker, *Life,* p. 143. Ernest to Ernest Walsh, Jan. 1925.

*Ernest meets Pauline Pfeiffer:* Baker, *Life,* p. 142. Kenneth S. Lynn, *Hemingway,* New York, 1987, pp. 300–301. Hadley tapes.

*Lady Duff Twysden:* Baker, *Life,* pp. 144–45, 156. Lynn, *Hemingway,* pp. 289–99. Author conversation with the current Lady Twysden, Knightsbridge, London, Feb. and April 1987.

*The Dingo Bar:* Author's correspondence with Holly Peterson, Sept. 3, 1987.

*Ernest's meeting with Scott:* Baker, *Life,* pp. 145–46. *A Moveable Feast,* pp. 147–50.

*Scott Fitzgerald on writing: A Moveable Feast,* pp. 151–54.

*Ernest's trip with Scott to Lyon: A Moveable Feast,* pp. 154–74.

*Ernest and Professor Gauss:* Baker, *Life,* p. 147.

## Chapter 7

*Ernest and Bumby in Paris: Islands in the Stream,* pp. 54–65.

*Duff Twysden's addictions:* Author's conversation with the current Lady Twysden, March and April 1987.

*Ernest on Joyce:* Ernest to Ezra Pound, July 19, 1924. Baker, *Life,* p. 148.

*Ernest and Hadley leaving for Pamplona:* Baker, *Life,* p. 148. Ernest to Ernest Walsh, June 25, 1925. Ernest to Scott Fitzgerald, July 1, 1925.

*Ernest and the Spaniard who showed him the "biggest trout":* Ernest to Bill Smith, Dec. 6, 1924.

*The Harold Loeb and Duff Twysden assignation:* Baker, *Life,* p. 148. Sarason, *Hemingway and the Sun Set,* pp. 136–44.

*Ernest's response:* Baker, *Life,* p. 150.

*Ernest from Bayonne to Pamplona: The Sun Also Rises,* pp. 103–9, 130, 198.

*Ernest fishing the Irati:* Baker, *Life,* p. 149. Ernest to Gertrude Stein and Alice B. Toklas, July 15, 1925. *The Sun Also Rises,* pp. 112–25. Sarason, *Hemingway and the Sun Set,* p. 121. Hadley tapes.

*Ernest to Scott Fitzgerald about Spain, 1925:* July 1, 1925.

*Ernest and Hadley in Pamplona, 1925:* Item 193, Hemingway Collection, 34 pages. Early draft of *The Sun Also Rises. The Sun Also Rises,* pp. 130 ff. Hadley tapes.

*Hadley's interest in Ordoñez:* Baker, *Life,* p. 149. Ernest to Gertrude Stein and Alice B. Toklas, July 15, 1925.

*The bullfights: The Sun Also Rises,* pp. 161–69. White, *Dateline: Toronto,* pp. 340–55. Ernest to Gertrude Stein and Alice B. Toklas, July 15,

1925. Baker, *Life*, pp. 149–50. *Death in the Afternoon*, pp. 40, 497–503. David B. Atkinson to author, June 9, 1987. David Sabel to author, March 19, 1987.

*Loeb and Ernest and Duff's black eye:* Sarason, *Hemingway and the Sun Set*, p. 124.

*Ernest apologizes to Loeb:* Ernest to Harold Loeb, July 12, 1925.

*Ernest's early love for Hadley:* Griffin, *Along with Youth*, pp. 161 ff.

*Ernest to "Dear Dad":* Aug. 20, 1925.

*Hadley returns to Paris:* Baker, *Life*, p. 153.

## Chapter 8

*Ernest's health after a long stretch of writing:* Ernest to Ernest Walsh, Sept. 15, 1925. Ernest to "Dear Mother," Dec. 14, 1925. Ernest to Scott Fitzgerald, Dec. 15, 1925. Ernest to Ernest Walsh, Jan. 2, 1926. Ernest to Scott Fitzgerald, Sept. 7, 1926.

*Gertrude Stein and "the Lost Generation":* A Moveable Feast, pp. 30–31.

*Ernest leaves Liveright over* The Torrents of Spring: Ernest to Horace Liveright, Mar. 31, 1925. Ernest to John Dos Passos, April 22, 1925. Ernest to Horace Liveright, May 11, 15, 1925. Ernest to Horace Liveright, June 21, 1925. Ernest to Horace Liveright, Dec. 7, 1925. Ernest to Scott Fitzgerald, Dec. 31, 1925. Ernest to Horace Liveright, Jan. 19, 1926.

*Maxwell Perkins's interest in Ernest:* Ernest to Maxwell Perkins, April 15, 1925.

*Ernest and Sherwood Anderson:* Ernest to Sherwood Anderson, May 21, 1926.

*Pauline Pfeiffer:* McAlmon and Boyle, *Being Geniuses Together*, pp. 180, 183–84. Author's conversations with Ayleene Spence of Piggott, Arkansas, Summer 1987.

*Ernest in Shruns:* Baker, *Life*, pp. 160–63.

*Ernest and Pauline, the romance begins:* "Philip Haines was a writer . . . ," pp. 3–4. Baker, *Life*, pp. 163–64.

*Ernest in New York:* Baker, *Life*, pp. 164–65. Ernest to Ernest Walsh, Feb. 1, 1926. Ernest to Isabel Simmons Godolphin, Feb. 10, 25, 1926. Ernest to Louis and Mary Bromfield, March 8, 1926.

*Ernest back in Paris with Pauline:* Baker, *Life*, pp. 165–66. Author's conversation with Sunny Hemingway, October 1983.

*Meeting Bumby and Hadley in Schruns:* A Moveable Feast, p. 208.

*Ernest on Dos Passos:* A Moveable Feast, pp. 296–307. Author's conversation with Sunny Hemingway, October 1983. Dos Passos to Ernest, Jan. 22, 1926; July 7, 1926.

*Gerald and Sara Murphy:* Calvin Tompkins, *Living Well Is the Best Revenge*, New York, 1971, pp. 9–21.

*Dos Passos and the Murphys in Schruns:* Baker, *Life*, p. 166. *A Moveable Feast*, pp. 206–7.

*Avalanche:* Baker, *Life*, p. 167.

## Chapter 9

*Hadley confronts Ernest about Pauline:* Baker, *Life,* p. 168. Hadley tapes. Author's interview with Sunny Hemingway, October 1983.

*Bumby's illness begins:* Baker, *Life,* p. 168. Kurt V. Isselbacher et al., eds., *Harrison's Principles of Internal Medicine,* New York, 1980, pp. 654–56.

*Ernest writing in Madrid:* Ernest to Scott Fitzgerald, May 20, 1926.

*Ernest in defense of self to Sherwood Anderson:* Ernest to Sherwood Anderson, May 21, 1926.

*Ernest hints at future to Clarence Hemingway:* Ernest to "Dear Dad," May 23, 1926.

*Hadley and Bumby in Juan-les-Pins:* Telegram, Hadley to Ernest, May 21, 1926. Letter from same day, arrived May 25. Telegram, Hadley to Ernest, May 24, 1926 Hadley to Ernest, "Tuesday Afternoon," from Juan-les-Pins. Hadley to Ernest, "Saturday Noon," Juan-les-Pins. Hadley to Ernest, "Monday Afternoon," Juan-les-Pins. Hadley to "Don Ernesto Hemingway, Hotel Aguilar, 34 Carrera de San Jeronimo, Madrid, Espagne." Baker, *Life,* pp. 169–71.

*Ernest witnesses death of influenza patient:* Griffin, *Along with Youth,* p. 94.

*Gerald and Sara Murphy:* Tompkins, *Living Well Is the Best Revenge,* pp. 9–21.

*Life at the Villa America:* Tompkins, *Living Well Is the Best Revenge,* pp. 93–100.

*Ernest, Hadley, and Pauline in the South of France:* Hadley tapes. *The Garden of Eden,* pp. 4, 128–37.

*Scott Fitzgerald's criticism of* The Sun Also Rises: Frederic Joseph Svoboda, *Hemingway and The Sun Also Rises,* Lawrence, Kan., 1983, pp. 137–40.

*Pamplona, 1926: Death in the Afternoon,* pp. 497–503. Baker, *Life,* pp. 172–73.

*Ernest and Ernest Walsh:* Ernest to Ernest Walsh, July 20, 1925. Ernest to Ernest Walsh, Jan. 1926.

*Ernest and Hadley return to Paris:* Baker, *Life,* p. 173. *Short Stories,* pp. 339–42.

## Chapter 10

*Hadley and Ernest spend first night back together:* Hadley to Ernest, Aug. 20, 1926.

*The "hundred days" agreement:* Hadley to Ernest, Sept. 17, 1926.

*Keeping apart and Bumby's future:* Hadley to Ernest, Oct. 16, 1926.

*Hadley's attitude toward the "hundred days" demand:* Hadley tapes.

*Pauline with her parents:* Pauline to Ernest, Oct. 14, 1926.

*Pauline and losing allowance:* "Philip Haines was a writer . . . ," p. 6.

*Ernest assigns royalties for* The Sun Also Rises: Ernest to Hadley, Nov. 18, 1926.

*Ernest's studio in Rue Froidevaux:* "Philip Haines was a writer . . . ," p. 7.
"James Allen lived in a studio . . . ," pp. 1–4.

*Ernest's characterization of his early work:* "Philip Haines was a writer . . . ,"
p. 2.

*The "value of small happinesses":* Hemingway quoted in *Playboy,* January
1964, p. 226.

*Unreal existence of living alone:* "James Allen lived in a studio . . . ," pp.
17, 18.

*Ernest's reading:* James Allen lived in a studio . . . ," p. 25.

*Ernest's trips to café:* "James Allen lived in a studio . . . ," pp. 8–11.

*Echo of "A Clean Well-Lighted Place":* James Allen lived in a studio . . . ,"
pp. 7–8, 38, Gerogiannis, *Complete Poems,* p. 88.

*Ernest upset about his wet shoes:* "James Allen lived in a studio . . . ,"
pp. 23–25.

*Something fatal "advancing" on Ernest:* "James Allen lived in a studio . . . ,"
p. 18.

*Pauline's "improvements":* Pauline to Ernest, Oct. 15, 1926. Author's conversation with Laura Huxley, Aug. 16, 1987.

*Ernest on death of grandfather:* Ernest to "Dear Dad," Oct. 22, 1926.

*Maxwell Perkins responds to Ernest's work:* Perkins to Ernest, Feb. 1, 1926;
April 12, 1926; May 18, 1926. Perkins to Scott Fitzgerald, May 29,
1926.

*Pauline at home in Piggott, Arkansas*—To Ernest Oct. 14, 1926; Oct. 15, 1926;
Oct. 16, 1926; Oct. 17, 1926; Oct. 19, 1926; Oct. 21, 1926; Oct. 22,
1926; Oct. 23, 1926; Oct. 25, 1926; Oct. 29, 1926; Nov. 1, 1926; Nov.
15, 1926; Nov. 26, 1926; Nov. 27, 1926; Nov. 28, 1926; Nov. 29, 1926;
Nov. 30, 1926; Dec. 1, 1926; Dec. 3, 1926; Dec. 4, 1926; Dec. 10, 1926;
Dec. 12, 1926; Dec. 13, 1926; Dec. 15, 1926; Dec. 18, 1926; Dec. 27,
1926. Author's conversations with Ayleene Spence of Piggott, Arkansas, Summer 1987.

*Ernest's feeling about Pauline's letters:* "Philip Haines was a writer . . . ,"
pp. 11–12.

*Ernest meeting Hadley in café:* "Philip Haines was a writer . . . ," pp. 27–28.
"James Allen lived in a studio . . . ," pp. 27–41.

*Hadley wants reconciliation:* Hadley to Ernest, Nov. 16, 1926.

*Ernest on times unfaithful to Hadley:* "James Allen lived in a studio . . . ,"
p. 42.

*Ernest loses faith in Pauline:* Ernest to Pauline, Dec. 2 and 3, 1926.

*Ernest's brief trip to Spain:* Hadley to Ernest, Oct. 18, 1926. Lynn, *Hemingway,* p. 351.

*Hadley in Chartre with Winifred and Paul Mowrer:* Hadley to Ernest, Nov. 8,
10, 11a, 11b, 15[?], 1926.

*Perkins and* The Sun Also Rises: Maxwell Perkins to Ernest, July 20, 1926;
Oct. 30, 1926; Nov. 26, 1926. Ernest to Maxwell Perkins, June 5,
1926; July 24, 1926; Aug. 21, 1926; Aug. 26, 1926; Sept. 7, 1926; Nov.
16, 1926; Nov. 19, 1926; Dec. 7, 1926.

*Ernest's work on "A New Slain Knight":* Maxwell Perkins, Sept. 8, 1926. Ernest to Mother, Feb. 5, 1927.

*Dos Passos's review of* The Sun Also Rises: John Dos Passos to Ernest, Nov. 10, 1926.

*Ernest visits Hadley just before Christmas, 1926:* "Philip Haines was a writer . . . ," p. 25.

*Ernest meets Hadley again at café:* "Philip Haines was a writer . . . ," pp. 26–27.

*Hadley has new love:* Pauline to Ernest, Nov. 16, 1926.

*Ernest cables "Harrison Happy":* "Philip Haines was a writer . . . ," p. 27.

*Pauline sails for France:* Pauline to Ernest, Dec. 27, 1926.

*Ernest goes to meet Pauline:* "Philip Haines was a writer . . . ," pp. 27–30.

*Ernest and Pauline make plans:* Baker, *Life,* p. 180. Pauline to Ernest Feb. 26, 1927; March 15, 20, 21, 23, 1927.

# Epilogue

*Everybody loses all the bloom":* Ernest to Scott Fitzgerald, September 13, 1929.

*Ernest in defense of himself and his work:* Ernest to "Dear Mother," February 5, 1927.

*Wife's death in childbirth scene: A Farewell to Arms,* pp. 331–32.

*Clarence Hemingway to his son, Ernest:* September 10, 1928; September 11, 1928; September 26, 1928; October 10, 1928; October 23, 1928.

*Ernest's behavior at his father's wake in the Hemingway home:* Sterling S. Sanford, Marcelline Hemingway's husband, a witness, conversation with author, March 1983.

# *Index*